Relationship Marketing Management

Relationship Marketing Management

Edward Little
and
Ebi Marandi

THOMSON

Australia • Canada • Mexico • Singapore • Spain • United Kingdom • United States

THOMSON

™

Relationship Marketing Management

Copyright © Thomson Learning 2003

The Thomson logo is a registered trademark used herein under licence.

For more information contact, Thomson Learning, High Holborn House, 50–51 Bedford Row, London WC1R 4LR or visit us on the World Wide Web at: http://www.thomsonlearning.co.uk

British Library Cataloguing-in-Publication Data
A catalogue record for this book is available from the British Library

ISBN 1-86152-931-7

First edition published by Thomson Learning, 2003

Typeset by Saxon Graphics Ltd, Derby, Great Britain

Printed in Great Britain by TJ International

Dedicated to

Michell Littlegray,
and
Roxie and Davood Marandi

Acknowledgement

The authors wish to thank Julie Ratcliff and Lawrence Marshall for reading the manuscript and making useful suggestions.

6

Contents

Figures

Tables

Introduction

The rise of relationship marketing

The 1980s and 1990s witnessed the growing popularity of the Relationship Marketing (RM) concept, with significant growth in the number of academic papers being published in the field. Early work on the subject related to the business-to-business sector.

Interaction and network approaches to marketing

Much of contemporary RM theory originates from earlier work on the so-called interaction and network approaches, which were developed from studies of marketing in business-to-business relationships. Gronroos (1997) attributes the conception of this approach to Uppsala University, Sweden, in the 1960s, but it was popularised (in academic circles at least) by the International Marketing and Purchasing (IMP) Group, which was formed in 1976 to coordinate work on a new approach. Previous research in industrial contexts had focused on discrete transactions, analysing the steps by which a particular decision was made, and seeking to categorise different types of purchase decision. The IMP group conducted studies in various European countries, examining the nature of ongoing interaction between a buying organisation and its supplier, and the relational context within which selling/purchasing decisions were made (Turnbull *et al.*, 1996).

As a result of its early studies, the IMP group developed a new model for the analysis of marketing activities, based on the interaction process between the following elements of the two organisations (MacDonald, 2000):

- social systems
- structures
- strategies
- technologies
- resources
- individuals (experience, attitudes and aims).

This was proposed as a new marketing paradigm, which became known as the interaction approach (Turnbull *et al.*, 1996).

Network theory is an extension of the interaction approach which again has been strongly influenced by the IMP group (Healy *et al.*, 2000). It recognises the fact that the study of dyadic relationships cannot capture the complexity of marketing decision-making or organisational behaviour in complex commercial environments. As the term suggests, network approaches to marketing are based on the existence of a number of complex interrelationships, rather than the simple buyer–seller dyad (e.g. Ford, 2002; Hakansson and Snehota, 1990).

According to Healy *et al.* (2000) there is an intermediate path between the interaction and network approaches. They use the term 'neo-relationship' marketing to describe an approach in which the market is analysed in terms of a number of related dyadic relationships – not just buyer–seller, but also dyadic relationships between other parties, such as management – employees and competitor–competitor relationships. This approach is perhaps most famously represented in Gummesson's (1999) 30Rs model, in which he outlines 30 such dyads.

RM in consumer markets

More recent research, however, has attempted to apply the RM concept to mass consumer markets. It is mainly with reference to this sector that this book has been written. There is, however, much confusion as to what RM is, particularly in its application to consumer markets. Gummesson points out that most of the literature on RM is a

> [s]tack of fragmented philosophies, observations and claims which do not converge in the direction of an emerging RM theory. For example, RM is often presented as a new promotional package to be sold to the customer, or a new type of marketing made possible thanks to information technology.
>
> (Gummesson, 1997: 267)

Practitioners have also embraced the concept and many of the larger companies now have a RM Manager or Director in place. Bejou and Palmer (1998) assert that RM has become the focal point of business strategy. Companies providing software packages and RM solutions are increasing in number almost daily, as RM gains acceptance by practitioners as well as by academics. Within the practitioner field the situation can be disappointing. A visit to a typical RM exhibition will reveal stand after stand staffed by salespeople who are now 'selling' RM in the same way that they have sold other products in the past, using gimmicks and buzzwords to lend credibility to their pitch. These companies are often selling what is at best a software package for tracking customers, profiling them and contacting them in order to sell more products to them without an understanding of, and provision for, any of the key requirements of successful RM. This frequently results from a lack of understanding of the RM concept, combined with false pretences by some database and direct marketers.

The rationale for this book

This book seeks to find a way through the maze of RM by bringing together the writings of numerous academics and researchers. It offers the student of marketing at undergraduate and postgraduate level a platform from which to work and conduct further research. This is felt to be necessary as more universities and colleges are offering RM as an independent unit rather than as part of another unit or module. It may also be useful to practitioners who are looking for practical advice rather than inspirational rhetoric.

There have been a number of books published on the subject of RM, but disagreements and differences remain. Texts tend to approach the subject either from a business-to-business or a services marketing perspective, often portraying RM as a tactical issue. Although this book draws much from services marketing, it takes a strategic management approach to RM. This book's contribution to the subject is, therefore, to bring together current work on services, business-to-business marketing and organisational management into a coherent framework for the management of RM.

The structure of the book

This book assumes, at least, a basic understanding of marketing concepts by the student, and approaches RM from the perspective of the management tasks that must be performed in order to develop RM within an organisation. These are illustrated, step by step, in the Figure shown on page 5. Although this structure cannot accommodate some of the more complex and ambiguous interrelationships between the various elements of RM, it nevertheless provides a robust framework around which to build an understanding of the subject, and how it may be applied in practice. Each chapter fits into the framework as follows:

Making the case for RM

Whether embarking on academic study, or seeking to develop RM in a business, it is important to understand the rationale for the subject and be able to explain its key tenets. The opening chapters, therefore, outline the theory of RM, and its differences from 'traditional' approaches to marketing.

Chapter one, Criticisms of traditional marketing, deals with developments in the field of marketing over the past 50 years, which have rendered the traditional approach to marketing inappropriate, at least in some markets. The main aim of the chapter is to justify the need for an alternative to traditional marketing.

Chapter two, Characteristics of RM, defines RM and its constituent elements, and examines the key underlying principles. This chapter should help the reader to understand the distinction between RM and the traditional marketing paradigm. It also discusses the main characteristics of RM and explains how the adoption of RM requires a change of strategic perspective.

Identifying critical RM success factors

The adoption of RM requires a fundamental shift in the philosophy of the organisation. Long-term orientation needs to replace the short-term perspective of transactional marketing. For this to happen, a fundamental change in the focus and values of the organisation needs to occur.

Chapter three, Key concepts in RM, provides a detailed study of the three crucial concepts in RM – satisfaction, trust and commitment – and examines their role in the formation and maintenance of relationships.

Developing RM practices

The primary concern of the book is the practical application of RM theory. Chapters four to eight outline the methods by which the philosophy of RM can be brought to life in the organisational arena. These chapters draw on familiar frameworks of planning and implementation, adapting them to address the implementation of RM. While the main focus will be on consumer markets, chapters four to seven will also address the management of relationships with other stakeholders.

Chapter four, Planning RM programmes, paints a road map for the adoption of a relational approach to strategy. In particular, it identifies criteria for the identification of strategic relationships and the formulation of realistic goals.

Chapter five, Implementing RM programmes – strategy, structure and systems, examines those elements of RM that are defined and manipulated by senior management – the so-called 'hard issues' of implementation. A proactive approach to the allocation of organisational resources is crucial to the success of any managerial endeavour, and this chapter sets out the mechanisms by which the RM manager can anticipate changes in the demands of their various stakeholders.

Chapter six, Implementing RM programmes – shared values, staff, skills and style, deals with the 'soft' issues of RM, focusing on the creation of a corporate culture that supports RM. No strategy will be successful without the support of the people who operate it. Chapter six looks at the task of inculcating the organisation with the skills and attitudes necessary to effect relational strategies.

Chapter seven, Monitoring and controlling relationships, focuses on maintenance issues. It identifies and evaluates the tools available for monitoring and measuring relationships, both at the strategic and tactical levels.

Chapter eight, Ethical considerations in RM, deals with the two-way channels of communication between customer and supplier and the creation and maintenance of databases on customers. It is essential that an ethical approach is taken to the gathering, utilisation and sharing of information on customers in order to maintain the trust that is required for a successful long-term relationship. The handling of such information may also be subject to legal restrictions.

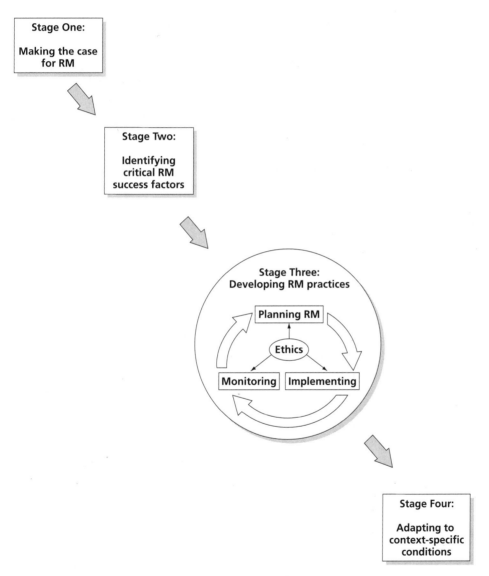

The RM Process

Adapting to context-specific conditions

Up to this point, the book addresses general issues and techniques that could be applied in a variety of commercial environments. The remaining chapters look at research and practice in specific organisational contexts, illustrating how the principles of RM may be adapted and applied in different situations. In particular, contemporary approaches in business-to-consumer and business-to-business markets are compared and contrasted.

Chapter nine, Key account management, looks at the application of RM in a business-to-business context by examining the mechanics of strategic partnership building.

Chapter ten, Customer relationship management, examines the enormous potential offered by the Internet and associated technologies to create and maintain successful relationships in markets where the number of customers are large and/or there is a considerable physical distance between the customer and supplier.

In addition to the short case studies at the end of each chapter, there are four main case studies in the book which may be used to explore the practical implications of RM within various types of organisation. One of the cases deals with RM within the leisure industry, another with retailing on the Internet. The third case deals with the intentions of a firm of solicitors to manage relationships with its clients, whilst the fourth deals with RM in a not-for-profit context. All of these case studies are based on real life organisations. In two of the cases, Tennyson and Paris, Downey and Jagger, the names of the organizations and some details have been altered.

Terminology

Throughout this book the word customer is used to mean both buyers of products and end-users; this is in order to be consistent with the sources of reference used.

Furthermore, throughout this book the word product is used to mean both goods and services. Also, the word supplier is used to mean supplier/manufacturer of goods as well as provider of services. Finally, where the word he or his has been used, it is merely to keep the writing simple and to avoid using he/she, his/hers.

References

Bejou, D. and Palmer, A. (1998) 'Service failure and loyalty: an exploratory empirical study of airline customers', *Journal of Services Marketing*, 12, 1, 7–22.

Ford, D. (2002) *Understanding Business Marketing and Purchasing*, 3rd edn, London: Thomson Learning.

Gronroos, C. (1997) 'From marketing mix to relationship marketing – towards a paradigm shift in marketing', *Management Decision*, 35, 4, 322–339.

Gummesson, E. (1997) 'Relationship marketing as a paradigm shift: some conclusions from the 30R approach', *Management Decision,* 35, 4, 264–272.

Gummesson, E. (1999) *Total Relationship Marketing: from the 4Ps – product, price, promotion, place – of traditional marketing management to the 30Rs – the thirty relationships – of the new marketing paradigm,* Oxford: Butterworth-Heinemann.

Hakansson, H. and Snehota, I. (1990) 'No business is an island', in O. Ford *Understanding Business Network,* London: Academic Press.

Healy, M., Hastings, K., Brown, L. and Gardiner, M. (2000) 'The old, the new and the complicated – a trilogy of marketing relationships', *European Journal of Marketing,* 35, 1/2, 182–193.

MacDonald, M. (2000) 'Key account management – a domain review', *The Marketing Review,* 1, 15–34.

Turnbull, P., Ford, D. and Cunningham, M. (1996) 'Interaction, relationships and networks in business markets: an evolving perspective', *Journal of Business and Industrial Marketing,* 11, 3/4, 44–62.

Stage One:

Making the case for RM

Stage Two:

Identifying critical RM success factors

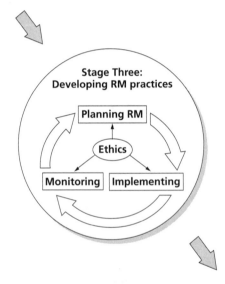

Stage Three:
Developing RM practices

Planning RM

Ethics

Monitoring | Implementing

Stage Four:

Adapting to context-specific conditions

1 Criticisms of traditional marketing

Learning objectives

After reading this chapter, you should be able to:

- Analyse the main assumptions of the marketing mix framework.

- Critically evaluate the relevance of the marketing framework in today's markets.

- Discuss the importance of customer retention.

Introduction

This chapter will examine the marketing mix framework, which has dominated the teaching and practice of marketing for the last 50 years. It will trace the development of marketing during that period and highlight the changes which have taken place; for example, studies on the profitability of customer retention, globalisation and increased competition, and developments in new technology. These render the framework relied upon by traditional marketing largely redundant as an approach to the discipline, at least in some sectors. The chapter will discuss criticisms of the framework for treating customers as passive agents as well as for being transaction orientated. It will propose that today marketing is increasingly about gaining competitive advantage and that RM is the best way to achieve that objective in the long run.

The inadequacy of the marketing mix framework of marketing

The development of the marketing concept

There were different schools of marketing in the first part of the twentieth century, but there is no universal agreement as to the origins of marketing theory. It is, however, generally agreed that marketing as it is known today – the marketing mix approach – began to take shape during the 1950s and 1960s in the mass consumer goods markets of the USA.

The original architects of the concept were authors such as Levitt, Borden, McCarthy and Kotler. They helped to create the marketing mix or marketing management approach to marketing as an alternative to the production and sales concepts, stressing that business success depended on identifying and satisfying customer needs.

Marketing mix management

Borden (1964) proposed that the component activities of marketing could be explained and understood within a framework which he termed the *marketing mix*. The mix consisted of twelve ingredients:

1. Product planning
2. Pricing
3. Branding
4. Channels of distribution
5. Personal selling
6. Advertising
7. Promotions
8. Packaging
9. Display
10. Servicing
11. Physical handling
12. Fact-finding and analysis.

Borden called the marketing executive a *mixer of ingredients*, and suggested that the marketing manager mixed the ingredients within the limitations of the market forces. Borden did not, however, offer the mix as a universal formula for conducting marketing, and stated that the list of the elements was one that he had observed and used in his teaching, but that others might build a different list.

McCarthy (1960) later simplified the mix into one that contained only four ingredients: Product, Price, Place and Promotion. This was a seductively simple and easily understood framework for both teaching and learning of marketing and has since formed the basic framework and structure of virtually all marketing textbooks. It has also been widely adopted by practitioners.

According to the marketing mix approach, marketing is said to be about selling the right product, at the right price, at the right place with the right promotion, i.e. management of the marketing mix. Hence, marketing taught on this basis is also known as the marketing management theory of marketing. Various authors have since proposed the addition of further Ps to the list. This is illustrated in Table 1.1.

Criticisms of the marketing mix framework

In the late 1970s and early 1980s a number of writers began to criticise the marketing mix theory. Some of these criticisms, for example by Gronroos, were rather harsh, considering that Bordon and McCarthy were writing when the field of knowledge was beginning to take shape and the technology for enabling a more sophisticated approach to marketing was unavailable.

Nevertheless, the advances in technology combined with further academic research have revealed a number of shortcomings in the marketing mix approach. These are discussed below.

Theoretical limitations

One of the main criticisms of the marketing mix, or the 4Ps framework, is that it is neither a theory nor a model but rather a tool, with much of its value depending on how it is used. In practice this tool has tended to emphasise the ingredients and the structure at the expense of the processes (Kent, 1986).

Gronroos (1997) has, in a similar vein, stated that marketing has never had a general theory and referred to the marketing mix paradigm as a straitjacket that fosters toolbox thinking. Instead, he proposes, marketing should be viewed as a multifaceted social process requiring a more relational approach. Gronroos has argued that the marketing mix is merely a list of variables, which is not a valid way of defining or describing a phenomenon.

Table 1.1

The marketing mix and proposed extension of the 4Ps

4Ps

McCarthy (1960) — Product, Price, Promotion, Place

5Ps

Judd (1987) — Product, Price, Promotion, Place, People

6Ps

Kotler (1984) — Product, Price, Promotion, Place, Political power, Public opinion-formation

7Ps

Booms and Bitner (1981) — Product, Price, Promotion, Place, Participants, Physical evidence, Process

15Ps

Baumgartner (1991) — Product/service, Price, Promotion, Place, People, Politics, Public relations, Probe, Partition, Prioritise, Position, Profit, Plan, Performance, Positive implementations

Source: Gummesson, E. (1994: 8) Making Relationship Marketing Operational', *International Journal of Service Industry Management*, 5, 5, 5–20.

This is because a list cannot possibly include every relevant element applicable in every situation. This is one of the main reasons why academics have tried to add further Ps to the list.

Practical limitations

Gronroos (1997) argues that the marketing mix approach is inadequate for operating according to the marketing concept, which advocates satisfying customer needs and wants. He believes that the four Ps approach constitutes a production-oriented definition of marketing. Gronroos postulates that, perhaps, Borden's original idea of marketing mix ingredients acquired popularity as an easy way of teaching, and also because it fitted the environment that was typical of North America in the 1950s and 1960s. This environment was characterised by the marketing of consumer packaged goods in mass markets, with a highly competitive distribution system and a mass media that was hugely commercial. This is clearly representative of a limited aspect of the domain and process of marketing (Baker, 2000). Furthermore, the development of industrial and services marketing in the 1970s and 1980s has exposed the limited applicability of the mix (Gummesson, 1993).

Gummesson (1999) has proposed that the marketing mix approach is supplier oriented as opposed to customer oriented, and has pointed out that it excludes or treats marginally such things as complaints handling, invoicing, design and production. He has further argued that the marketing mix is narrowly limited to functions and not a base for marketing oriented management.

Others (see for example, Baker, 2000) have further stressed that the marketing mix approach treats customers as persons to whom something is done rather than persons for whom something is done. Whether or not this view of consumers was workable in the last century, it clearly underestimates the sophistication of today's consumer.

Limitations on the scope of marketing within the organisation

Baker (2000) has argued that the marketing mix approach treats marketing as a functional activity in its own right and so creates the potential for conflict with other functional areas, discouraging others in the organisation from participating in marketing because it is the preserve of the marketing department. This hinders the adoption of the marketing concept by the whole organisation. In any case, it is doubtful if the marketing manager can always exercise full control over the four Ps. For example, variables such as sales, market share, profitability, labour and material costs are variables that a marketing manager can only hope to control indirectly. The responsibility for such factors may be shared with others outside the marketing function (Kent, 1986). Additionally:

> There may be market, parent company, legal or other constraints on the price or prices that may be charged for a product. The price for any

individual product may be determined by the prices charged for other products in the firm's range; prices charged in the shops to the final customers may be largely outside the firm's control.

(Kent, 1986: 148)

Kent (1986) has further argued that the marketing mix approach focuses attention on decisions relating to individual products, and assumes that such decisions can be taken in isolation from what is happening to a company's other products. Put simply, marketing managers often do not have as much control over the variables of the mix as the textbooks suggest.

Limitations on long-term focus

Peppers and Rogers (1995) have offered further criticism of the traditional approach to marketing. They have argued that growth driven by mass marketing encourages businesses to chase short-term profits based on transaction volume, hence possibly forgoing the opportunity for long-term prosperity.

Studies on the profitability of customer retention

Various studies show that it is more beneficial to retain existing customers than to recruit new ones. The benefits come in the form of increased profits (Reichheld and Sasser, 1990) and reduced costs and lower expenditure on marketing (Evans and Laskin, 1994). This is partly because it costs money, in advertising and promotional offers, to get new customers. It makes good business sense to keep existing customers happy instead of devoting high levels of marketing effort to stemming customer turnover, when every customer who leaves has to be replaced so that the company can merely stand still (Barnes, 1994). Additionally, it is often easier to persuade existing customers who know and trust a company to spend a bigger share of their purse with that company, buying both more of the original product which they bought and also other products; for example selling life insurance to a customer who originally bought car insurance from the company. Hence, there is a better opportunity for cross-selling if one retains customers. These customers are also more likely to promote a company's products by word of mouth. However, one must be cautious about the figures that are produced in books which claim that the figure quoted is applicable to all industries, to all companies and at all times. Each company must carry out its own investigation to determine the possible savings to be made. Some companies may find that the cost of a RM programme is far higher than the benefits that they may accrue from it.

Changes in the marketing environment

Further reasons for the inadequacy of the marketing mix relate to environmental factors which have developed since the 1960s.

Globalisation and internationalisation of markets

Globalisation refers to the convergence of demand across the world and attempts by companies to offer the same, or very similar, products across national boundaries. Encouraged by the World Trade Organisation (WTO), as well as the International Monetary Fund (IMF) and the World Bank, most countries are increasingly eliminating trade barriers and opening their doors to foreign companies. Coupled with the demise of the Eastern European communist bloc and China recently joining the WTO, the flow of goods and services across national boundaries is greater than it has ever been. Russia has now expressed a desire to join the WTO.

The trend has resulted in a massive choice for customers around the world and intensified the competition in the marketplace. Suppliers are faced with a customer who no longer has to contend with local or national products when a typical store carries products from hundreds of suppliers from around the world. Hence, acquiring and retaining customers has become more difficult than it was in the previous decades.

New developments in technology

Businesses have sought to have an ongoing relationship with their customers for centuries. Mass marketing and the huge growth in the size of many businesses since the 1950s and the fact that they were targeting thousands, sometimes millions, of customers took them away from the practice. Customer traffic (the number of customers coming through the door), the number of hits scored (number of sales made) and share of the market became the main preoccupation of marketers. Relationship building was either forgotten or thought to be impossible with the large number of customers that companies were courting and doing business with. Recent developments in technology, however, have made it possible for even the largest of companies to build individual relationships with their customers. If the best marketing could offer thus far was a product for a particular segment of hundreds or thousands, today a product can be customised for microsegments and even for segments of one.

> The marketplace of the future is undergoing a technology driven metamorphosis – made possible by interactive television, consensual databases, electronic couponing, fax machines in the home and more opportunities for electronic interactions with individual customers... The new marketing system enables marketers to mass-customise products, tailor services and personalise dialogue with consumers.
>
> (Peppers and Rogers, 1995: 48)

Increasing brand promiscuity among customers

Various factors have contributed to customers becoming more sophisticated and demanding. These include the considerable increase in competition in consumer markets resulting in increasing choice among customers, coupled with increasing affluence in the last two to three decades. Even when the products offered are satisfactory, customers still exercise their right to go from one supplier to another in order to purchase the products they need at a better price, or merely to experience change and variety. Consequently, suppliers are having to think of different ways of keeping customers loyal in order to survive and prosper. While some suppliers are turning to such tactical devices as loyalty cards, others adopt a more strategic and philosophical approach to gaining customer loyalty through designing genuine RM programmes.

The idea of engaging in RM and earning customer loyalty is particularly important in mature industries, where the core products offered by the various suppliers are similar, and therefore not an effective basis for creating differential advantage. Bowen and Shoemaker (1998) refer to the example of general managers from ITT Sheraton in Asia, who when shown pictures of hotel rooms from their own chain and three of their competitors, could not identify the brand of one room – not even their own.

In such a competitive environment customer satisfaction is essential for a company's survival. Unless a company is in a monopoly situation, it has to constantly strive to satisfy its customers, indeed to exceed customer expectations, and delight them, in order to be successful. However customer satisfaction, though a necessary step towards achieving customer retention, does not on its own guarantee customer retention and many firms lose customers along the way (see Chapter three).

Mattson (1997) has argued that the discussion of service quality has often been reduced to trivial problems of measuring service quality and debating whether quality or satisfaction comes first. The writer proposes that more time and effort ought to be spent on relationships.

The realisation that satisfaction does not lead to loyalty

As discussed above, it is increasingly recognised that customer satisfaction does not equal customer loyalty. Discussing the luxury hotel industry sector, Bowen and Shoemaker (1998) give a number of reasons as to why a satisfied hotel guest may not wish to come back to the hotel, i.e. may not become loyal. They argue that a traveller may never visit the area again and hence may never have the opportunity to come to the hotel again. Additionally, some guests seek variety and wish to visit different hotels on different occasions, while others remain price sensitive and will look for the best deal. Similar reasons apply to most markets.

Fragmentation of the media

In the 1960s and 1970s most countries had a few radio stations and an even smaller number of TV channels. Today in the developed, and even in the developing, world the average listener or viewer is faced with endless choices thanks to satellite TV, deregulation of radio services, radio on the Internet, etc. The number of newspapers, magazines, free papers, specialist publications and so on has also increased considerably. This means that the media are segmenting audiences more narrowly, and hence making it more difficult to reach a wide audience through the same medium. Peppers and Rogers (1995) point out that potential customers are now scattered into a variety of media audiences and that the overall effectiveness of advertising is declining.

It is argued therefore that to inform and persuade customers as well as to retain them, methods other than mass advertising ought to be given prominence.

The continuing search for added value and competitive advantage

Increasing competition, similarity in core products and lack of customer loyalty is leading companies to search for new ways of gaining competitive advantage over their rivals. It is generally accepted that products can be marketed at three levels of product: the core, the actual and the augmented product (see for example, Kotler *et al.*, 2001). The *core product* consists of the basic benefit for which the product is purchased, or the main need that the product satisfies. For example, the basic need fulfilled by the motor car is that for personal transport. Henry Ford's approach to the marketing of the model T focused on the core product; a standard, mass-produced offering. The *actual product* was based on styling, packaging, brand image, quality and price benefits.

As competition intensifies, improvements in production and marketing intelligence facilitate the launch of 'me-too' products and the actual benefits become increasingly similar. This can lead to customer confusion and disillusionment, forcing companies to compete at the third level; the *augmented product*. This level involves the provision of benefits that support the purchase or consumption experience, but are not part of the actual product. Examples include sales support, guarantees and after sales care. Daewoo's early success in establishing a foothold in the UK car market can be attributed to the brand's focus on the augmented product. In a market where products offered similar functional benefits, Daewoo stressed not the product attributes, but the measures in place to enhance the purchase and ownership experience.

It is widely accepted now that concentrating on the core product is not an effective way of gaining and sustaining competitive advantage. It is suggested that RM offers a vehicle for product augmentation which can lead to sustainable competitive advantage. Effective relationships, unlike core or actual product benefits, are difficult to copy. Since they are based on trust and commitment (this is discussed in Chapter three) it is difficult to lure away a company's customers. This is understandable in that customers often commit themselves to a particular supplier in order to reduce, through familiarity, the degree of risk and anxiety in purchasing, and to obtain customised products for their particular needs. Also, many customers distrust advertising and large firms. Hence a new approach to marketing, that creates an opportunity to build trust and confidence between the supplier and the customer to increase retention rates, is needed. Barnes (1994) has said that strategic competitive advantage can no longer be based on the core product offering and that corporate profitability is now clearly linked to satisfying existing customers.

It should be stressed that whilst RM is a vehicle for augmenting the total offer, it should not be viewed as something that can be 'bolted on' to existing offerings. The successful delivery of RM benefits requires fundamental changes in the way that the organisation approaches marketing management. The nature of these changes will become apparent in the following chapters.

Summary

The marketing mix theory of marketing, as taught and practised in the last fifty years or so, has come under increasing criticism of late. Limitations have been identified in the theoretical and practical scope of this approach to marketing. In addition, recent studies on the profitability of retaining existing customers, developments in technology and the globalisation of markets coupled with increasingly demanding customers has rendered the approach inadequate. It is argued that the theory began to acquire popularity because it was easy to use as a framework for teaching and practising the subject. It was also probably more relevant to the mass consumer goods markets of the USA in the 1950s. In today's increasingly competitive marketing environment, with services dominating the advanced countries' economies, a short-term transactional approach to dealing with customers is thought to be inadequate. There is a need for a new approach to retain customers, to gain their loyalty and to establish competitive approach. This is the subject of the next chapter.

Case Study   *A letter to the bank manager*

Although this case is a letter from a customer of an American bank, it highlights the frustrations commonly experienced by customers of British banks. In July 2002 British Members of Parliament heavily criticised the high street banks for running a monopoly, overcharging and giving poor customer service.

This letter was received by a bank and printed in an American newspaper.

I am writing to thank you for bouncing the cheque with which I endeavoured to pay my plumber last month. By my calculations some three nanoseconds must have elapsed between his presenting the cheque and the arrival in my account of the funds needed to honour it.

I refer, of course, to the automatic monthly deposit of my entire salary, an arrangement which, I admit, has only been in place for eight

▶

years. You are to be commended for seizing that brief window of opportunity and also for debiting my account with $50 by way of penalty for the inconvenience I caused to your bank.

My thankfulness springs from the manner in which this incident has caused me to rethink my errant financial ways. You have set me on the path of fiscal righteousness. No more will our relationship be blighted by these unpleasant incidents, for I am restructuring my affairs, taking as my model the procedures, attitudes and conduct of your very bank. I can think of no greater compliment and I know you will be excited and proud to hear it.

To this end, please be advised about the following changes. First, I have noticed that whereas I personally attend to your telephone calls and letters, when I try to contact you I am confronted by the impersonal ever-changing, pre-recorded, faceless entity which your bank has become. From now on I, like you, choose only to deal with a flesh and blood person.

My mortgage and loan repayments will, therefore and hereafter, no longer be automatic, but will arrive at your bank by cheque, addressed personally and confidentially to an employee of your branch, whom you must nominate.

You will be aware that it is an offence under the Postal Act for any other person to open such an envelope. Please find attached an application for contact status which I require your chosen employee to complete. I am sorry it runs to eight pages, but in order that I know as much about him or her as your bank knows about me, there is no alternative.

Please note that all copies of his or her medical history must be countersigned by a Justice of the Peace, that the physician signature be legible and that the mandatory details of his/her financial situation (income, debts, assets and liabilities) must be accompanied by document proof.

In due course I will issue your employee with a PIN number which he/she must quote in all dealings with me. I regret that it cannot be shorter than 28 digits but, again, I have modelled it on the number of button presses required to access my account balance on your phone bank service. As they say, imitation is the sincerest form of flattery.

Let me level the playing field even further by introducing you to my new telephone system which you will notice is very much like yours. My authorised contact at your bank, the only person with whom I will have any dealings, may call me at any time and will be answered by an automated voice. By pressing buttons on the phone, he/she will be guided through an extensive set of menus:

1. To make an appointment to see me.
2. To query a missing repayment.
3. To make a general complaint or inquiry.
4. To transfer the call to my living room in case I am there, extension of living room to be communicated at the time the call is received.
5. To transfer the call to my bedroom in case I am still sleeping, extension of bedroom to be communicated at the time the call is received.
6. To transfer the call to my toilet in case I am attending to a call of nature, extension of toilet to be communicated at the time the call is received.
7. To transfer the call to my mobile phone in case I am not at home.
8. To leave a message on my computer a password to access my computer is required. Password will be communicated at a later date to the contact.
9. To return to the main menu and listen carefully to options 1 to 8. The contact will then be put on hold, pending the attention of my

automated answering service. While this may on occasion involve a lengthy wait, uplifting music will play for the duration. This month I've chosen a refrain from The Best Of Woody Guthrie.

Oh, the banks are made of marble
With a guard at every door
And the vaults are filled with silver
The miners sweated for.

After 20 minutes of that, our mutual contact will probably know it off by heart.

On a more serious note, we come to the matter of cost. As your bank has often pointed out, the ongoing drive for greater efficiency comes at a cost, a cost which you have always been quick to pass on to me.

Let me repay your kindness by passing some costs back. First, there is the matter of advertising material you send me. This I will read for a

fee of $2.00 per page. Inquiries from your nominated contact will be billed at $5 per minute of my time spent in response. Any debits to my account, as, for example, in the matter of the penalty for the dishonoured cheque will be passed back to you.

My new phone service runs at 75 cents a minute (even Woody Guthrie doesn't come for free), so you would be well advised to keep your inquiries brief and to the point. Regrettably, but again following your example, I must also levy an establishment fee to cover the setting up of this new arrangement.

May I wish you a happy, if ever-so-slightly less prosperous, New Year.

Your humble client

Discussion questions

1. What are the real problems that the customer is highlighting?
2. How can banks increase the quality of service they offer and increase customer satisfaction?
3. Why are the big banks, despite their massive annual profits, seen by most customers as giving poor service; and why, often, can these customers not be bothered to change banks?

Suggested reading

For a deeper analysis of the marketing mix and its shortcomings, interested students could read the following:

Kent, R.A. (1986) 'Faith in four Ps: an alternative', *Journal of Marketing Management*, 2, 2, 145–154.
Brownlie, D. and Saren, M. (1991) 'The four Ps of the marketing concept: Prescriptive, Polemical, Permanent and Problematical', *European Journal of Marketing*, 26, 4, 34–47.
For an analysis of the historical development of marketing see various papers contained in:
Baker, M.J. (ed.) (2000) *Marketing Theory – A Student Text*, London: Thomson Learning.

References

Baker, M.J. (2000) 'Marketing – philosophy or function?' in M.J. Baker (ed.) *Marketing Theory – A Student Text*, London: Thomson Learning.

Barnes, J.G. (1994) 'Close to the customer: but is it really a relationship?', *Journal of Marketing Management,* 10, 561–570.

Borden, N.H. (1964) 'The concept of the marketing mix', *Journal of Advertising Research,* June, 2–7.

Bowen, T. and Shoemaker, S. (1998) 'Loyalty: a strategic commitment', *Cornel Hotel and Restaurant Administration Quarterly,* 39, 1, 12–24.

Evans, J.R. and Laskin, R.L. (1994) 'The relationship marketing process: a conceptualisation and application', *Industrial Marketing Management,* 23, 5, 439–452.

Gronroos, C. (1997) 'From marketing mix to relationship marketing – towards a paradigm shift in marketing', *Management Decision,* 35, 4, 332–339.

Gummesson, E. (1993) 'Broadening and specifying relationship marketing', invited paper, *Monash Colloquium on Relationship Marketing,* Monash University, Melbourne, Australia, 1–4 August.

Gummesson, E. (1994) 'Making relationship marketing operational', *International Journal of Service Industry Management,* 5, 5, 5–20.

Gummesson, E. (1999) *Total Relationship Marketing – Rethinking Marketing Management: From 4Ps to 30 Rs,* Oxford: Butterworth-Heinemann.

Kent, R.A. (1986) 'Faith in four Ps: an alternative', *Journal of Marketing Management,* 2, 2, 145–154.

Kotler, P., Armstrong, G., Saunders, J. and Wong, V. (2001) *Principles of Marketing,* Harlow: Pearson Education.

Mattson, J. (1997) 'Beyond service quality in search of relationship values', *Management Decision,* 35, 4, 302–303.

McCarthy, E.J. (1960) *Basic Marketing,* Homewood, IL: Irwin.

Peppers, D. and Rogers, M. (1995) 'A new marketing paradigm: share of customer, not market share', *Managing Service Quality,* 5, 3, 48–51.

Reichheld, F.F. and Sasser, W.E. (1990) 'Zero defections: quality comes to services', *Harvard Business Review,* Sep.–Oct., 105–111.

2 Characteristics of RM

Learning objectives

After reading this chapter, you should be able to:

- Explain what is meant by a relationship in marketing.

- Distinguish the main characteristics of RM from those of TM.

- Define RM and analyse the main components of the concept.

- Identify the main aim of RM.

- Evaluate the applicability of RM to different markets and customers.

Introduction

RM is offered as an alternative strategy to the traditional marketing mix approach, a means of obtaining sustainable competitive advantage and the best way to retain customers in the long run. This chapter begins by defining RM and proceeds to what is meant by a relationship and with whom the company should have a relationship.

The main characteristics of RM are then identified and compared and contrasted with those of marketing mix or transaction marketing (TM). This is followed by a discussion of different levels of RM and its benefits for customers and companies as well as a discussion of the relationship continuum.

Although the content of this chapter is largely theoretical, it provides the rationale for the more practical techniques discussed in later chapters.

RM defined

Two decades have passed since Berry (1983) first used the term RM, and longer since the concept has been studied under different names. Indeed, Culliton (1948: 26) used the term 'customer relationships' well over fifty years ago. Yet there is still no universally agreed definition of RM, let alone a universally agreed theory. According to Buttle (1996) RM has yet to acquire uncontested status and meaning. Palmer (1996) has argued that discussion of RM has failed to position the concept, and that consequently interpretations range from sales incentives to a core business philosophy.

The processes involved and how far within the micro and macro environments of a company RM should be applied are under debate, and will continue to be so for some time to come.

There are, however, indications that a consensus is on the horizon, based on the definition of RM by Gronroos and the commitment–trust theories of RM as proposed, among others, by Morgan and Hunt (1994). Harker (1999) has examined 26 random definitions of RM and pointed to the differing opinions about what should and should not be at the core of what constitutes RM. He has pointed out that one of the main reasons for the difference of opinion is that those who have contributed to the development of RM theory come from an extremely varied socio-political heritage and academic background. He rightly concludes that Gronroos's definition is the best in terms of its coverage of the underlying conceptualisations of relationship marketing and its acceptability throughout the RM community.

According to Gronroos, marketing in relational terms means:

> To establish, maintain and enhance relationships with customers and other partners, at a profit so that the objectives of the parties involved are met. This is achieved by mutual exchange and fulfilment of promises.
>
> (Gronroos, 1997: 327)

This book adopts this definition, and the framework it follows is largely built around this definition.

What is a relationship?

In order to understand that direct marketing and database marketing per se and many other types of interaction between suppliers and customers are not RM, and to gain a better understanding of the concept, a discussion of the meaning of the word relationship in a marketing context is required. The marketing context is emphasised here because a philosophical or socio-psychological examination of what constitutes a relationship would require a significant volume of its own and is not, in any case, necessary for the purposes of this book.

Does a relationship exist merely because a supplier and a customer do business with one another from time to time, or can it only exist when both parties perceive a relationship to exist between them and conduct business according to certain obligations and mutual understandings? Does repeat purchase mean there is a relationship between a supplier and a customer?

It is generally accepted that a series of transactions where the supplier and buyer do not really know each other does not constitute a relationship. Belois (1998) points out that in consumer markets the term RM is often employed because a database is being used to underpin a supplier's marketing activities. In such cases customers are usually not conscious that they are participants in what is meant to be a RM campaign.

For the purposes of RM the term relationship refers to voluntary repeat business between a supplier and a customer where the behaviour is planned, cooperative, intended to continue for mutual benefit and is perceived by both parties as a relationship. This approach means that repeat purchase through lack of alternative suppliers or the operation of lock-in programmes and loyalty schemes cannot be defined as RM.

Relationships with different stakeholders

In this text it is the relationship between a company and its customers which is the focus of attention, but for RM to be successful, a long-term and mutually trusting and committed relationship with other stakeholders is also required.

Morgan and Hunt (1994) discuss four categories and ten types of relationship, while Gummesson (1999) outlines thirty types of relationship. The six markets model by Christopher *et al.* (1991: 21–31), however, seems to have gained a wider acceptance. The model includes customer markets, internal markets (treating individuals and departments within an organisation as customers and suppliers), referral markets (referral and advocate sources), supplier markets, potential employee markets (those who may potentially work for the company) and 'influence' markets (government, financial organisations, etc.) (Figure 2.1).

Figure 2.1

The Six Markets model

Source: Christopher, Payne and Ballantyne (1991). Reprinted by permission of Elsevier Science Ltd.

Based on the six markets model, the emphasis of this book will be on the customer markets. Chapters four to seven, however, will also deal with supplier and internal markets in some depth, while brief references will be made to the other three. This apportions discussion according to the relative significance of these markets to the task of RM.

Deciding who to have a relationship with

RM is not advocated in all situations and with all customers; only where it would be profitable for the company and with those customers who wish to engage in such a relationship.

Gummesson (1994) points out that *some marketing is best handled as TM.* Gronroos adds:

> In some situations, if the customers are not in a relational mode or if a relational strategy cannot be justified from an economic standpoint, it may be more profitable and suitable to adopt a transactional intent and create a marketing strategy that is transactional in nature.
>
> (Gronroos, 1997: 409)

Palmer (1996: 18) proposes that 'Although relationship marketing may be very attractive for many products and markets, its adoption may be inappropriate in others.' He suggests four main reasons for this:

- Parties in a transaction may not necessarily wish to forgo the chance for opportunistic behaviour.
- One or both parties may view the relational exchange as a short-term means of acquiring those competencies that will allow them to bargain from a position of strength in the future.
- The cost of loyalty schemes could make them uneconomical.
- Buyer–seller relationships could develop to a point where they become anti-competitive.

Table 2.1 Relational and transactional customers	Customer mode	Customers' expectations and reactions
	Transactional mode	Transactional customers are looking for solutions to their needs at an acceptable price, and they do not appreciate contact from the supplier or service provider between purchases.
	Active relational mode	Active relational customers are looking for opportunities to interact with the supplier or service provider in order to get additional value. A lack of such contacts makes them disappointed, because the value inherent in the relationship is missing.
	Passive relational mode	Passive relational customers are looking for the knowledge that they could contact the supplier or service provider if they wanted to. In this sense they too are seeking contact, but they seldom respond to invitations to interact.

Source: Gronroos, 2000: 36. Reprinted with permission of John Wiley & Sons, Ltd.

Gronroos (2000: 36) distinguishes between those customers who wish to have a transactional exchange with suppliers and those seeking either an active or passive relationship with them (Table 2.1).

Conditions that are conducive to RM

The question of who a supplier pursues a relationship with and the conditions that are conducive to RM are interrelated. Szmigin and Bourne (1998) argue that the value of the relationship, and by implication the desire to commit to it, will depend on the nature of the service, the nature of the consumer and the nature of the situation.

Berry (1983), discussing the service sector, identifies three conditions for the applicability of RM:

1. The customer ought to show a continuing and periodic desire for the service;
2. The service customer must be able to select the service provider;
3. There must be a choice of suppliers available to the customer.

Berry adds that very few service firms sell one-time services and in most cases the above conditions apply. This lends itself to building relationships with customers. He further asserts (1995) that where there is a demand for services which are continuously or periodically delivered and that are 'personally important, variable in quality, and or/complex' there is potential for RM. Additionally, he points out that high involvement services, such as banking, insurance and hairstyling services, have the characteristics which lend themselves to relationship building – importance, variability, complexity and involvement. Berry believes that generally the intangibility of services and the heterogeneity of labour-intensive services encourages customer loyalty. He gives auto repair business as an example – the firm would want loyal customers and those customers also would want to find a repair firm to whom they could stay loyal.

Contrast with TM

A useful aid to understanding RM is to contrast it with TM, so called because the traditional marketing mix approach to marketing deals mainly with customer *getting* rather than customer *keeping*. In TM companies have focused on single sales and closing individual deals. Mass advertising and sales promotion campaigns have been aimed at selling as many products as possible to as many customers as possible. In most cases, as long as customers have walked through the door, little concern has been shown as to whether they are new customers or existing ones. In many business sectors, for example insurance services, historically a heavy emphasis has been placed on customer getting rather than customer keeping. This situation has been made worse by the typical reward structures existing in many companies, in which sales staff are given low basic salaries which can only be topped up by commission earned from making sales to new customers. Consequently, marketers have put greater effort into attracting prospects and turning them into customers. Product features, gimmicks and sales promotion are the main tools used to win customers, but once the sale has been made the customer is often regarded as a nuisance unless he wishes to make another purchase.

RM focuses on customer *keeping*, rather than purely customer *getting*. Importance is attached to the lifetime value of a customer to a company rather than the value of a single sale. In consequence, a high level of importance is attached to customer service, quality and product benefits rather than product features and gimmicks. Contact with customers is encouraged and provision of quality and adherence to customer orientation is regarded as a concern for the entire organisation. RM attempts to satisfy customer needs and wants as closely as possible by trying to get to know customers individually, or at least in much smaller segments than in the past, and to tailor products for them accordingly rather than offer 'one size fits all' products.

Transaction marketing	Relationship marketing
● Focus on single sale	● Focust on customer retention
● Orientation on product features	● Orientation on product benefits
● Short timescale	● Long timescale
● Little emphasis on customer service	● High customer service
● Limited customer commitment	● High customer commitment
● Moderate customer contact	● High customer contact
● Quality is primarily a concern of production	● Quality is the concern of all

Adapted from Christopher *et al.* (1991: 9). Reprinted with permission of Elsevier Science Ltd.

Customer retention and RM

For the reasons discussed in Chapter one, customer retention is a major concern of many companies. Advocates of RM believe that adherence to a genuine customer orientation philosophy and operating from a platform of RM can enable businesses to retain their customers by gaining their loyalty and commitment. Hence, it is suggested that RM is the most effective way to retain customers on a mutually beneficial basis and over a period of time. Retention devices such as coupons, loyalty schemes, exit penalties, tie-ins and other structural ties which make exit difficult (see Figure 2.2) are regarded as weak variations of RM or as not RM at all, even though their operators may claim that they are. The main objective of RM, for compa-

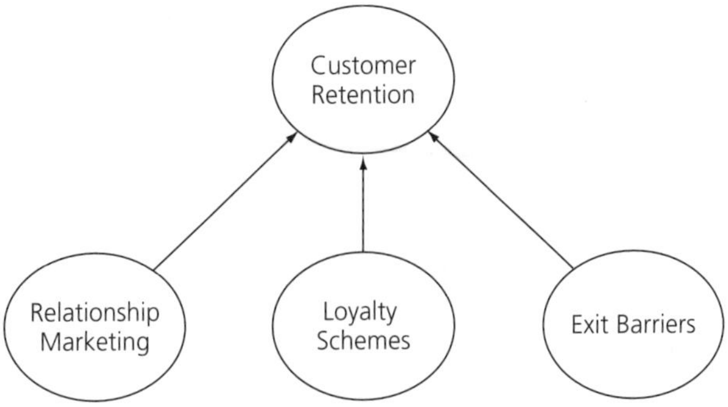

Figure 2.2

Methods of
customer retention

nies adopting it, is to retain customers by gaining their loyalty based on mutual commitment. Due to the similarity of core products and the difficulty of differentiating them on the basis of physical attributes, organisations are adopting RM in an attempt to encourage key customers either to stay with them or to come back. In other words, the objective is to create loyal customers by means other than economic factors and product attributes. Thinking of marketing in terms of *having customers*, not merely *acquiring customers* is crucial for service firms (Berry, 1983).

Loyalty is taken here to mean a commitment by a customer to a supplier which is based on choice. According to Lovelock *et al.* (1999), in a business context loyalty describes

> A customer's willingness to continue patronising a firm over the long term, purchasing and using its goods and services on a repeated and preferably exclusive basis, and voluntarily recommending the firm's products to friends and associates.
>
> (Lovelock *et al.*, 1999: 183)

Bowen and Shoemaker (1998: 13) assert that 'In essence, relationship marketing means developing customers as partners, a process much different than traditional transaction-based marketing'. Peppers and Rogers (1995: 48) add: 'The objective of this new marketing paradigm – called "one-to-one" marketing or "relationship marketing" is to give an enterprise the capacity to treat its customers as individuals and thereby develop a continuing business relationship with them.'

It is suggested that in today's competitive environment and with customer choice prevailing, RM offers the best route to gaining competitive advantage by offering customers added value in the form of customised solutions.

On the other hand, RM has been hailed as a paradigm shift (Gronroos, 1994; Gummesson, 1999). According to Gummesson

> A paradigm shift implies that a science or discipline is given a new foundation, with new values, new assumptions, or new methods. The accepted and established must be set aside.
>
> (Gummesson, 1999: 252).

Hence today RM is regarded as a more relevant approach in the present world of marketing – one that has more logical underpinnings and is more in tune with the basic philosophy of marketing, i.e. customer orientation.

The RM approach presents key strategic and tactical implications for the firm and major changes in the philosophy of the business are required. Using direct marketing techniques and developing partnerships alone are not sufficient (Gronroos, 1996).

Based on Gronroos's definition the following are the main characteristics of RM.

Characteristics of RM

Long-term orientation/horizon

Long-term orientation is a key feature of RM. It assesses success in terms of how long a customer is kept in the relationship and the share of 'customer wallet'. RM involves estimating customer lifetime value and engaging in relationships based on the value of those relationships over a number of years.

Gummesson (1999) highlights long-term collaboration and *win–win* as a key feature of RM. That means viewing suppliers, customers and others as partners rather than opposite parties. This view promotes collaboration and the creation of mutual value, RM should bring about a win–win rather than a win–lose situation created by the adversarial nature of transactional marketing.

Commitment and fulfilment of promises

RM implies a long-term relationship and forsaking of other suppliers by the customer, as well as mutual exchange of information. This suggests that there ought to be trust between the parties; that each party believes in the integrity of the other to keep their promise and to deliver on promises; also that each party believes the relationship to be valuable enough to invest in and to commit to. Nurturing of trust and commitment is particularly important as it is clear now that satisfaction alone does not necessarily lead to customer loyalty. Satisfied customers may still wish to look elsewhere for bargains, change/novelty, etc. RM relies on fostering a bond between the customer and the supplier which is glued with empathy. Bonding is the result of the customer and supplier acting in a unified way towards the achievement of desired goals (Callaghan *et al.*, 1995) and empathy is the dimension of a business relationship that enables the two parties involved to see the situation from the other's perspective and to understand their desires and goals (Yau *et al.*, 2000).

Satisfaction, trust and commitment are important and key concepts within RM and will be discussed separately in Chapter three.

Customer share not market share

RM shifts the emphasis from concentrating on gaining share of market and rewarding its employees for the new business which they bring in. Instead, it concentrates on keeping customers and attempting to gain a bigger share of their 'wallet' by selling more of the same product or by cross-selling to them. This is a very important shift, because traditional marketing puts the emphasis on market share and success is usually measured in a short timescale, i.e. growth in market share per annum. For example, Day *et al.* (1979), in what is regarded as a 'classical' paper, and from a traditional platform, say that share of market is a crucial tool for the evaluation of performance and for using as a guide for advertising, sales force and other budget allocations.

Concentrating on customer share implies a long-term orientation and requires that success is measured and rewarded differently. According to Peppers and Rogers (1995), this approach implies that a customer with high potential is treated as an individual whose needs are addressed and an attempt is made to persuade him to buy more of the company's products during the lifetime of the relationship.

Customer lifetime value

The lifetime value of a customer is a key element in the practice of RM. It is not economical for a supplier to invest in long-term relationships with all customers – not that all customers would necessarily want such a relationship. The supplier has to identify those customers who are willing to enter a long-term relationship with his company, forecast their lifetime with the company, and then calculate those customers' lifetime values in order to identify the ones with whom it will be profitable for the company to have a relationship. RM costs money and maintaining a customer can be expensive, hence long-term customers should be selected carefully. Calculating a customer's lifetime value is not a precise science, and each company will need to experiment and improve those techniques that are used to predict how much business a customer is likely to do with them.

Generally, a customer's purchase profile, as well as the purchase profile of the segment to which the customer belongs, are studied and an estimate is made of the amount of purchases which the customer is likely to make over a given period and therefore the profit the company can expect from the customer. An estimate of the possible referral business by the customer is added to that figure. Then, on the minus side, the cost of products to be sold to the customer as well as the cost of keeping him in the relationship are calculated. This is subtracted from the first figure to show if the lifetime value will be attractive to the company.

Two-way dialogue

A further requirement of RM is the facilitation of a two-way dialogue between the supplier and the customer in order to identify needs and to find solutions. Indeed, RM is ultimately about partnering and partnerships are built on, and maintained by, dialogue and communication. A properly designed RM system should provide ample opportunity for the customer to initiate communication with the supplier. The flow of information must be a two-way process. While this happens frequently in industrial and business-to-business sectors, it ought to be a part of RM in mass consumer goods and services markets too. This is now possible with the continuous improvements in technology. Gummesson (1999), viewing RM as relationships, networks and interaction, proposes that 'This initiative to action cannot be left to a supplier or a single party of the network, everyone in a network, can, and should, be active.'

Wolfe (1998: 449) has argued that if dialogue is not to ring hollow and to be fully satisfying to all parties involved there are three conditions which must be fulfilled:

- Conversational reciprocity: each party allowing the other to condition its responses, i.e. 'I influence you; you influence me.'
- Reciprocal empathy: each party reaches out to identify with and understand the other party's circumstances, feelings and motives.
- Reciprocal vulnerability: both sides in a relationship let down their guard to some level that remains safe and comfortable yet allows information to flow and trust to build.

The conditions set out above are in line with Berry's (1983) writings, and show that database and direct marketing, with their characteristic one-way flow of communication from supplier to customer, are not RM, even though 'relationship building' has now become a buzz phrase for the practitioners in those fields.

Customisation

Berry (1995) asserts that through RM service providers gain a better knowledge of the customer's requirements and needs. This knowledge can then be combined with social rapport built over a number of service encounters to tailor and customise the service to customer's specifications. An important requirement or feature of RM is that of customisation of product and communication for each customer. Customisation in mass markets, however, is rarely a totally unique offering for one customer and no other. Often it takes the form of using basic designs both for products and communication and adapting them to the requirements of individual customers, or microsegments of the markets. Hence, the term mass-customisation is used. Mass customisation is a recognition of the fact that today increasing competition and customer power is fragmenting mass markets into smaller markets, and that the 'one size fits all' strategy of traditional marketing no longer applies. It is an attempt to create added value, and many companies, utilising improvements in technology and flexible processes, are able to engage in the practice profitably. Mass customisation is an important advantage of RM to customers and one of the rewards they can expect in return for their commitment to a supplier.

Gilmore and Pine (1997) propose four approaches to customisation which companies can adopt in order to make it economically viable:

1. *Collaborative customisation* – this approach involves the company engaging in a dialogue with the customers, helping them to articulate their needs. The company then, through continued dialogue, identifies the offering that would precisely satisfy those needs and develops customised products for each individual customer. Gilmore and Pine suggest that this is most appropriate where customers cannot easily articulate their requirements, and where size, fit, functionality, performance, etc. are highly desirable features, e.g. a bridal dressmaker or a garden designer.

2. *Adaptive customisation* – an offering that is standard, but so designed that the customer can alter or customise it. This is appropriate where customers want to use the product differently on different occasions, e.g. interchangeable mobile phone covers, or a Mercedes Smart Car whose exterior panels may easily be changed to different styles.

3. *Cosmetic customisation* – customisation of the packaging of a standard offering, e.g. printing of the customer's name or logo on a standard product such as a T-shirt.

4. *Transparent customisation* – a situation where unique goods or services are offered to customers without informing them explicitly that the offering has been customised. This is appropriate where customers' needs are predictable, or when customers do not wish to repeat their requirement at every transaction, e.g. catalogue clothing retailer Lands End Inc. operates an intelligent website which uses information about the customer's previous purchases and those of customers with a similar profile to recommend product offers.

The relationship continuum

RM has a substantial record and history of acceptance and practice in the field of business-to-business and industrial marketing, where the number of people involved in the interaction is smaller than, and the nature of decision-making different to, the mass consumer markets to which RM is now being applied. The large number of customers in mass consumer markets and the variations in consumer needs and behaviour begs the question: Should a company attempt to have a relationship with all of its customers? The answer is a definite no. RM is very expensive and requires a great deal of effort. The company should concentrate on those customers with whom it would be profitable to have a relationship. This has to be further narrowed down to those customers who are willing to have a relationship with the company.

To help with this task, the company should identify where on the continuum of interaction its business and customers lie, and calculate customer lifetime values (Table 2.2).

Table 2.2	*RM*	*RM–TM continuum*	*TM*
	⇐		⇒
The RM–TM continuum	High customer anxiety		Low customer anxiety
	High degree of contact		High contact unnecessary
	Confidence, social and special benefits valued highly		Standard products
	Customers in favour of having a relationship with the supplier		Customers do not seek a relationship with the supplier

Levels of RM

Palmer (1996) identifies three levels of RM in which a supplier may engage:

1. *Tactical.* At this level RM is used as a tool for sales promotion. This is best exemplified by the numerous loyalty schemes which were introduced in the 1990s and, in practice, created loyalty to the incentive rather than to the supplier. These were easily copied and quickly lost their competitive advantage.

2. *Strategic.* At this level which, as with tactical level RM is supplier led, customers are tied in by a mixture of legal, economic, technological, geographical and time bonds. This type of strategy depends for its success on no legal or technological changes occurring so that the customer, through either lack of power or knowledge, stays with the supplier. Obviously this can easily turn into a form of detention, which is not what real RM is about.

3. *Philosophical.* Palmer proposes that, focusing on customer needs and operating from a genuine customer orientation platform, a philosophical commitment to RM turns away from products and product life cycles and focuses on customer relationship life cycles. A philosophical dedication to RM implies 'using all employees of an organisation to meet profitably the lifetime needs of target customers

better than competitors'. This approach to RM does not try to 'lock in' customers but to gain their affective commitment by giving the same in return. RM at its highest and most effective level requires a genuine customer orientation and the facilitation of partnering. It is important to recognise that there is a big difference between RM and mere customer retention.

Benefits of RM

Benefits for suppliers

We saw earlier how some regard RM as the best way to retain customers in the long run by creating added value for them and in so doing gaining competitive advantage in an increasingly competitive world. Bejou *et al.* (1998) refer to a number of studies which show that *where there is a heavy reliance on credence qualities* development and maintenance of satisfactory long-term relationships with customers could result in increased customer loyalty, and that this is particularly useful in intangible service industries. It has also been suggested that loyal customers created through RM strategies are more likely to respond favourably to cross-selling efforts by suppliers (Reichheld 1996; Mittal and Lassar, 1998), enabling companies to gain a bigger share of customer wallet. Additionally, Reichheld (1996) has pointed out that loyal customers take less of a company's time in personal selling, are less price sensitive, bring the benefit of word of mouth advertising and have no acquisition or set-up costs, e.g. lower interest rates offered by credit card companies to new customers who transfer their accounts from other credit card companies, or gift vouchers offered by insurance companies to new customers. Mittal and Lassar (1998) have argued that loyal customers mean spending less money on advertising, personal selling and the setting up of new accounts. Similarly, greater profitability is identified as an advantage of loyal customers because the cost of recruiting new customers and other marketing expenditure, e.g. advertising, is reduced.

Benefits for customers

RM requires customers to commit themselves to a particular supplier and to divulge a great deal of information about themselves to that provider. This means the customers have to trust the supplier and believe that the information they provide will be treated with confidence and sensitivity. More importantly this commitment means forgoing the benefits of acting opportunistically and not looking for bargains, discounts and better deals elsewhere, preferring instead the possible long-term benefits of doing business with the same supplier. The benefits which customers might thus expect, e.g. high quality service, customised products, feeling valued, reduction of anxiety, are often implicit in the literature. In fact, the majority of academic literature and research focuses on the benefits of RM for businesses.

One of the few studies which makes the benefit for customers its major focus of attention is that by Gwinner *et al.* (1998). Assuming that the customer has a choice among service providers and hence the option of switching, they posed the following questions from the customer's perspective:

1. What are benefits of maintaining a relationship with a service firm?
2. Which relational benefits are greatest?
3. Can predictions be made about relational benefits on the basis of the type of service?

Briefly, their conclusions were that:

1. Consumers engaged in long-term relationships with service providers experience three primary types of benefits: confidence, and social and special treatment. These benefits are experienced in addition to the core service benefits, and are applicable in all types of service relationships.
2. Confidence benefits are the most important. These relate to a reduced sense of anxiety, trusting the provider and reduced perceived risk and anxiety.
3. Confidence benefits are rated highly regardless of the type of service. Social (friendship/fraternisation with the provider) and special treatment benefits (economic and customisation) were more highly rated in services where there is a high degree of employee–customer contact, and rated least important in moderate contact situations and the standardised type of services where the opportunity for customisation and personal service was low.

Bejou *et al.* (1998) also refer to reduced perceived risk as a benefit of RM for customers.

Disadvantages of RM

Belois (1998: 256–270) summarises the five possible negative factors or disadvantages of engaging in a relationship put forward by Hakansson and Snehota (1995) as follows:

- *Loss of control* – developing a relationship inevitably results in some loss of control over matters such as resources, activities and intentions.
- *Indeterminateness* – a relationship is subject to continuous change, with an uncertain future which is, in part, determined by its history but also by current events and the parties' expectations of future events.

- *Resource demanding* – effort is required to build and maintain a relationship. This can be viewed as an investment and a maintenance cost.

- *Preclusion from other opportunities* – there is always a need to prioritise the use of limited resources and, hence, it may not be possible to pursue all of the individually attractive opportunities. Additionally, some relationships may be irreconcilable with an existing relationship.

- *Unexpected demands* – given that the two parties in a relationship will also have other relationships, establishing a relationship means being linked, if only passively, into a network of relationships. Such linkage to or membership of a network may bring with it obligations or expectations by others of specific behaviours.

It is clear, therefore, that engaging in a relationship requires time, cost and effort on the part of the parties involved and that these have to be weighed against the expected gains.

Further considerations

While enthusiasm for RM is shared by many, there are some who are sceptical and others who advise caution. RM is expensive, more suitable to some markets than others and not all customers want a relationship with suppliers. Additionally, courting of most valuable customers and giving them preferential treatment could create resentment on the part of the remaining customers, whose business could be a source of income that a business may not wish to forgo.

Fournier *et al.* (1998) have highlighted some of these concerns; the following is a summary of the points they made. Although they were concerned with the US market the same could be said to be true in the UK and in other European markets too.

- RM is in vogue – academics extol its merits while practitioners claim they are engaged in it.
- In the real world, however, consumers talk about the confusing, stressful, insensitive, and manipulative marketplace in which they feel trapped.
- Companies are taking 'delight' in increasingly using information about customers and adding 'features and services' to their offerings. 'But customers delight in neither. Customers cope.'
- Customer satisfaction is lower than ever before.
- Companies are rushing in to reap the rewards of RM while 'skimming over the fundamentals of relationship building', i.e. building customer trust and operating from a platform of customer orientation.

- The number of companies wishing to build a relationship with customers is too large, an overkill, and untenable for customers.

- A good relationship enjoys a balanced give and take, but all too often companies ask customers for 'friendship, loyalty, and respect' without giving them in return. The focus often seems to be on the company rather than on the customer.

- There are times when the treatment a company gives its valued customers leaves others, who also generate revenues and may be loyal but don't spend enough money, feeling unappreciated.

- Companies must start to behave in a way that enables them to regain customers' trust by treating them as valued partners. This is necessary because in the past marketers have generally acted to destroy customer respect and confidence.

- Additionally, customer intimacy and the way information about customers is handled must be thought through carefully and with sensitivity.

- Ongoing research and attempts to understand customers by everyone in the organisation are crucial to the success of RM.

Summary

In this chapter Gronroos's definition of RM was adopted for the book, and the characteristics of RM were highlighted. We discussed how a genuine RM programme has a long-term orientation and is based on a relationship for mutual benefit, nurtured by fulfilment of promises and kept going by trust and commitment. Two-way dialogue was also identified as crucial for the success of RM.

It was further pointed out that not all customers want a relationship with suppliers and that it is not profitable to have a relationship with all customers. The concept of lifetime value and the importance of the right conditions for RM were presented. For example, it was stated that where there is continuous demand for a service which is variable in quality and personally important there is the potential for RM. Additionally, the benefits of RM for both suppliers and customers were discussed; for example, that customers could benefit from reduced anxiety while suppliers could benefit from increased profits and lower costs.

Case Study *Intimacies*

They stroke you, caress you, and you pay them to do it.

Sarah Ebner on the roots of a woman's relationship with her hairdresser.

It has been almost a year, but Monjana Biswas is still trying to avoid her hairdresser. 'When you live in a small place like Cheltenham, it's so easy to bump into someone you don't want to', she says. 'I sometimes see him in a local wine bar and try not to make eye contact. You feel so guilty when you move on and it's not as if you can break the news in a sympathetic way. It feels like such a betrayal.'

Biswas, 29, is suffering from an affliction that can hit us all – hairdresser guilt. The reason is simple; our cut has made us unhappy, it's time for a change, but breaking the ties that bind us – long chats, intimate moments, gentle caressing of your locks – can be painful.

The relationship between a woman and her hairdresser is unique. There aren't many people a woman visits regularly, confides in and trusts enough to alter her physical appearance, sometimes radically. After 20 years with long hair, Jo Greene thought it might be time for a change. 'My hairdresser convinced me that it was right to cut my hair,' she says. 'She told me I should go for it and she was right. It really made me feel good about myself.'

'I love my hairdresser!' she adds, laughing. 'I really enjoy going to see her. We're at different phases of our lives – I'm a married thirty something and she's a single twenty something – and it's good fun to catch up with each other.'

Traditionally women found a hairdresser and stuck with them through thick and thin. But times are changing, says Franco Della Grazia, head of two central London salons called Franco & Co., 'British women have become a lot more savvy. They won't simply stick around if they don't think you are providing what they want.'

But Biswas argues that the fate of your tresses isn't everything. 'I enjoy the whole experience of going to the hairdresser,' she explains. 'The cut isn't the important thing. I like to have a proper chat, too.'

Hairdressers have to be instant psychologists as well as confidantes. Working on this assumption, American campaigners against domestic violence have taken their crusade into the hairdressing salon. The idea originated in Connecticut where local women's centres trained stylists to spot signs of abuse and gently hint to their clients that help was available. The idea has since been picked up across the US.

Nicole Singer, 24, works in London and is Greene's hairdresser. 'When I started out,' she says, 'I was amazed when some people told me really personal things. Hairdressers are good to speak to because they are completely separate from their clients' lives. There can definitely be a special relationship between a woman and her hairdresser.'

The place hairdressers occupy in our lives regularly makes it to the big screen. Warren Beatty not only cut women's hair, but made more intimate acquaintances in *Shampoo*. Craig Ferguson's gay crimper featured in 1999s *The Big Tease* and Alan Rickman has recently snipped away in *Blow Dry*. All three, obviously, are men. Around 70 per cent of all hairdressers are women, but the most famous – Trevor Sorbie, Nicky Clarke and Vidal Sassoon – are men.

This fact has caused some female hairdressers angst and it has been explained away by reasons that verge on the sexist. One male hairdresser insisted that men were better businessmen and sold themselves better and that women weren't really committed for the long haul and were in it for 'pin money'.

Meanwhile, one female hairdresser, who had her own problems making it to the top and has now closed down her salon, says it is harder for women to break through. 'It's ironic,' she says. 'If you walk down any high street, you will see that most of the hairdressers are women, but it's men who own the salons and men who get to be famous. A lot of that is because of other women. They like to have their hair done by men – and to flirt with them.'

Some women are breaking through, though. Beverly Cobella was nominated for Hairdresser of the Year last year and other respected female hairdressers include Zöe Irwin at Stage Door (once described as the 'Stella McCartney of hairdressing'), Sally Brookes (artistic director of Trevor Sorbie) and doyenne Jo Hansford.

Greene finds no difference between male and female hairdressers. 'It's the personality that's important,' she says. 'They have to be empathic and make you feel good about yourself.'

Although Monjana Biswas is currently going to a female hairdresser, she usually prefers to see a man. 'Women are very reliable, but I don't think they are as daring or dynamic as men,' she says. 'Men style your hair in a way the opposite sex are attracted to. It's not to do with them fancying you, it's just because blokes look at you in a different way.'

Nevertheless Biswas thinks that gay men make the best coiffeurs. 'You get the best of both worlds with a gay hairdresser,' she says. 'They have that slightly intuitive feminine side, but they also have the ability to see how the hair will look from the male perspective.'

The men's sector is the fastest growth area in hairdressing and that creates its own irony. 'I have a different relationship with my male customers,' Singer says. 'The conversations are more superficial and there's lots of flirting. Some women see male hairdressers to feel good about themselves. Now men seem to like female hairdressers for the same reason.'

Guardian, 11 June 2000

Discussion questions

1. Why is hairdressing a suitable business sector for RM? Relate the issues raised in the case study to the issues and concepts discussed so far?

2. How much do you think factors such as price, distance to travel, etc., bear on the decision to remain loyal to a hairdresser/stylist? Why?

3. As far as RM is concerned, what are the similarities and differences between a hairdresser's service, a car repair garage and an insurance broker?

4. Do you think that gender and/or age influence one's propensity to be loyal to a retailer or service supplier? Explain your answer.

References

Bejou, D., Ennew, C.T. and Palmer, A. (1998) 'Trust, ethics and relationship satisfaction', *The International Journal of Bank Marketing*, 16, 4, 170–175.

Belois, K. (1998) 'Don't all firms have a relationship?', *Journal of Business and Industrial Marketing*, 13, 3, 256–275.

Berry, L.L. (1983) 'Relationship Marketing', in L.L. Berry, G.L. Shostack and G. Opah (eds) *Emerging Perspectives on Services Marketing*, Chicago, Il: American Marketing Association, 25–28.

Berry, L.L. (1995) 'Relationship Marketing of Services, Growing Interest, Emerging Perspectives', *Journal of the Academy of Marketing Science*, 23, 4, 236–245.

Bowen, T. and Shoemaker, S. (1998) 'Loyalty: a strategic commitment', *Cornel Hotel and Restaurant Administration Quarterly*, February 39, 1, 12–25.

Buttle, F. (1996) *Relationship Marketing: Theory and Practice,* London: Paul Chapman.

Christopher, M., Payne, A. and Ballantyne, D. (1991) *Relationship Marketing – Bringing Quality, Customer Service, and Marketing Together,* Oxford: Butterworth-Heinemann.

Callaghan, M., Mc Phail, M. and Yau, O.H.M. (1995) 'Dimensions of a relationship marketing orientation', *Proceedings of the Seventh Biannual World Marketing Congress,* Melbourne, 6, 2, 10–65.

Culliton, J.W. (1948) *The Management of Marketing Costs,* Boston: Harvard University Press.

Day, G.S., Shocker, A.D. and Srivastava, R.K. (1979) 'Customer oriented approaches to identifying product-markets', *Journal of Marketing,* 43, 8–19.

Evans, J.R. and Laskin, R.L. (1994) 'The relationship marketing process; a conceptualisation and application', *Industrial Marketing Management,* 23, 439–452

Fournier, S., Dobscha, S. and Mick, G. (1998) 'Preventing the premature death of relationship marketing', *Harvard Business Review,* January/February, 42–51.

Gilmore, J.H. and Pine, B.J. (1997) 'The Four Faces of Mass Customisation', *Harvard Business Review,* January/February, 91–101.

Gronroos, C. (1997) 'From marketing mix to relationship marketing – towards a paradigm shift in marketing', *Management Decisions,* 35, 4, 322–339.

Gronroos, C. (1996) 'Relationship marketing: strategic and tactical implications', *Management Decision,* 34, 3, 5–14.

Gronroos, C. (1997) 'Value-driven relational marketing: from products to resources and competencies', *Journal of Marketing Management,* 13, 407–419.

Gronroos, C. (2000) *Service Management and Marketing – A Customer Relationship Approach,* 2nd edn, Chichester: John Wiley and Sons.

Gummesson, E. (1994) 'Making relationship marketing operational', *International Journal of Service Industry Management,* 5, 5, 5–20.

Gummesson, E. (1999) *Total Relationship Marketing – Rethinking Marketing Management: From 4Ps to 30Rs,* Oxford: Butterworth-Heinemann.

Gwinner, K.P., Gremler, D.D. and Bitner, M.J. (1998) 'Relational benefits in services industries: the customer's perspective', *Journal of Academy of Marketing Science,* 26, 2, 101–114.

Hakansson, H. and Snehota, I. (1995) 'The burden of relationships or who's next?', *Proceedings from the IMP 11th International Conference,* Manchester, 347–360.

Harker, M.J. (1999) 'Relationship marketing defined? An examination of current relationship marketing definitions', *Marketing Intelligence and Planning,* 17, 1, 13–20.

Lovelock, C., Vandermerwe, S. and Lewis, B. (1999) *Services Marketing – A European Perspective,* Harlow: Pearson Education.

Mittal, B. and Lassar, W.M. (1998) 'Why do customers switch? The dynamics of loyalty', *Journal of Services Marketing,* 12, 3, 177–194.

Morgan, R.M. and Hunt, S.D. (1994) 'The commitment-trust theory of relationship marketing', *Journal of Marketing,* 58, July, 20–38.

Palmer, A. (1996) 'Relationship marketing: a universal paradigm or management fad?', *The Learning Organisation,* 3, 3, 18–25.

Peppers, D. and Rogers, M. (1995) 'A new marketing paradigm: share of customer, not market share', *Managing Service Quality,* 5, 3, 48–51.

Reichheld, F.F. (1996) 'Learning from customer defections', *Harvard Business Review,* March–April, 56–69.

Szmigin, I. and Bourne, H. (1998) 'Consumer equity in relationship marketing', *Journal of Consumer Marketing,* 15, 6, 544–557.

Wolfe, D.B. (1998) 'Developmental relationship marketing (connecting messages with mind: an empathic marketing system)', *Journal of Consumer Marketing,* 15, 5, 449–467.

Yau, H.M., Chow, P.M., Lee, J.S.Y., Sin, L.Y.M. and Tse, A.C.B. (2000) 'Is relationship marketing for everyone?', *European Journal of Marketing,* 34, 9/10, 1111–1127.

Stage One:

Making the case
for RM

Stage Two:

Identifying
critical RM
success factors

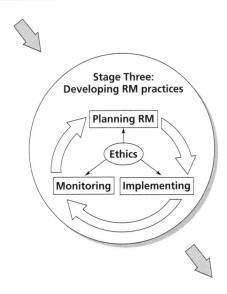

Stage Three:
Developing RM practices

Planning RM

Ethics

Monitoring   Implementing

Stage Four:

Adapting to
context-specific
conditions

3 Drivers of RM

Learning objectives

After reading this chapter, you should be able to:

- Define the concepts of satisfaction, trust and commitment.

- Identify the causes of satisfaction, trust and commitment.

- Be able to discuss how satisfaction, trust and commitment may be created, maintained and used to gain customer loyalty.

Introduction

In the previous chapter satisfaction, trust and commitment were identified as the core values in RM. This chapter explains the theories behind those values, and lays out a framework for building relationships with customers. This framework is set out in Figure 3.1. The chapter begins by looking at the challenges of creating customer satisfaction during an isolated transaction or consumption experience. It then proceeds to outline the difference between a satisfactory transaction and a satisfactory relationship. The chapter argues that, by understanding customer expectations and perceptions of quality, an organisation may deliver a satisfactory transaction. In order to create customer loyalty, however, mechanisms must exist for the development of trust and commitment. Since these can only be developed through consistent treatment of the customer over a period of time, the key to RM lies in the creation and management of systems for interacting with the customer over time.

Satisfaction

The importance of satisfaction

For a long time satisfaction was regarded as the key to customer loyalty. More recently this notion has come under scrutiny, and researchers are questioning the role of satisfaction as the key for customer retention. Writers such as Reichheld *et al.* (2000) suggest that a high proportion of satisfied customers do in fact defect to competitors, and that suppliers must achieve 'high satisfaction' or 'customer delight' in order to promote customer retention. Indeed, customer delight has become something of a buzzword. Before making a judgement we will examine the concept of satisfaction.

Satisfaction defined

Oliver (1981) defines satisfaction as 'a summary psychological state resulting from the emotion surrounding expectations [which] is coupled with the consumer's prior feeling about the consumption experience'.

This definition has two important elements:

- Satisfaction results from an emotional state: the causes of satisfaction differ widely between individual customers, since they arise from the emotional state of the individual.

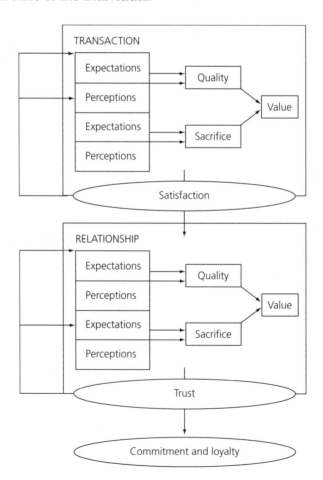

Figure 3.1

A framework for understanding relationships

- Expectations influence satisfaction: further subjectivity arises from the fact that satisfaction arises from expectations; the higher the customer's expectations, the harder they will be to satisfy. Since these expectations are formed through unique personal experience, they will vary greatly from customer to customer.

The disconfirmation model

The disconfirmation model describes the mental processes that lead to attitude change. It asserts that an individual's attitude towards a product will only change if his experience disconfirms (i.e. differs from) his expectations of the experience. This role of expectations explains the difference between satisfaction and delight. Customers are satisfied when the consumption experience meets their expectations and delighted when it exceeds them.

Rising expectations

Customers' expectations are based on product norm experience – their understanding of the value they should receive from the average supplier. As markets become increasingly competitive, so these expectations rise. Hence suppliers must continuously improve the value offered through their products if they are to maintain customer satisfaction.

Relationship quality

Satisfaction and quality

Satisfaction, then, is the reaction of the customer to a consumption experience. Product quality is one of the factors that create satisfaction, and must therefore be monitored by an organisation that wishes to create satisfied customers. The problems surrounding the definition of quality are similar to those of satisfaction.

Mechanistic vs humanistic quality

Holbrook and Corfman (1985: 15) make the distinction between mechanistic and humanistic quality: 'mechanistic involves an objective aspect of a thing or event; humanistic involves the subjective response to objects and is therefore a highly relativistic phenomenon that differs between judges'.

Juran and Gryna (1988) accommodate a degree of subjectivity in their definition of quality as 'Fitness for purpose'. Behind this definition is the assumption that producers must understand the use to which products will be put by the customer, since the product's ability to fulfil that use will form the basis for judgements on quality.

Although Juran's definition allows for some subjectivity, the quality of most consumer goods cannot be defined in easily measurable terms. Subjective criteria such as design, brand reputation and corporate image play a significant role in customers' perceptions of quality. When the product is a service, the lack of tangible evidence on which to base judgement and the inherent variability of the product allow for still greater subjectivity.

Work on the management of service quality, notably by Parasuraman, Zeithaml and Berry (1985), supports the view that customers' judgements about product quality are made in the same way as those on satisfaction, i.e. that disconfirmation directly influences perceived quality. Parasuaraman *et al.* developed a method, known as SERVQUAL, for measuring service quality. This is a research tool involving two questionnaires, one measuring customers' expectations before a specific transaction, the second measuring perceptions of performance afterwards. The difference between the scores on the two questionnaires provides perceived quality scores. SERVQUAL has been used in a number service sectors and found to accurately measure levels of quality and identify the nature of quality failures.

Dimensions of quality

Researchers into service quality have also found that there are generic criteria which customers apply in making judgements on service quality. These criteria relate to broad aspects of the service design, delivery or setting, and are commonly referred to in the literature as dimensions of service quality. The specific number and nature of service quality dimensions vary between researchers (e.g. Carman, 1990). However, there is considerable overlap between the various lists. This, together with the lack of clarity with which the various dimensions are defined, makes it difficult to establish the superiority of one set of dimensions or criteria over another. The five dimensions below, however, seem best supported by research findings:

- *Reliability*: the ability to perform the promised service dependably and accurately;
- *Assurance*: the professionalism, knowledge and courtesy of employees and their ability to inspire trust and confidence;
- *Tangibles*: physical facilities, equipment and the appearance of personnel;
- *Empathy*: the caring, individualised attention the firm provides its customers;
- *Responsiveness*: willingness to help customers and provide prompt service (Parasuraman *et al.*, 1988).

It has been found that these dimensions are generally consistent across service sectors. Other authors, however, suggest that service *fairness* should constitute a further dimension (Seiders and Berry, 1998). This is defined as a customer's perception of the degree of justice in a service firm's behaviour. There is compelling evidence that unfair service is likely to be judged as substandard in quality and that customers' sensitivity to fairness increases with purchase risk and customer vulnerability.

Quality, then, is a complex, subjective and ever-changing perception in the mind of the customer. In order to deliver a good quality product, the provider must constantly refer to the customer in order to know the criteria against which product quality will be judged. As if this were not complicated enough, quality is only half of the satisfaction equation.

Customer value

Satisfaction and value

Quality represents the benefits that the customer derives from a transaction, but it must not be forgotten that these benefits come at a cost to that customer. If the costs outweigh the benefits, satisfaction will disappear. Abbott (1955: 123) summarises this important point:

> When price tags are attached to ideas, services or products, it is the best bargain that wins. How good a bargain anything is depends upon both quality and price; these two elements together form the basis for evaluation of winning contestants in the market place.

It is not sufficient, therefore, to measure and improve quality as a strategy for creating satisfaction. Providers must understand that considerations of quality must be balanced against those of cost to the customer. Those providing the greatest quality in return for the least cost will create the greatest satisfaction. This balance between cost and quality defines the concept of value.

The subjectivity of value

Once again, there are problems of subjectivity when trying to define and measure value. Zeithaml (1988) defines perceived value as: 'The consumer's overall assessment of the utility of a product based on a perception of what is received [i.e. quality] and what is given'.

Customer sacrifice

It is important to stress that what is given is not limited to money. Ravald and Gronroos (1996) coin the phrase 'consumer sacrifice' to indicate that transactions may involve both financial costs and psychological costs.

Psychological costs are defined as the mental effort spent in worrying that the product will not offer adequate benefits, and time spent in rectifying product errors. A customer will often be prepared to pay more for a product if that added expenditure buys peace of mind. The extent to which a customer is prepared to bear financial and psychological costs in return for a perceived benefit will depend on their individual circumstances. Obviously, customers with a lack of disposable income will tend to be more sensitive to financial loss. In the same way, customers who feel stressed by a high-risk purchase decision will be more sensitive to psychological costs. As with satisfaction and quality, the specification of a good value product cannot be determined by the producer alone. Customers' perceptions of value must be monitored constantly if the producer hopes to satisfy its customers.

Transactions vs relationships

Transaction and relationship models

Teas (1993) proposes a model for the relationship between quality and satisfaction which is supported by Parasuraman, Zeithaml and Berry (1994). The model separates customer responses at the transaction and relationship level. For each transaction, viewed in isolation, satisfaction is caused by a favourable comparison of the perception of quality with expectations. The outcome of each transaction influences the customer's attitude towards his overall relationship with the supplier. Parasuraman *et al.* offer a similar model, but propose that satisfaction arises from value (a comparison of costs incurred and quality received) rather than quality alone. If transactions consistently result in satisfaction, trust will develop. Trust in turn results in loyal and committed behaviour (see below).

Loyalty

Satisfaction and loyalty

Attempting to satisfy customers is a necessary first step in building customer loyalty, but that is only a start. It is now generally agreed that satisfaction alone does not necessarily lead to loyalty, and that satisfaction indices are not a reliable indication of the number of customers who will return. In today's highly competitive markets, numerous suppliers are chasing the same customers with similar offerings, and many customers are playing the field and seeking satisfaction from different suppliers on different occasions. Brand promiscuity is a problem facing many suppliers at present. So while satisfaction surveys ought to be carried out, having a high percentage of satisfied customers must not give suppliers a false sense of security. Satisfied customers can, and do, exit.

The debate about satisfaction has now moved on to whether it is a high degree of satisfaction, complete satisfaction or delight, as opposed to mere satisfaction that leads to customer loyalty. A survey by British Airways, however, found that 13 per cent of its 'completely satisfied' customers did not intend to fly British Airways again (Weiser, 1995). Hence it is suggested in this book that satisfaction must be coupled with trust and commitment and that it is the added value associated with that which creates customer loyalty.

There are, nevertheless, many situations in which dissatisfied customers continue to stay loyal to a supplier simply because there is no better alternative. This situation is clearly characterised by banking services in the UK, and the helplessness felt by most customers caught in an oligopolistic competition. High bank charges, the reduced number of branches and the increasing difficulty of speaking to a personal banker in one's own branch as opposed to someone unfamiliar at a call centre are some of the common problems for UK bank customers. Yet the alternatives, at present, are no more attractive. So most customers remain with their banks. This could be regarded as *apathetic* loyalty; others have referred to this type of customer as a *hostage* (Jones and Sasser, 1995). It should be remembered that hostages and advocates have one thing in common: word of mouth. While advocates spread positive words about the company, hostages or apathetic loyals will often take the opportunity to complain and criticise. This increases the cost of complaints handling and damages the corporate image – and these customers will look for the first real opportunity to exit. This is obviously not wise long-term business planning.

Although satisfaction does not guarantee loyalty, in most cases where one is a willing participant in a relationship one will experience a high degree of satisfaction. Consequently, suppliers must ensure that they research satisfaction levels amongst their customers and adjust their total offerings to maximise customer satisfaction. High satisfaction is an important component in the loyalty formula. This is particularly so where intense competition exists in the marketplace and customers have easily obtainable alternatives. It is necessary to remember that what satisfies customers today may not, will not, satisfy them in the future. The competitive environment of the markets, at present, requires continuous innovation and improvements to be made to a producer's augmented offering. It is also necessary to remember that satisfaction alone will not create loyalty.

Satisfaction + Trust + Commitment ⟶ Loyalty

Figure 3.2

The loyalty formula

A business that focuses exclusively on customer satisfaction runs the risk of becoming an undifferentiated brand whose customers believe only that it meets the minimum performance criteria for the category. Long term customer retention in competitive markets requires the supplier to go beyond mere basic satisfaction and to look for ways of establishing ties of loyalty that will help ward off competitor attack.

(Clark, 2001: 160)

Trust

The growing importance of RM has directed the attention of many marketing researchers to the concept of trust, which has long been of interest to several other disciplines including human resource management, communication and law. In the business-to-business sector, trust is considered to be an important requirement for a successful relationship. Business buyers do not change suppliers as often as do consumers, and prefer to find reliable suppliers on whom they can depend, i.e. trust, for delivering the right order, at the right time and in good condition. The growth in the use of such practices as just-in-time purchase management creates an anxiety that can only be alleviated by a trust in the relational partner and in their commitment to the success of the relationship. RM in consumer markets, particularly in services due to the intangibility of the product, relies on the same principles. 'Effective services marketing depends on the management of trust because the customer typically must buy a service before experiencing it' say Berry and Parasuraman (1991: 144).

Additionally, RM requires investment in time and resources as well as emotional bonding and forsaking of others which can only be facilitated by mutual trust between the parties involved.

Trust defined

There is no universally agreed model of trust, nor an agreed definition. Moorman, Deshpande and Zaltman (1993) define trust as 'a willingness to rely on an exchange partner in whom one has confidence'. This definition is an attempt to marry different definitions of trust which broadly either emphasise a psychological disposition toward a partner (confidence) or reliance on the partner.

The role of trust

The general view, however, is that trust and commitment are necessary attributes in a successful relationship. Morgan and Hunt (1994) identify trust and commitment as the key mediators in their model of RM. They argue that trust and commitment encourage marketers:

1. To work at preserving relationship investments by cooperating with exchange partners,

2. To resist attractive short-term alternatives in favour of the expected long-term benefits of staying with existing partners,

3. To view potentially high risk actions as being prudent because of the belief that their partners will not act opportunistically (Morgan and Hunt, 1994: 21).

That trust should be important in relational exchanges is understandable in terms of what has been suggested in this book so far – the higher the degree of risk, anxiety and customer involvement the higher the need for relational exchange – i.e. reliance on and confidence in a trusted partner.

In a study of service industries, Gwinner *et al.* (1998) identify three main types of benefit which consumers expect from their relationship with a producer: confidence, social and special treatment. According to their findings, confidence benefits are received more and rated as more important than the other relational benefits by consumers. Confidence in the relational partner is an ingredient of trust, and signifies the role of trust in RM. A UK-wide survey conducted amongst a sample of British businesses on behalf of BT shows that almost two-thirds of the respondents considered customer service and contact as an important factor in future success, but only one-third of participants researched their customer's views of the services provided (BT CiB, 2000). The survey concludes that

> Poor service keeps levels of trust in many UK companies low [and that by only] paying lip service to the importance of customer service whilst failing to deliver it, many businesses are destroying the essential ingredient for long-term customer loyalty: trust.

In discussions of trust integrity, honesty and credibility are often used either as components or drivers of trust. Other adjectives used are sincerity, consistency, information sharing and equality of power. Trust is also related to the concept of source credibility.

Commitment

Commitment defined

Commitment follows trust and is defined as 'an exchange partner believing that an ongoing relationship with another is so important as to warrant maximum efforts at maintaining it' (Morgan and Hunt, 1994). Implicit in this definition is the perceived importance and high value of the relationship to the committed partner.

Garbarino and Johnson (1999) propose that customer satisfaction, perceived service quality, perceived value, trust and commitment are generally regarded as the basis of consumer behaviour with respect to marketing organisations. Their research amongst visitors to a New York off-Broadway repertory theatre company, however, reveals that for high relational customers (consistent subscribers), trust and commitment, rather than satisfaction, are the mediators between component attitudes and future intentions.

How is commitment created?

According to Hocutt (1998), commitment may be regarded as a function of:

1. Satisfaction with the service provider (bonding),
2. Quality of alternative providers,
3. Investments in the relationship.

Commitment is stronger when satisfaction levels are high, the quality of alternatives is perceived to be poor and when the investment is large.

How can trust and commitment be encouraged and nurtured?

A survey of the literature suggests that trust and commitment can be encouraged and nurtured by a combination of factors which will be discussed fully in the following chapters. Briefly these are:

A genuine customer orientation

The terms marketing and customer orientation can be used interchangeably. Customer orientation implies achieving organisational goals through a genuine concern and motivation to satisfy customers. This requires a clear understanding of customers through marketing research and, where appropriate, through empathy, dialogue and proximity within a RM framework. This also requires the development of systems, structures and a culture around customer needs and wants.

An efficient customer care and service mechanism inspired, and run, by well-trained staff

In order to create mutual understanding between supplier and customer, mechanisms must exist for efficient and effective contact between the two parties. The use of Total Quality Management (TQM) techniques and the empowerment of customer-facing staff can ensure that this contact can promote satisfaction.

Clear safeguards and redress mechanisms

Companies must accept that it is inevitable that transactions will occasionally fail and dissatisfaction will result. Proper mechanisms for recovery, which incorporate fairness and promptness, should be in place. Also any guarantees and warranties must be clearly communicated to customers, and 'small print' must be avoided.

Sharing of and confidentiality of information

RM implies the customisation of products, which depends on a good understanding of the customer's situation and requirements. This requires the sharing of information and knowledge which must be treated as confidential. Many customers are reluctant to pass on their details to producers for fear of the information being passed on to other companies or generating junk mail. This book contains a chapter on ethics (Chapter eight) which discusses these issues in detail.

Sharing of power

By committing resources to the acquisition and retention of customers, the supplier surrenders some of its freedom, or power to discontinue the relationship, if the customer becomes increasingly difficult to satisfy. This in turn gives the customer greater power to negotiate the terms of the relationship. It is important to stress, however, that this works both ways. As the relationship continues, the customer will also see a greater risk in switching to a new producer, and the customer's stake in the relationship will grow.

Avoidance of opportunistic behaviour

At various stages of the relationship there may be opportunities for either party of short-term gain by engaging in behaviour which will harm the other. For example, a supplier may be tempted to increase prices as a result of short-term changes in the marketing environment. If this happens, trust may disappear.

Keeping of promises

Trust and commitment help reduce anxiety because of the belief that a trusted and committed partner will not jeopardise the relationship by knowingly breaking promises. This is an important factor for customers entering a long-term relationship with a producer. Through mutual dialogue and based on a realistic assessment, the supplier must promise only what can be delivered and deliver what has been promised. Sometimes it may be beneficial to decline an order.

The concept of satisfaction and efforts to keep promises and build trust between supplier and customer sit closely with the concept of 'moments of truth' in services marketing. According to Lovelock *et al.* (1999), from the customer's point of view the most obvious evidence of the quality of service occurs when the customer interacts with the firm (the moment of truth). Negative customer experiences during moments of truth include lost customers, negative word of mouth and reduction in employee morale. During the moment of truth the life of the relationship between the supplier and customer is at stake.

Shared values

Shared values refer to: 'the extent to which partners have beliefs in common about what behaviours, goals and policies are important or unimportant, appropriate or inappropriate, and right or wrong' (Morgan and Hunt, 1994: 25). The chances of a successful partnership and commitment to a long term relationship will be significantly reduced if the two parties do not share the same values. Disappointments and disagreement are bound to arise sooner or later.

Additional considerations

So far in this chapter the emphasis has been on the external customer, but the role of trust and commitment in building successful long-term relationships with employees, intermediaries and other stakeholders must not be forgotten. RM programmes aimed solely at external customers will be incomplete and have a reduced chance of success. Internal marketing and a belief in the value of a long-term relationship with customers and other stakeholders must be incorporated into the organisational culture.

Finally, trust and commitment have to be genuine and born of choice in order to be at their most effective in building long-term relationships. Some of the current literature, particularly that written by practitioners, over-emphasises the role of creating economic ties, or even proposes exit barriers to make exit too expensive or difficult for customers (see the three levels of RM in Chapter one). Whilst RM is not a welfare exercise, the original advocates of RM in consumer markets – e.g. Berry, Gronroos and Gummesson – wrote from customer orientation platform and a genuine belief in the value of creating mutually beneficial relationships.

Figure 3.3

A model of trust and commitment

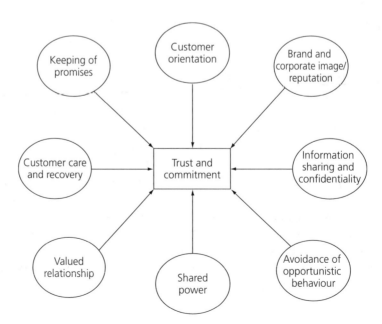

Entrapment was not part of the original concept. It is regrettable that references are made to customers as, for example, terrorists and mercenaries (Jones and Sasser, 1995) in the RM literature.

The systems approach

It will be clear from this chapter that customer loyalty cannot be won from a single sale or transaction, but rather from a series of satisfactory transactions over a period of time. This is perhaps the fundamental difference between RM and traditional target marketing. Whilst the latter focuses on the task of designing products in accordance with customer needs, it does not extend beyond the perspective of an isolated transaction. RM views the task of winning a customer as an ongoing process, developed gradually over a period of time. The implementation of the RM concept, therefore, focuses on systems rather than products. This has significant implications for the way that an organisation is managed. This is explored in more detail in the following chapters. Gronroos (1996) proposes that in strategic terms, RM's aim is to redefine the business as a service business. It also aims to look at the organisation from a process management point of view, and to create partnerships and a network for dealing with the full service process.

Summary

Customer satisfaction, while a key first step towards gaining customer loyalty, does not on its own guarantee it. Customer commitment based on trust is the next hurdle to cross in order to gain customer loyalty. The development of such trust and commitment depends on a variety of factors, which are summarised in Figure 3.3. In services, in particular, where products are intangible and also where there is high customer involvement as well as anxiety, trust assumes an even greater significance. This process require a philosophical and strategic commitment to RM based on a platform of genuine customer orientation and a belief in the long-term benefits of RM. Structured systems also need to be put in place. These will be the subject of the next section of the book.

Case Study   *Promises, promises*

In order to win and keep customers, many organisations make promises to their customers. These promises are meant to reassure customers and create a differential advantage for the organistaion. Examples of such promises are given below:

US Air

Flying with an airline these days is straightforward on most occasions. However, on some occasions flights are delayed or even cancelled due to bad weather or general maintenance problems with the plane; such events can cause upset, misery and long waiting times for the customer. According to the Department of Transport, customers registered 1,248 complaints about airline services with them in February 2001, a 43.8 per cent decrease from the 2,221 complaints filed in January and 37.3 per cent below the 1,992 filed in February 2000. This may be an indication of the fact that airlines are taking customers more seriously in an increasingly competitive world, where also political events have caused a drop in passenger numbers.

US Air operate by a Customer Charter, which includes promises to reimburse customers for their travel to the airport if a flight is delayed or cancelled, guaranteeing travellers a hotel if they are not close to home and also putting them on the next flight within a certain time frame.

US Air try to solve problems faced by passengers quickly and often go beyond the Charter to satisfy their customers. For example, it is quite common for the airline to offer free travel and up to two thousand pounds' worth of travel vouchers to passengers whose flights are delayed for twenty-four hours or more.

Ibis Hotels

Every guest at an Ibis hotel will find a card titled Fifteen Minutes Satisfaction Contract in their rooms. These 'contracts' promise that guests can expect a solution within fifteen minutes to 'little' problems that the hotel may be responsible for, and that should the hotel not be able to solve the problem it will pick up the guests' bill.

Independent Financial Advisors

Independent Financial advisors (IFAs) search for financial products for their clients among the offerings of many companies and, hence, do not attempt to sell the products of a single company or institution. They provide advice on life assurance, pensions, unit trusts, mortgages, etc. Normally, a representative from an IFA company will visit clients in their homes and from the start provide the client with a brochure introducing the company and setting out general terms of business. The representative may verbally explain some of the content too. The information provided will often include: whether the company is registered with the Personal Investment Authority (PIA) and if so for which products, whether professional indemnity insurance is maintained by the company, how the information on the customer will be maintained, whether they will receive commission from the third party whose products they will sell to the client, etc.

Such a brochure may also contain a set of promises and assurances from the representative, among them for example:

- To give impartial, independent advice
- To be honest and transparent in all dealings with the client
- To supply written terms and conditions of business before engaging in the provision of advice
- To be deemed financially fit, and qualified, as a minimum, the Chartered Insurance Institute's full Financial Planning Certificate examinations
- To act on behalf of the client at all times.

RAC

RAC Motoring Services provide roadside assistance to millions of motorists whose cars have broken down. When the motorists call the RAC they are given a waiting time within which they can expect assistance on the scene. On occasions that the waiting time is noticeably longer than promised for a motorist, which may be distressing experience, a letter is sent to him shortly afterwards. A typical letter from the RAC, signed by the Customer Care Operations Manager, reads:

I would like to apologise for the delay that you experienced recently when you called for our assistance. Customer care is of the utmost importance to RAC and it is always disappointing when we fail to provide our normal high standards of service.

Whilst we always try to ensure that our resources match our expected demand, there may be occasions when we do not get the balance quite right, However, please accept my assurances that delays such as this are rare.

May I take this opportunity to thank you for being a loyal and valued customer of RAC. I am confident that should you require our help in the future you will receive outstanding service from us.

Case study by Yasmin Sekhon

Discussion questions

1. What are the important factors that companies should consider before making and promoting promises?
2. What should a company do when it breaks its promises and why?
3. What can companies do to ensure they reduce to a minimum the possibility of breaking promises to customers?

References

Abbot, L. (1955) *Quality and Competition,* New York: Columbia University Press.

Berry, L. and Parasuraman, A. (1991) *Marketing Services,* New York: The Free Press.

BT CiB (2000) *The Evolution of Customer Management*, London: CiB.

Carman, J.M. (1990) 'Consumer perceptions of service quality: an assessment of the SERVQUAL dimensions', *Journal of Retailing,* 66, Spring, 33–55.

Clark, K. (2001) 'What price on loyalty when a brand switch is just a click away?' *Qualitative Market Research: An International Journal,* 4, 3, 160–168.

Garbarino, E. and Johnson, M.S (1999) 'The different roles of satisfaction, trust and commitment in customer relaytionships', *Journal of Marketing,* 63 (April), 70–87.

Gronroos, C. (1996) 'Relationship marketing: strategic and tactical implications', *Management Decision,* 34, 3, 5–14.

Gwinner, K.P., Gremler, D.D. and Bitner, M.J. (1998) 'Relational benefits in service industries: the customer's perspectives', *Journal of the Academy of Marketing Science,* 26, 2, 101–114.

Hocutt, M.A. (1998) 'Relationship dissolution model: antecedents of relationship commitment and the likelihood of dissolving a relationship', *International Journal of Services Industry Management,* 9, 2, 189–200.

Holbrook, M. and Corfman, K. (1985) 'Quality and value in the consumption experience: Phaldrus rides again', in J. Jacoby and J. Olsen (eds) *Perceived Quality*, Lexington, Massachusetts: Lexington Books.

Jones, T.O. and Sasser, E.W. (1995) 'Why satisfied customers defect', *Harvard Business Review*, November/December, 88–101.

Juran, J. and Gryna, F. (eds) (1988) *Juran's Quality Control Handbook*, 4th edn, New York: McGraw-Hill.

Lovelock, C., Vandermerwe, S. and Lewis, B. (1999) *Services Marketing – A European Perspective*, Harlow: Pearson Education.

Morgan, R.M. and Hunt, S.D. (1994) 'The commitment-trust theory of relationship marketing', *Journal of Marketing*, 58 (July), 20–38.

Moorman, C., Deshpande, R. and Zaltman, G. (1993) 'Factors affecting trust in market research relationships', *Journal of Marketing*, 57, 81–101.

Oliver, R. (1981) 'Measurement and evaluation of the satisfaction process in a retail setting', *Journal of Retailing*, 57, Fall, 25–48.

Parasuraman, A., Zeithaml, V. and Berry, L. (1985) 'A conceptual model of service quality and its implications for future research', *Journal of Marketing*, 49 (September), 41–50.

Parasuraman, A., Zeithaml, V. and Berry, L. (1994) 'Reassessment of expectations as a comparison standard in measuring service quality: implications for further research', *Journal of Marketing*, 58, 1, 111–124.

Ravald, A. and Gronroos, C. (1996) 'The value concept and relationship marketing', *European Journal of Marketing*, 30 (February), 19–30.

Reichheld, F., Markey, J. and Robert, G. (2000) 'The loyalty effect – the relationship between loyalty and profits', *European Business Journal*, 12, 3, 134–139.

Seiders, K. and Berry, L. (1998) 'Service fairness: what it is and why it matters', *Academy of Management Executive*, 12, 2, 8–20.

Teas, K. (1993) 'Expectations, performance evaluation, and consumers' perceptions of quality', *Journal of Marketing*, 57, 4, 18–34.

Weiser, C.R. (1995) 'Championing the customer', *Harvard Business Review*, November/December, 113–116.

Zeithaml, V. (1988) 'Consumers' perceptions of price, quality and value: a means ends model and synthesis of evidence', *Journal of Marketing*, 52 (July), 2–22.

Stage One:

Making the case
for RM

Stage Two:

Identifying
critical RM
success factors

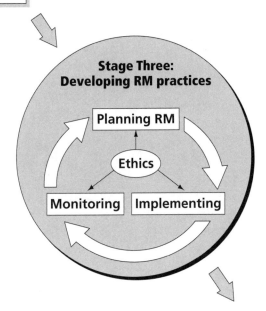

Stage Three:
Developing RM practices

Planning RM

Ethics

Monitoring   Implementing

Stage Four:

Adapting to
context-specific
conditions

4 Planning RM programmes

Learning objectives

After reading this chapter, you should be able to:

- Describe the RM planning process, and the interaction between its various stages.

- Explain the implications of the relationship life cycle to relationship portfolio planning.

- Outline the criteria that can be used to identify strategically significant relationships.

- Articulate useable RM objectives.

Introduction

This chapter is the first of five which look at the application of RM theory to practical management activities. RM planners can draw on a wealth of academic and professional material which presents established tools and methodologies for general marketing planning activities. These are well documented elsewhere, and will not be dealt with in great depth in this text. A brief reminder of the marketing planning process will be given, but this chapter will focus on the issues, principles and techniques specific to relationship marketing planning. This is not intended to imply that the established tools are irrelevant, but that they should be adapted to reflect the distinctive flavour of RM.

The RM plan

Planning, strategy and management

There is considerable variation in the definitions of planning, both explicit and assumed, offered in the marketing literature. The term is often used interchangeably with those of strategy and management and is usually prefaced by strategic or tactical. Rather than devote much-needed space in this text to the debate over the meaning of these various terms, this chapter will simply state the definitions on which its arguments are based, and explain the implications of these definitions for the way in which this and the following chapters have been structured.

The RM plan

The strategic plan is defined as a statement outlining an organisation's future direction, near-term and long-term performance targets, strategy, and monitoring and control mechanisms. The planning process may also involve the coordination of different plans governing different levels or parts of the organisation.

Strategic and tactical planning

The difference between strategic and tactical planning resides in the time horizon and the organisational scope of the plan. Strategic plans will generally deal with objectives, initiatives and events for several years into the future, and will impact on most areas of the organisation. Tactical plans, in contrast, generally cover time periods of up to a year, and impact only on specific parts of the organisation, such as the marketing department (MacDonald 1999). It will become evident from this and subsequent chapters that the successful implementation of RM requires a strategic approach. It should be stressed, however, that the successful implementation of a strategy depends on the use of appropriate tactics, and the planning process should cascade down through the organisation.

Marketing strategy

Strategy is frequently defined as the means by which objectives are achieved. Although this definition is technically accurate, it throws little light on the nature of strategy. In this text, strategy is taken to mean a set of constantly evolving operating principles or guidelines that coordinate the numerous activities and resources of an organisation over time, so that a predetermined outcome is achieved. This definition distinguishes strategy from planning in that the former is only one part of the latter. In the words 'constantly evolving' it also refers to the incremental nature of strategy development.

Whereas planning is a deliberate, analytical process, strategy results both from deliberate analysis and adaptation to unforeseen events. According to Mintzberg and Waters (1985), strategy is 'crafted' rather than planned, and strategy formulation cannot be separated from experience of implementation. A business unit may begin with an *intended strategy* based on the planning process, but experience of trying to implement this plan will quickly identify its good and bad elements. Success comes through recognising which aspects of the plan are working (and why) and updating the plan accordingly into a new *emergent strategy*. This process cannot happen in rigid, three-year cycles as envisaged in the classical five-year rolling plan, but must be an incremental process of interaction between the plan and its implementation. Planners must constantly receive and interpret information about the performance of the business and the behaviour of its environment, shifting the plan to accommodate changing circumstances or to leverage newly developed organisational skills or strengths.

Although this perspective on planning and strategy is only subtly different from the classical approach, it is nevertheless important, since it reduces the role of senior managers in the planning process. Whereas the classical planning process sees senior managers predicting future events and controlling the organisation and its behaviour, the concept of emergent strategy assumes that successful strategy depends on recognising and reacting to present events. Successful organisations take a structured approach to these tasks, and are able to consistently learn from implementation experiences, and disseminate such learning throughout the organisation. This concept has spawned a wealth of literature on learning organisations and how appropriate systems, structures and skills can be developed to facilitate the process.

This text adopts some aspects of the classical approach to planning. For example, the structure of the next four chapters is based on one version of the classical planning process. A major reason why the classical planning process forms the basis of most management texts is the fact that it is relatively easy to present and understand in theory. The practical application of the process, however, is more complex. It is proposed here that the concept of emergent strategy is more consistent with the systems, process and techniques necessary for successful RM. The RM concept implies the interplay between the goals and circumstances of the customer and those of the business unit. Although classical techniques can be applied, the key to RM is the recognition that organisational actions take place as a result of a dialogue with the customer, rather than following an internally developed plan. The planning techniques set out in the following chapters serve only as a starting point.

The components of the marketing plan

The classical marketing planning process consists of four questions which describe a journey (see Figure 4.1). The model forms the context for much of mainstream management writing, though some authors make minor changes. For example, Wilson and Gillighan (1997) add a fifth stage – strategic evaluation – between those of strategy formulation and monitoring and control. The need for strategic evaluation is based on the assumption that a range of possible strategies by which the organisation may meet its objectives will be identified. MacDonald (1999) offers a still more detailed model,

The marketing
planning process

consisting of ten stages. For the purpose of this book, however, the simple four-stage model will be used. This chapter looks at the situation analysis and marketing objectives in more detail, whilst the development of strategy and monitoring and control mechanisms are considered in the chapters on implementation.

The situation analysis

The role and content of the situation analysis

The purpose of the situation analysis, also known as the strategic audit, is to answer the question: *Where are we now?* This involves the detailed analysis of the organisation and its environment. A comprehensive analysis commonly involves the following elements:

- *The macro-environmental audit*: general external factors such as political, economic, sociocultural and technological trends must be analysed in order to identify current and future developments that are likely to affect the organisation.

- *The micro-environmental audit*: this examines external factors that are more localised, directly affecting the organisation and its market. The micro-environmental audit will review issues relating to intermediaries and other channel partners, as well as assess competitors.

- *The customer audit*: clearly, an analysis of current and future customers will form the central part of any marketing analysis. The customer audit is commonly concerned with establishing the state of the organisation's current customer base, as well as identifying opportunities for customer acquisition (see for example Wilson and Gillighan 1997).

- *The company audit*: the final dimension of the situation analysis is an assessment of the organisation's strengths and weaknesses. Here, tangible and intangible resources are reviewed and core skills or competences are assessed, usually in relation to competitors' strengths and weaknesses.

These analyses will provide information on the opportunities and threats facing the organisation, as well its strengths and weaknesses relative to competitors. The internal and external issues are commonly brought together in the Strengths, Weaknesses, Opportunities and Threats (SWOT) analysis. By identifying the convergence of threats and weaknesses, or opportunities and strengths, the planner can prioritise the issues facing the organisation and so develop the aims or general direction of its strategy.

Traditional marketing audit techniques are not dealt with in great depth here. Instead, the chapter concentrates on issues and analytical techniques that are specific to RM. For those students needing a broader understanding of marketing planning, Baker (2000) and Wilson and Gillighan (1997) are recommended as offering excellent coverage of established theory.

The RM audit

Figure 4.2 illustrates the questions which must be asked as part of the situation analysis that will form the basis of the development of a RM programme. It should be stressed that, in most cases, the scope of the analysis will not be limited to these questions; rather they will sit within a broader analysis. The importance of the RM-specific questions will depend on where the organisation's approach to marketing lies on the RM–transaction continuum (see Chapter two). Hence a useful starting point is to ascertain the degree to which RM is appropriate to the organisation, product category and market conditions. Chapter two provides a comprehensive discussion of the issues that must be considered in making this decision.

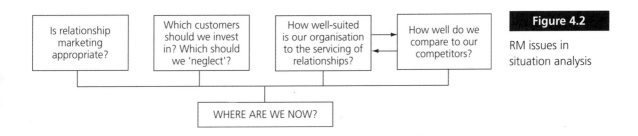

Figure 4.2

RM issues in situation analysis

The relationship portfolio

A key component of the situation analysis

Given its emphasis on customer retention, the analysis of current customers plays a central role in the relationship planning process. Traditional marketing techniques advocate the application of segmentation techniques in order to analyse current and potential earnings from customer segments. RM can borrow much from traditional techniques in its analysis of a business unit's customer base.

The relationship ladder

Payne *et al.* (1998) developed the concept of the 'relationship ladder', whereby customers could be moved from one level of loyalty to the next (see Figure 4.3). The task of relationship marketing strategy is to bring customers as high up the ladder as possible, since greater benefits accrue to the company at each level of loyalty. Although this model is an important one in terms of establishing the fact that relationships progress through different stages, it assumes that this progress is linear; that relationship marketers should aim to develop relationships to the highest possible level, and that the termination of a relationship at any stage is a failure. Subsequent research has indicated that relationships conform to a cycle, and that consideration of how and when to end a relationship is as important a consideration as which relationships should be developed.

The relationship life cycle

It is widely accepted that products have a finite life span which is characterised by distinct stages (Kotler, 2000). The concept of the Product Life

Figure 4.3

The relationship marketing ladder of customer loyalty

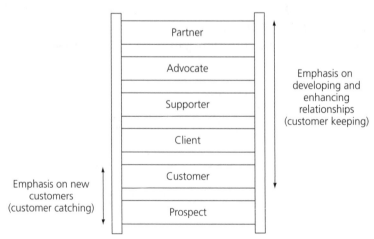

Source: Christopher, M., Payne, A., Peck, H. and Clark, M. (1998) *Relationship Marketing for Competitive Advantage – winning and keeping customers*, reprinted by permission of Elsevier Science Ltd.

Cycle (PLC) is used in marketing planning to make predictions of future demand, profit expectations and changes in the competitive environment. The PLC can even be used as a blueprint for strategy development, the introduction, growth, maturity and decline stages inviting launch, build, hold and harvest strategies respectively.

A number of writers have noted that business relationships also follow distinct phases as the relationship develops over time. Four contrasting models of the relationship cycle are summarised in Figure 4.4. The common themes in these works suggest that the relationship life cycle (see Figure 4.5) has at least four distinct stages, each requiring different actions on the part of the supplier, and each entailing different rewards.

The prospective phase

All relationships start with a single trial purchase, though the prospective phase may last indefinitely, with the customer making occasional purchases from a range of suppliers without committing to a particular one. These customers represent relationship prospects. Little investment is made on either side, with no attempt by the supplier to develop customised offerings, or to invest resources in an attempt to better understand the buyer. Similarly, the buyer makes no special demands on the supplier, being content to make occasional purchases from the supplier's standard listings. There is little or no trust between the two parties. The task for the supplier in this phase is to select those customers that offer the greatest potential for long-term relationships and seek to move them into the development phase.

The developing phase

A move to this phase requires a conscious effort on the part of the supplier, whether or not the move is prompted by the buyer. Relationship development requires the supplier to invest time and resources in better understanding the needs of a specific buyer and developing skills, products or processes to satisfy those needs. This stage, therefore, represents the biggest risk for the supplier. Whilst an investment is made in the hope of future benefits, the relationship is still in a relatively unstable state, and carries a high risk of failure. As business increases, so mutual understanding and joint systems develop between the two parties. These may be embodied in explicit contracts or agreements between the two parties, or reside in an increasingly strong relational norms.

The established phase

The established phase demands less of both parties, and offers much higher rewards. According to White (2000), the mature stage is characterised by lower costs, supported by open communication and mutual problem solving, whilst Zineldin (1996) states that in the final stage, customers are prepared to pay premium prices in return for superior perceived value.

Figure 4.4	Models of the relationship life cycle

	Ford (1984)	Jap and Ganesan (2000)	White (2000)	Zineldin (1996)
Stage *Characterised by:*	**1. Pre-relationship** *Buyer evaluates new supplier.*	**1. Exploration** *Uncertainty regarding future of and reluctance to invest in relationship, mutual mistrust.*	**1. Uncommitted** *Trust and commitment have not had time to develop.*	
Stage *Characterised by:*	**2. Early** *Buyer negotiates sample delivery or trial purchase.*			**1. Early** *Uncertainty about requirements and abilities of other party.*
Stage *Characterised by:*	**3. Development** *Formal contract agreed between supplier and buyer.*	**2. Build up** *Development of relational norms, growing trust investment and interdependence.*	**2. Developing** *Increased business, development of understanding and joint systems.*	**2. Development** *Mutual knowledge of norms, values and abilities. Supplier adapts to customer requirements.*
Stage *Characterised by:*	**4. Long-term** *Major purchases and large-scale deliveries made.*			**3. Long-term** *Supplier has majority share of customer. Mutual trust and satisfaction and close, frequent interaction.*
Stage *Characterised by:*	**5. Final** *Business between the two parties becomes habitual.*	**3. Maturity** *High level of tangible and intangible input to the relationship on both sides. Acceptable levels of benefit and satisfaction.*	**3. Mature** *Open communication and mutual problem-solving.*	**4. Final** *Mutual interdependence and complex social and commercial bonds, often institutionalised.*
Stage *Characterised by:*		**4. Decline** *Growth of mistrust, dissatisfaction, or erosion of benefits on one or both sides.*	**4. Decline** *Misunderstandings leading to conflict and deterioration of trust.*	

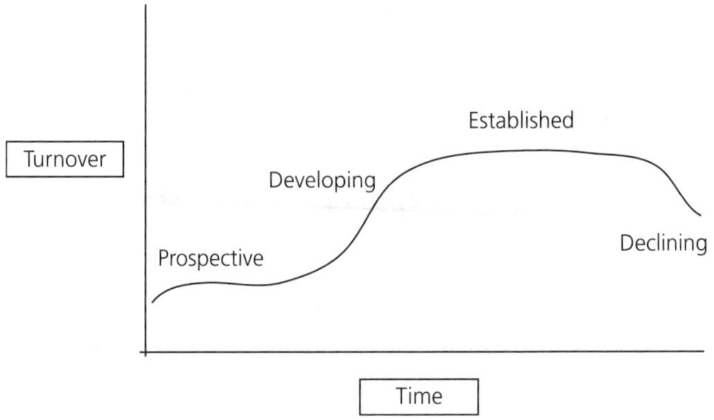

Figure 4.5

The relationship life cycle

Hence, turnover and profitability levels for the supplier peak in this stage. The task for the supplier in this phase is to maintain the relationship.

The declining phase

The declining phase may consist of a gradual deterioration, or a sudden exit on the part of either customer or supplier. Its onset may be stimulated by a failure (or repeated failures) on the part of the supplier, by competitor activity, or by circumstances beyond the control of either party, such as a dramatic change in the financial circumstances of one of the partners (Donaldson and O'Toole 2000). Whatever the causes, the decline phase involves a reduction in satisfaction, trust, and hence commitment on one or both sides, and a consequent reduction in business. It should be stressed, however, that the decline of a relationship is not always a negative event – managing the declining phase and having an exit strategy is just as much a part of RM as identifying and developing new relationships.

Managing the relationship portfolio

Since an organisation will simultaneously engage in a number of relationships with various partners, each of which may be at a different stage, it is essential that these are viewed as a portfolio rather than in isolation. Given the differing costs and benefits of respective stages of the cycle, it is important that the organisation is able to fund its development activities by maintaining a number of mature relationships. If the portfolio becomes unbalanced in favour of developing relationships, the organisation will experience cash flow problems. Similarly, a preponderance of mature relationships will make for a healthy profit and loss account, but without new relationships to replace these when they decline, the long-term future of the organisation is in doubt. Even prospective relationships have their place, providing the prospects from which future strategic relationships may be developed.

Donaldson and O'Toole (2000) provide a framework for classifying relationships for portfolio planning purposes. Although the model was developed from a study of industrial markets, there are obvious parallels with consumer markets. Donaldson and O'Toole define relationship strength by the level of belief and action components. Belief components are the attitudes towards the customer or supplier – the trust, commitment and loyalty that exists between the two parties. Action components are the more tangible measures of the relationship – the frequency and volume of transactions, the investment in resources specific to the relationship, etc. By separating these two components, Donaldson and O'Toole distinguished four types of relationship.

- *Bilateral relationships* are those in which there is a high level of both action and belief components. The relationship is important to both parties economically, and considerable trust and commitment to the long-term development of the relationship exists on both sides. The management focus of such relationships will be on the maintenance and development of these bonds, and the exploitation of the relationship for mutual benefit.

- *Hierarchical relationships* are those in which the economic content is high, but the belief components are not. Such relationships are characterised by either supplier or buyer dominance, where the junior partner is dependent on the senior for either sales or supplies, but this dependence is not reciprocated. The management task here is to either move the relationship onto a more equal footing, or to end it altogether.

- *Recurrent relationships*, in contrast, include a high belief and low action components. Though trust and commitment exists between the two parties, the economic content is low. It is tempting to recommend that managers seek to develop this into a bilateral relationship, by developing the action component on both sides. It must not be forgotten, however, that one or both parties may have no interest in developing such a relationship, or that the product or market conditions may limit such opportunities (see Chapter two). If Donaldson and O'Toole's framework were applied to consumer markets, for example, the majority of relationships would be classed as recurrent. Although consumers may trust a particular manufacturer or service provider, they are unlikely to make a significant economic commitment to it. Similarly, a manufacturer is unlikely to make a significant commitment to an individual consumer. Where there is no potential for developing a recurrent relationship, management should focus on maintaining the belief components as cost effectively as possible.

- *Discrete or opportunistic relationships* are characterised by low belief and action components. Again, such relationships are not necessarily a negative feature of a portfolio – by definition, all relationships must

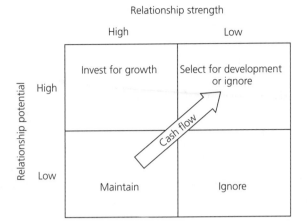

Figure 4.6

The relationship
strength–potential
matrix

begin as opportunistic ones – nor should it be assumed that the optimum strategy is to develop all opportunistic relationships into more solid partnerships. However, those relationships that are not to be developed should be granted a low priority in terms of the resources and strategic attention afforded them.

Although Donaldson and O'Toole's framework is a useful one, by looking at two different dimensions of relationship strength it captures information about the relationships in their current state only. It should be remembered that the planner's task is to manage future events. Product portfolio managers may draw on a range of portfolio analysis techniques such as the Boston Consulting Group, Shell and General Electric Matrices (see Wilson and Gillighan, 1997 for a full description of these models). Although these techniques differ in the specific criteria they use, they all use indicators of product strength and product potential in order to make portfolio management decisions. In the same way, relationship managers may classify relationships either by segment or by individual account, using the relationship strength–potential matrix described in Figure 4.6.

In order to apply the matrix, it is necessary to understand the criteria by which relationship strength and potential may be assessed. These are discussed in the following section.

Assessing relationship strength

Relationship strength defined

Views vary about the exact nature of relationship strength. As discussed above, Donaldson and O'Toole define it as 'Both the economic ties and the social bonding of the partners: belief in the spirit of cooperation and trust … and actions taken indicate the strength of the relationship' (Donaldson and O'Toole 2000: 494).

In this definition, they also provide a means of measuring the quality of relationship strength. Hausman offers a broader definition: 'Relationship strength … refers to the ties between relational partners and reflects their ability to weather both internal and external challenges to the relationship' (Hausman 2001: 602).

Hausman sees the economic content of the relationship as an outcome, rather than a dimension, of its strength. According to her, relationship strength comprises shared commitment, mutual trust and relationalism. In summary, Hausman proposes that relationship strength reflects the extent to which both parties will make an effort to maintain the relationship (commitment), has confidence in the other's reliability and integrity (trust) and believes that relationships are important to the success of the organisation (relationalism). Hausman further notes that relationalism consists of mutuality (the equity in the exchange relationship), solidarity (the perceptions of one party regarding the importance of their relationship with another), flexibility (the willingness/ability to alter the terms of the relationship) and duration (Hausman 2001).

Measuring relationship strength

Not only are there differences over the definition of relationship strength, but also about its antecedents, elements and consequences. For example, Patterson and Smith (2001) and Bove and Johnson (2000) suggest that relationship commitment arises indirectly from relationship duration – the longer the relationship, the greater the commitment or loyalty on the part of the customer. In contrast, Hausman (2001) argues that the long-term survival of the relationship is a consequence of relationship strength. A comprehensive model of the causes, components and effects of relationship strength cannot be developed from the literature. However, it is possible to identify a list of factors that are commonly associated with strong relationships. For planning purposes, these suffice as criteria for assessing relationship strength:

- *Economic content*: as identified by Donaldson and O'Toole (2000), economic content is perhaps the most easily applied measure of relationship strength. In view of the fact that mutuality is an important part of relationship strength, care must be taken to ensure that measures are taken on both sides of the relationship. It should also be remembered that economic content of a particular relationship should be assessed relative to that of the party's overall portfolio of relationships – hence a supplier must take measure both of share of turnover devoted to, or profits arising from a particular customer, as well as the share of the customer's spend devoted to the relationship.
- *Interaction*: besides the hard cash and resources that flow between the two parties, an important indicator of relationship strength is the amount of contact between customer and supplier. Such interaction

may take many forms, depending on the nature of the relationship and the sector. Bove and Johnson (2000) offer contact intensity, confining this factor to the quantity of interaction between the two parties. Hausman (2001) and Zineldin (1996) add qualitative elements, such as the openness of communication and the nature of institutional interfaces. Patterson and Smith (2001) note that interaction can take the form of social bonds as well as business transactions.

- *Loyalty, trust and commitment*: as discussed in Chapter two, loyalty, trust and commitment are key requirements of any long-term relationship. Loyalty is often taken to be synonymous with relationship strength (see for example Patterson and Smith 2001). It has been grouped here with its antecedents in view of the fact that all three are very strongly associated with relationship strength, but would be difficult to obtain reliable quantitative information about in a commercial setting. Inferences can be made, however, by observation of customers' buying patterns, complaints information and other feedback.

- *Alignment*: this term encompasses a range of characteristics relating to the ease with which the two parties interact – the fit between the corporate or individual personalities of the two parties. Hausman, for example, observes that similarity of internal relational norms (i.e. similar expectations of the other party regarding values and behaviour) between two parties is likely to contribute to relationship strength, whilst Bove and Johnson (2000) identify the importance of the customer and service worker's interpersonal orientations.

- *Relationship history*: obviously, the history of any dealings between the two parties should be carefully reviewed in order to provide the information needed to make judgements on the criteria listed above. Care should be taken, however, to interpret the significance of any past conflicts in the context of the relationship conditions at the time. Jap and Ganesan (2000) note that conflict often increases with mutual interdependence, and can therefore be a feature of strong, mature relationships. Relationship duration in itself is also associated with relationship strength – the longer the relationship, the stronger it is likely to be.

Consumer vs business-to-business markets

Although much of the work referred to above is based on business-to-business markets, it should be noted that these criteria for measuring relationship strength apply equally well to consumer markets. Measures such as share of customer and behavioural loyalty can apply to individual customers as well as corporate buyers. In some cases, reinterpretation is needed. For example, in business-to-business relationships, considerable scope exists for different forms of interaction, at various levels of the organisation, and with different levels of formality or institutionalisation.

In a business-to-consumer environment, there is less scope for complex interactions. Nevertheless, Bove and Johnson (2000) stress that it is important to identify the number of different service workers with whom a customer interacts. Strong relationships with the organisation are characterised by frequent interaction with a range of service personnel.

Assessing customer potential

The need to assess relationship potential

The management of a relationship portfolio will require the marketer to make decisions as to which relationships to develop, which to continue and which to end. Frameworks of portfolio analysis such as that outlined by Donaldson and O'Toole (2000) provide useful insights into the overall state of the organisation and the nature of the strategic task, but do not offer help in choosing which relationships would best be developed or discontinued. This section therefore identifies the factors that should be considered in determining whether a prospective relationship has the potential to develop into a long-standing partnership.

Commitment

As discussed in Chapter three, commitment is a feature of all stable relationships. When looking for relationships with development potential, the manager should therefore favour those customers or suppliers that have made, or are willing to make, a commitment to the business relationship. Hocutt (1998) providers an even clearer guide, by noting that commitment arises from a satisfaction and investment in the relationship:

- *Satisfaction*: various studies (e.g. Cronin and Taylor 1992, Patterson and Johnson, 1997) have shown what common sense predicts: customer satisfaction is a prerequisite of commitment (see Chapter three). This means that the planner must gather feedback about customer satisfaction on a regular basis – this can then be used to determine which customers offer the most potential for development. Mechanisms for measuring satisfaction are discussed in Chapter seven.

- *Investment*: where the customer has made a significant investment in the initiation or maintenance of the relationship, that customer will be committed to the relationship. It is important to stress here that commitment may not only be in the form of money or hard resources. Thibault and Kelley (1959) noted that the time and effort expended in finding new service suppliers influences customers to continue business relationships. This means that the planner should not only seek out information about the economic resources that the customer devotes to the relationship, but also the time and effort that the customers perceive themselves to have spent in this respect.

Power

The balance of power between the two parties has implications for the length and profitability of the relationship. Gaski (1984) produced evidence that in distribution channel relationships where one partner is dependent on another, the dependent party has a greater interest in maintaining the relationship. Hocutt (1998) argues that the same is true in the case of expert services, such as medical or legal services. Providers of specialist expertise create power over the consumer, placing them in a dependent role. The greater this dependence, the greater is their commitment to the relationship. It should be stressed that this is not the same as the coercive power referred to in Chapter two, which is characterised by the creation of barriers to customer exit. The power here is a natural consequence of the provider's expertise, not one that has been created artificially in order to trap the customer.

The power of each customer relative to the supplier is an important consideration in planning relationships. Power may derive from a number of sources, which are reviewed below:

- *Access to markets*: whether because of its brand strength, geographical location, size, or skills, an organisation with the ability to generate customer sales will have power over those that do not. For example, after Goodyear started selling tyres in the USA through Sears, its traditional independent outlets retaliated by adopting additional brands (Munson, Rosenblatt and Rosenblatt 1999). UK supermarkets are able to exert influence on the sale of branded products by controlling shelf-space allocation, product location within the store and merchandising support. The New Covent Garden Soup Company believed that much of its early growth was hampered by the lack of merchandising support given to the product by the major supermarkets. Retailers will also attempt to reduce the power of brands by introducing cheap own-label products. These not only increase competition in the brand's market, but also tend to devalue the product category as a whole, further reducing the influence of the manufacturer brands.

- *Access to information*: information is power, and marketing information is marketing power. In manufacturer–supplier relationships, Munsen *et al.* (1999) note that the introduction of Electronic Data Interchange (EDI) systems and the practice of Vendor Managed Inventory (VMI) can shift the channel's power in favour of the supplier. Both are systems by which the supplier or manufacturer takes responsibility for maintaining the retailer's stock levels. Information about the retailer's sales is wired direct to the supplier, which makes just-in-time deliveries of the necessary stock. This obviously brings considerable benefits for the retailer in terms of the reduction of stock-holding costs, and many systems of this type have been introduced by reluctant suppliers under pressure from retailers. However, Munson *et al.* (1999) point out that such a system will give the supplier far greater power over inventory systems, as well as providing them with valuable information about customers' purchasing patterns. On the other hand, the installation of EDI systems can lock both partners into the relationship, since the cost of switching either the supplier or the retailer is the sacrifice of the system.

- *Resource investment*: the greater the proportion of resources that an organisation devotes to a business relationship, the greater the interest that organisation will have in continuing that relationship. Retailers such as Wal-Mart consolidate their power by requiring suppliers to develop unique production processes or product ranges for them. The supplier must sacrifice this investment in order to switch retailers, and will therefore bear heftier price cuts. A retailer that relies on the unique offerings of one supplier for a large proportion of its turnover is similarly bound. An organisation should therefore be wary of committing resources to meeting the requirements of a single partner that does not reciprocate this level of commitment. The same principle applies in consumer markets, though commitments on either side will be on a much smaller scale. A customer may commit to a bank by placing all his financial affairs within its control, or spread the risk across a number of credit, mortgage and investment providers. The investment here is in the time and effort spent in providing information and the disruption to the customer's affairs whilst new arrangements are made. Nevertheless, it represents a significant indicator of reluctance of the customer to go elsewhere.

Organisational culture/personality

A review of the past behaviour of either an organisation or an individual will reveal patterns of behaviour. Naturally, the relationship planner should look for loyalty to suppliers in those customers that they seek to develop.

Nature of the bonds

Yau *et al.* (2000) observe that Westerners generally see business and social relationships as separate. Where the two types of interaction do coincide, it is the business relationship that gives rise to the social. The Chinese business philosophy of *Guanxi* (relationships) holds that commercial bonds should develop out of personal friendship (Yau *et al.*, 2000). Whatever the order of development, there is considerable evidence to support the view that the existence of social bonds strengthens business relationships (Czpiel

1990). The customer audit should therefore include an analysis of the social and commercial interaction between the organisation and its respective customers.

Goal congruence

This final factor is more relevant to organisational customers than to consumers. In order for the relationship to remain stable over time, the two organisations must have compatible objectives regarding growth, market entry or other matters of strategic focus. An organisation with ambitious growth objectives will remain committed to its supplier only as long as they can keep pace with the increasing demands of this expansion. Where possible, therefore, the planner must gain information about the customers' objectives, to check for compatibility with their own plans.

Company audit

Organisational processes and the value chain

The concept of the customer value chain provides a valuable framework for analysing the organisation. The theory may be applied either to a single organisation, or to a group of organisations working together to deliver the product to a customer. The theory presents the marketing channel as a set of processes through which the product passes, each of which adds value in the eyes of the customer and means that the customer is willing to pay a higher price for the finished product. The typical value chain for consumer goods might be as follows:

Inbound logistics

This stage might be handled by the suppliers, who would be responsible for delivering raw materials or components as required. By offering services such as just-in-time delivery, the supplier could add value to its contribution, by reducing the manufacturer's need for an expensive stock buffer. Alternatively, the supplier could add value in terms of the quality of the goods it delivers.

Manufacturing and operations

As the name suggests, the manufacturer would be responsible for this stage. Here value can be added by attention to production quality, research and development or offering services that reduce costs for the next stage member of the marketing channel. Manufacturers can help retailers, not only by improving systems for delivery, but also by developing mechanisms that help the retailer to deliver good customer service, such as an efficient system for repairing or replacing products returned because of defects. The manufacturer may also seek to increase its power by contributing to the marketing and sales stage (see below).

Outbound logistics

This part is usually played by the wholesaler – getting the finished products to the point were the customer can most easily buy them. Larger manufacturers, or those serving a small, accessible market, may handle this stage themselves.

Marketing and sales

This function is traditionally handled by the retailer, which conducts the resource-intensive business of persuading the customer to buy the products. Specific services that facilitate this process include bulk breaking, accessibility, sales advice, after-sales support, the provision of an enjoyable purchase environment etc.

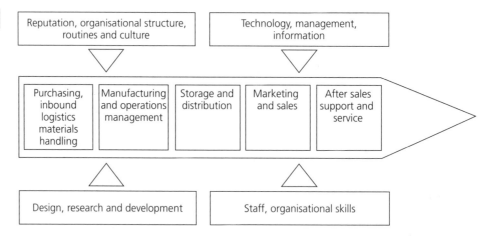

Figure 4.7

The value chain

Reprinted with the permission of The Free Press, a division of Simon & Schuster Adult Publishing Group, from *Competitive advantage: creating and sustaining superior performance* by Michael E. Porter. Copyright © 1985 Michael Porter

Uses of the value chain

The value chain can be used in a number of ways. First, it can form the basis for analysing a single organisation, identifying the systems that support the creation of the product, evaluating their importance in creating customer value and looking for ways to improve efficiency or enhance customer value. It can also be used to analyse the operation of marketing channel, evaluating the contribution of each member to the value delivered to the final customer. This can provide a guide to relationship development by identifying complementary processes. The real power of the value chain model is in forcing the analyst to view the organisation as a set of processes – this engenders the systems thinking that is crucial to the success of RM.

Ethics and RM

Given RM's emphasis on trust and commitment, the adoption of an ethical approach to the treatment of customers and other stakeholders must receive overt attention in the planning process. According to Vinten, the ethical organisation is the only viable form of organisation in the long term:

> An organisation that creates a negative ethical impact may find the withdrawal of public approval and of the market for its products. It may benefit in the short term but the nemesis is always potentially just around the corner.
>
> (Vinten, 1998)

Quality awards such as ISO9000 and the Malcolm Baldridge National Quality Award include criteria regarding the contribution to the well-being of staff, customers and the wider community. In short, corporate ethics have a significant impact on the sustainability of a business strategy, and the perceptions of organisational quality. (See also chapter eight)

The social audit

Vinten provides a definition of the social audit, which he argues, should form part of the planing process:

> A review to ensure that an organisation gives due consideration to its wider and social responsibilities to those both directly and indirectly affected by its decisions, and that a balance is achieved in its corporate planning between these aspects and the more traditional business-related objectives.
>
> (Vinten, 1991)

He identifies the work of Social Audit Ltd as a model of practice. Social Audit Ltd is a not-for-profit organisation concerned with improving public accountability of government and private business. The work in question examined the Avon Rubber Company Ltd, and reported on the following aspects of the business:

- Organisation, management style, resource use, investment;
- Employee relations, pay and conditions, job security;
- Customer relations and product benefits;
- Community relations;
- Environmental impact (Vinten, 1998).

The above forms a comprehensive list of the issues that should be covered by the social or ethical audit.

In terms of measuring the organisation's impact under these headings, Natale and Ford (1994) suggest a number of approaches:

- The inventory approach: a simple list of programmes the organisation has implemented to deal specifically with social problems;
- The process audit approach: a systematic assessment of costs, benefits and achievements of the firm's activities from the perspective of its various stakeholders;
- Cost-benefit approach: an attempt to quantify costs and benefits of the company's activities in money terms;
- Social indicator approach: the use of social criteria (e.g. the provision of employment, contribution to the economy etc.) to evaluate the impact of corporate activities.

Whatever method is used, the effectiveness of the social audit can be enhanced by the involvement of all stakeholders in the process. Planners should, therefore, seek to engage customers, suppliers, employees and the wider community in the process of analysing the company's ethical performance and developing plans for future improvements.

RM planning objectives

The importance of RM objectives

Objectives are the yardsticks by which the plan's progress may be measured. They serve a number of key functions:

- *Motivation*: objectives provide an organisation and its constituent departments a goal at which to aim.
- *Monitoring*: progress towards a given objective is the criterion by which the success of the organisation's strategy can be judged.
- *Coordination*: objectives ensure that all parts of the marketing organisation are working together towards the same goal.
- *Communication*: objectives are a clear statement of what the organisation seeks to achieve. They therefore communicate the strategic direction throughout the organisation.
- *Control*: by providing a basis for measurement, objectives enable managers to control the activities of the organisation. In some companies, corporate objectives are directly linked to senior managers' appraisal targets, and used as basis for salary review.

Clearly, then, the flavour of marketing objectives is significant, so RM should contain different objectives to those used in traditional marketing plans.

Formulating measurable RM objectives

To be of value, planning objectives must be both specific and measurable (MacDonald, 1999). One of the difficulties with RM programmes is that key indicators of success, such as relationship strength, satisfaction and commitment, are difficult to define and measure. Hence Chapter seven is devoted solely to issues of performance monitoring, and provides some useful insights into the development of workable objectives.

At this stage, however, it is worth stressing that objectives should not relate solely to the outputs of the plan, but also to the inputs and process elements. Alongside objectives which specify outcomes such as target share of customer spending, the plan should include *enabling* objectives that direct how this outcome should be achieved (e.g. increase number of consultation visits to twelve per year to maintain interest and collect feedback on specific product/service requirements), and input objectives, which set out the resources or other inputs required to enable the strategy (e.g. £X to be invested in product/service development for X account). In terms of outcome-based objectives, Gordon (1998) suggests the following:

- Revenues and costs by customer;
- Customer retention rates;
- Share of customer for products and services now made;
- Share of customer for products and services that the organisation could supply;
- Progression up the relationship ladder.

However, it will become evident in Chapter seven that, in terms of enabling objectives, it is necessary to define objectives relating to customer satisfaction, service quality and other important components of relationship performance.

Summary

The chapter began its review of planning issues by setting out the traditional marketing planning process. Although RM is distinct in many ways from traditional marketing, the planning process for RM programmes can draw extensively on conventional techniques. Having decided that RM is appropriate for the organisation and its environment, the RM plan is likely to focus on three key questions.

Which relationships should be developed and which neglected?

The planner must focus the use of limited resources on those relationships that offer the greatest returns. The planner should also manage the organisation's various relationships as a portfolio, initiating, developing and terminating relationships in order to maximise the long-term profitability of the whole portfolio. The model of the relationship life cycle was introduced at this point, to illustrate the fact that relationships will vary in strength and potential. A key task of the planner is to assess both relationship strength and relationship potential, as a prelude to identifying whether development, maintenance or termination strategies are appropriate for each relationship.

How well-suited is the organisation to the servicing of relationships, and how do we compare to our competitors?

These two questions are related, since the strengths and weaknesses of the organisation can only be judged in relation to those of its competitors. Given the importance of the process approach to the RM paradigm, Porter's value chain analysis (see p. 78) is recommended as an audit tool for RM planning purposes. By conducting such an analysis, the planner can not only evaluate the extent to which the organisation can service its customer needs, but also identify synergies between the processes of the customer and those of the supplier. It is also recommended that an ethical audit form a significant part of the RM audit, given the importance of trust and alignment of corporate values in the development of relationships.

Case Study   *Chapter One Books*

The business

Chapter One Books is an independent book-shop specialising in children's books. The business is run by a husband and wife team; John and Mary Baker. As well as making sales through their shop in Wokingham, the Bakers sell direct to primary schools in the area. Having worked as a primary school teacher, Mary has taken the decision to join the business full time. The business has been struggling in recent years, so the couple are keen to enhance sales by taking a more proactive approach to marketing planning.

The children's book market

The book market has been largely static over the last ten years, with children's book sales falling in volume for four years in a row. In 2001, children's books represented 20 per cent of the total book market, with a value of £425m. Only about 30 per cent of these sales were made though traditional retailers, with the bulk of sales being through supermarkets,

door-to-door, book clubs and other non-store-based channels.

Intense competition arises from other specialist children's bookshops, high street chains, direct suppliers of schools and a range of alternative channels such as book fairs, book clubs etc. The shop competes for sales mainly on a local level with high street chains such as Blackwells, Waterstones and Ottakars, whilst the school supply side of the business comes up against national suppliers.

Chapter One's strengths

The Bakers believe that Chapter One offers the best children's selection in the Thames Valley region, and both have considerable expertise in children's literacy. Rather than simply selling books, therefore, they are able to offer children, parents and schools a range of specialist advisory services to complement their product range. Examples of this are their Book Fair service, through which they provide a range of books to meet a school's specific requirements, and their book box service, in which they pre-select a range of suitable titles from publishers' catalogues for the school to evaluate. Both these services save teachers and literacy coordinators from wasting time looking through a large number of unsuitable texts. The same expertise is applied to the shop sales, both in selecting stock and advising parents and children on specific purchases.

Direct sales

As shown in the figure below, direct sales to schools accounts for around half of Chapter One's income. The high sales figure for 2000, however, suggests that there is considerable potential for increasing this arm of the business. The success of two years ago was largely based on a special booklist, designed to tie in with Radio Four's literacy hour.

Promotion to schools is conducted mainly via direct mailing, though personal visits are also made. Mary, in particular, has personal contacts in a number of schools from her days as a teacher. The Bakers also attend professional conferences, such as the London Book Fair, the Education Show in Birmingham and the Children's Book Fair in Bologna. Such events present the opportunity to make useful contacts both with teachers and publishers.

Book retailers such as Chapter One compete with publishers in making direct sales to schools. The Bakers have found, however, that many schools prefer the greater expertise and range of titles that they offer, since publisher

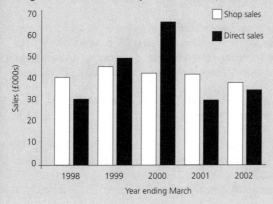

representatives are primarily sales people rather than educationalists, and must confine their range to their own catalogue. The publishers, too, are aware of these shortcomings, and maintain ties with retailers as well as pushing their own sales to schools.

The business currently has around eighty regular school customers, though income per school varies widely (see the table below). A database contains contact details for 350 primary schools, which serves as the basis for regular mailshots. By using their expertise to develop innovative booklists supporting the needs of schools, the Bakers hope to recreate the success of 2000.

Shop sales

Shop sales have remained fairly steady, though the recent year's performance was disappointing. The Bakers see the success of the two arms of their business as linked – whilst their marketing schools provides spin-off business from teachers, parents and children through the shop, so the shop served as a commercial base and a tangible manifestation of the direct sales business.

Marketing in support of shop sales centres on raising local awareness both of the shop, and of the expertise of its owners. Book reviews in local papers, local radio appearances and evening presentations have all figured in raising the profile of the shop, whilst establishing the credibility of the Bakers. Publicity is supplemented with advertising in local media, and shop-based promotions – for example, the shop opened at midnight to sell its first copies of the latest Harry Potter book. Attention to merchandising ensures that passers-by and casual visitors find the shop appealing and professional.

The future

The Bakers believe that there is considerable potential to improve both arms of the business. While Mary has devoted her attention full time to the running of the shop, John has invested in

▶

hardware, software and training to support direct mailing activities. They have also identified nurseries and playschools as a segment offering high potential for sales, and relatively little competition.

Table 4.1		Number of schools each year in sales value range		
Chapter One sales per schools		*1999–2000*	*2000–2001*	*2001–2002*
	Over £5000	3	0	2
	£4000–4999	1	0	0
	£3000–3999	2	2	0
	£2000–2999	3	1	0
	£1000–1999	6	6	4
	£500–999	10	26	10
	£100–499	55	0	32
	Under £100	0	20	33
	Average sales per school	825	540	450
	Total number of schools	80	55	81

References

Baker, M. (2000) *Marketing Strategy and Management*, 3rd edn, London: Macmillan.

Bove, L. and Johnson, L. (2000) A customer–service worker relationship model', *International Journal of Service Industry Management*, 11, 5, 491–511.

Christopher, M., Payne, A. and Ballantyne, D. (1991) *Relationship marketing – Bringing quality, customer service and marketing together*, Oxford: Butterworth-Heinemann.

Christopher, M., Payne, A., Peck, H. and Clark, M. (1998) *Relationship Marketing for Competitive Advantage – winning and keeping customers*, Oxford: Butterworth-Heinemann.

Cronin, J. and Taylor, S. (1992) 'Measuring service quality: a re-examination and extension', *Journal of Marketing*, 56, 3, 55–68.

Czpiel, J.A. (1990) 'Service encounters and service relationships: implications for research', *Journal of Business Research*, 20, 1, 13–21.

Donaldson, B. and O'Toole, T. (2000) 'Classifying relationship structures: relationship strength in industrial markets', *Journal of Business and Industrial Marketing*, 15, 7, 491–506.

Gaski, V. (1984) 'The theory of power and conflict in channels of distribution', *Journal of Marketing*, 48, 3, 9–29.

Gordon, I. (1998) *Relationship marketing: new strategies, technologies and techniques to win customers you want and keep them forever*, Toronto, Canada; Chichester, UK: Wiley.

Hausman, A. (2001) 'Variations on relationship strength and its impact on performance and satisfaction in business relationships', *Journal of Business and Industrial Marketing*, 16, 7, 600–616

Hocutt, M.A. (1998) 'Relationship dissolution model: antecedents of relationship commitment and the likelihood of dissolving a relationship', *International Journal of Service Industry Management*, 9, 2, 189–200.

Jap, S. and Ganesan, S. (2000) 'Control mechanisms and the relationship life cycle: implications for safeguarding specific investments and developing commitment,' *Journal of Marketing Research*, 37, May, 227–245.

Kotler, P. (2000) *Marketing Management (Millennium edition)*, Upper Saddle River, New Jersey: Prentice Hall.

MacDonald, M. (1999) *Marketing Plans*, Oxford: Butterworth-Heinemann.

Mintzberg, H. and Waters, J. (1985) 'Of strategies deliberate and emergent', *Strategic Management Journal*, 6, 257–272.

Mitchell, V. (1998) 'Segmenting purchasers of organisational professional services: a risk-based approach', *Journal of Services Marketing*, 12, 2, 83–97.

Munson, C., Rosenblatt, M. and Rosenblatt, Z. (1999) 'The use and abuse of power in supply chains', *Business Horizons*, 42, 1, 55–60.

Natale, S. and Ford, J. (1994) 'The social audit and ethics', *Managerial Auditing Journal*, 9, 1, 29–33.

Patterson, P. and Johnson, L. (1997) 'Modelling the determinants of customer satisfaction for business to business professional services', *Journal of the Academy of Marketing Science*, 25, 1, 4–17.

Patterson, P. and Smith, T. (2001) 'Modelling relationship strength across service types in an Eastern culture', *International Journal of Service Industry Management*, 12, 2, 90–113.

Payne, A., Christopher, M., Clark, M. and Peck, H. (1996) *Relationship marketing for competitive advantage, winning and keeping customers*, Oxford: Butterworth-Heinemann.

Porter, M.E. (1985) *Competitive Advantage: creating and sustaining superior performance*, New York: Free Press.

Thibault, J. and Kelley, H. (1959) *The Social Psychology of Groups*, New York: John Wiley and Sons.

Vinten, G. (1998) 'Putting ethics into quality', *The TQM Magazine*, 10, 2, 89–94.

Vinten, G. (1991) 'The social auditor', *International Journal of Value-based Management*, 3, 2, 125–136.

White, H.M.F. (2000) 'Buyer–supplier relationships in the UK fresh produce industry', *British Food Journal*, 102, 1, 6–17.

Wilson, R. and Gillighan, C. (1997) *Strategic Marketing Management*, 2nd edn, Oxford: Butterworth-Heinemann.

Yau, O., Lee, J., Chow, R., Sin, L. and Tse, A. (2000) 'Relationship marketing the Chinese way', *Business Horizons*, 43, 1, 16–24.

Zineldin, M. (1996) 'Bank–corporate client "partnership" relationship: benefits and cycle', *International Journal of Bank Marketing*, 14, 3, 14–22.

5 Implementing RM programmes Strategy, structure and systems

Learning objectives

After reading this chapter, you should be able to:

- Explain the nature of RM strategy.

- Recognise the interrelationship between strategy, structure and systems.

- Recommend appropriate strategies for each stage of the relationship cycle.

- Identify structural and systems issues arising from changes in RM strategy.

- Evaluate the role of TQM in RM programme implementation.

Introduction

In the last chapter, the ways by which the planner can establish the current state of the organisation were examined. By auditing current and potential customers, the competition and its own strengths and weaknesses, the supplier can establish its current situation before deciding on the direction of future progress. This chapter looks at how this information may be used, and the range of activities that must be undertaken if a RM strategy is to be successful.

Research by Colgate and Stewart (1998) suggests that poorly implemented RM programmes actually do more harm than good, creating customer dissatisfaction and stimulating negative word of mouth. Clearly, then, issues of implementation deserve serious attention. This chapter starts with a look at the nature of RM strategy itself, before discussing the organisational changes that must be made to support such a strategy.

Figure 5.1

The McKinsey Seven
S framework

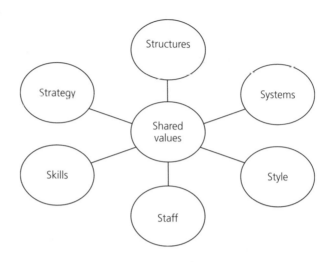

The McKinsey 'Seven S' framework

On the basis of their work at McKinsey and Co, Waterman, Peters and Philips (1980) argue that organisational change has seven dimensions (see Figure 5.1):

- **Strategy** is the senior management's plan of action with which the efforts of the staff are coordinated;
- **Structure** denotes the way in which resources and responsibilities are allocated;
- **Systems** are the mechanisms, procedures and processes by which tasks are completed;
- **Style** is more commonly referred to as culture, though Waterman *et al.* put heavy emphasis on management style in determining the 'personality' of the organisation;
- **Skills** refers to corporate strengths or core competencies;
- **Staff** means not only the human resources commanded by the organisation, but also the policies by which they are managed;
- **Shared values** are the overarching goals, beliefs and values of the organisation.

Waterman *et al.* used the framework to illustrate the range of activities needed to effect change in an organisation. Since all elements are connected, any change in strategy, for example, must be accompanied by corresponding changes in the other elements of the framework. A business initiative will only be successful if all seven elements work in harmony. This chapter considers strategy, structures and systems. These are often called the 'hard' elements of the framework, since they can be defined, measured and manipulated relatively easily.

Strategy

The nature of RM strategy

RM is a strategy in itself, and one that affords little scope for the organisation to follow a predetermined strategic direction. Having decided on its strategic partners, the way in which the organisation develops its resources, product range and skills will emerge from dialogue with the customer, not from a unilateral plan. It is the choice of customer, and the strategic importance placed on each customer, that forms the predictive component of RM strategy. In the previous chapter, it was shown how relationships follow a life cycle equivalent to the product life cycle, with different costs and rewards at each stage, and that different customers offer differing returns. The RM strategist must, therefore, manage the portfolio of customers to ensure an even flow of profits in the long term, and to determine when relationships should be initiated, developed, maintained or discontinued. Key strategy considerations are discussed below. As Gronroos (1996) points out, however, the essence of RM is in the organisation's processes, rather than its planning. The bulk of the two chapters on implementation will therefore focus on systems, and the structures and mechanisms that must support those systems, rather than the strategy itself.

Initiating relationships

Target marketing techniques

This stage of the relationship cycle involves the supplier in target marketing activities. For the smaller or less well-established company, initiation will usually involve the recruitment of new customers through advertising, sales promotion or personal selling. Identifying, evaluating and targeting new customers comes from arm's length research, and dialogue begins only when the new customer has been recruited. For organisations that already have a good base of occasional customers, relationships may be initiated with existing uncommitted customers, for example by using predictive modelling techniques as described later in the chapter. Whatever the method, this is commonly the most expensive stage of the relationship cycle, since success rates will be low (Johnson, 1999).

Avoiding the common mistakes

Some common mistakes to avoid at this stage are:

- A relationship is more than just repeat custom and, as discussed in Chapter three, more than a series of transactions. It is the presence of trust and commitment that bring the financial rewards, through positive word of mouth and the willingness to pay premium prices in

Figure 5.2

Four steps to initiating relationships

return for a customised product. It is the customer's willingness to commit that should form the basis of prospect evaluation.

- It should not be assumed that the customer would welcome a relationship – indeed, it is possible that customers are becoming increasingly cynical about RM, as the term is bandied about with increasing carelessness. The programme must be able to communicate relevant value from the outset.

- Although sales promotions based on financial incentives are a good way of recruiting new customers, the marketer must be careful not to confuse loyalty with self-interest. Like all mercenaries, customers attracted purely by economic benefits will defect as soon as a better offer comes along.

- Finally, the marketer should not expect all relationships to be successful. Just as new product launches suffer from a 90 per cent failure rate (Dibb *et al.*, 2000), so the vast majority of relationships fail in the early stages (Johnson, 1999).

Reducing the risk

In Chapter four we discussed the effect of risk in deterring customers from entering into a business relationship that involves a significant commitment but offers little reassurance in the form of search attributes. Figure 5.2 identifies a range of tactics that can be used to counteract the negative effects of such risk.

Simplifying the service offer

Lack of clarity regarding the benefits received from the supplier, the conditions of use or the terms of payment will increase the risk perceived by the customer. For example, Berry and Yadav (1996) claim that flat fee pricing increases the competitiveness of a service by reducing the risk of escalating costs. In the 1990s, the motorcycle training school CSM used this principle to increase the competitiveness of its courses by offering, for a set fee, unlimited tuition until the rider passed his test.

Guaranteeing the core benefit

Product guarantees must home in on the most valued aspect of the product in order to be effective. A simple example of such a strategy is the 'no win no fee' guarantee commonly offered by the growing number of solicitors offering injury claims representation. Just as with the overall service offer, the guarantee must be simple and unequivocal; one solicitor's advert promised that, if unsuccessful, the client 'may not pay a penny', and found that prospective customers were overly suspicious of the use of 'may'. Berry and Yadav give the example of Bank One, a small Texas-based trust bank, which managed to create a positioning of superior customer service by offering an unconditional service guarantee. The bank promised 'If you are not satisfied with our service quality in any given year, we will return to you the fees paid, or any portion thereof you feel is fair' (Berry and Yadav, 1996).

In its first six years of operation, just seven of the bank's 4,500 clients invoked the guarantee and received refunds. In 1996, Bank One was the fastest growing trust bank in the USA. It should be noted that money-back guarantees do not recompense the customer for psychological or emotional stress, and sometimes an organisation must promise compensation above the price of the service in order to pre-empt these types of risk – hence software supplier Quicken's promise regarding its home bank account management software. If the customer was dissatisfied, not only were they not asked to pay for the product, but they were also invited to keep it.

Encouraging trial

No-commitment trials are virtually undeliverable, since the time, effort and stress of trying the product is in itself a commitment on the part of the customer. For those products high in experience qualities, customers will often be reassured by the opportunity of a free trial prior to purchase. It is difficult, for example, for the customer to be confident about the quality of most service products without actually trying the service out. For this reason, it is common for health clubs to offer a trial membership period before asking the customer to commit to a year's membership and pay the joining fee. Where such trials are offered, it is again important that the conditions of the trial simply and clearly state the (limited) nature of the commitment the customer is asked to make.

Developing relationships

At this stage of the cycle the emphasis is still on investment, but the focus shifts to the identification of opportunities for increased business, and the development of systems that support the relationship. If the new customer represents a significant proportion of the supplier's business, new systems and structures must emerge to meet their requirements.

For suppliers operating in consumer markets, the changes to the organisation will be less significant – the new customer's requirements will usually be dealt with through existing systems. Nevertheless, the costs will still be relatively high in relation to the returns. For a customer to open a new bank account, for example, requires the processing of the application, credit checks, recording contact details, and the dispatch of new cards and cheque books. When viewed against the revenue generated by an average customer, the costs of these activities is significant. The supplier should ensure that the customer also makes a commitment to the relationship at this stage. There are a number of ways to encourage this, which are discussed below.

Increasing the scale or scope of the business relationship

Donaldson and O'Toole's (2000) research indicates that a relationship grows stronger as economic content increases. Colgate and Stewart (1998) also found that the more frequent the contact between the customer and the supplier, the more positive the view of the former towards the latter. The first and most obvious way of increasing the relationship is, therefore, to increase the volume and/or variety of products sold to the customer. In business-to-business markets, opportunities to do this will be revealed through dialogue with the individual customer. In mass consumer markets, due to the number of customers, the marketer may have to identify micro segments with which to target new product offers (Grossman, 1998). Johnson (1999) describes how banks use a predictive modelling technique called the Next Logical Product. The process segments household types according to buyer behaviour, product ownership and, where possible, response to product offers. The data is then used to predict the probability that a given household would respond positively to an offer of a given product. Those with the highest scores are then targeted. Although success rates are not high, they are nevertheless better than random mail-shots, and less likely to annoy existing customers with offers of unwanted products.

Legal/financial agreements

It is common practice for mobile phone operators to insist on a minimum of a year's initial contract in return for special offer, usually a cheap handset. Many 'Pay as you talk' services involve an element of commitment, the customer being required to maintain a minimum spending level. For example, in 2000 BT Cellnet followed a policy of deactivating accounts if the customer failed to top up within a set time period – in this case, however, the benefit to the customer is less clear. In order to be viewed positively by the customer, the request for a commitment on their part must be accompanied by a benefit, and preferably one that the customer can appreciate for the length of the relationship to which he commits. The use of special offers to trap customers in an exploitative relationship will not be successful in the long term (see Chapter two).

A good example is provided by Mi8 Corp, a small, Manhattan-based application provider, which in 2001 rented and serviced Microsoft server software. When it found that Microsoft Corporation was planning to raise its prices, it was faced with the necessity of upping its own rates by 14 per cent. Mi8 took the opportunity to select some long-term partners. It wrote to its customers, explaining the circumstances behind the planned rise, offering them a 90-day grace period, and offering them a lower price if they signed a one-year contract. Only a few took the contract, but none of them defected.

Resources and information

A customer that has invested resources, whether tangible or intangible, will have a greater stake in the continuation of the relationship. Still greater commitment will exist if resources or valuable information are shared between the two parties. Munsen *et al.* (1999) note that the introduction of Electronic Data Interchange (EDI) systems and the practice of Vendor Managed Inventory (VMI) can affect the commitment of both supplier and the buyer organisations (see Chapter four).

Time, effort and involvement.

Time, physical exertion or mental effort all represent an investment on the customer's part in the relationship with the supplier. The greater the investment in these terms, the greater the commitment will be. As one financial services customer put it: 'At the moment I want to continue with my present [financial] adviser though I am not fully satisfied with the service. It is very difficult for a small investor to find a new, good adviser' (in Sharma and Patterson, 2000).

As discussed in the previous chapter, the level of customer involvement in the buying decision and consumption of the product is to some extent dictated by the nature of the product type. In high involvement, extended problem-solving buying situations, the task of the marketer is to make the process as pleasurable (or painless) as possible, so that the customer follows through to a final purchase decision. In the case of low risk, low involvement products, however, encouraging the customer to expend greater psychological effort and time can increase loyalty.

Maintaining relationships

Importance of maintenance

Neglecting existing relationships is a common mistake. Although the maintenance of mature relationships often requires fewer resources than initiating and developing new ones, they are clearly critical to the success of RM strategy, since this stage represents the 'pay-off' from efforts to build the relationship. With well developed systems in place, the focus at this stage is on monitoring and control, safeguarding the customer's satisfaction with, and trust in, the supplier.

Communicate

Communication is a crucial requirement for building successful long-term relationships, by fostering trust and creating customer satisfaction. For example, the Danish Food Company Flensted Catering A/S attributed much of the success of its relationship marketing programme to frequent, effective communication. Among other things, newsletters, site visits and personal sales contacts were used to keep customers informed of current and planned progress (Lindgreen and Crawford, 1999). Similarly, but in a consumer environment, Sharma and Patterson (2000) found that communications had a greater impact than technical or function quality on the degree of relationship commitment exhibited by customers of financial advisers. The study suggested that effective communications served a number of functions, including shaping customers' expectations of the service and influencing their perceptions. Regular contact also helped in creating empathy with the customer by showing that the adviser cared about the state of their affairs, and valued their custom. Communication methods are discussed in more detail later in this chapter. It is important to strike a balance between regular meaningful communication and pestering the customer.

Reward loyalty

Customers will remain loyal to the supplier for as long as the perceived benefits outweigh the perceived sacrifice – the major cost being the lack of freedom to take advantage of short-term gains arising from competing offers (Sheth and Parvatiyar, 1995). In their attempts to win new customers, many organisations reinforce this perceived sacrifice by themselves targeting new customers with introductory deals that offer better terms than those afforded to existing customers. In 1991 it was estimated that the credit card company, MBNA, spent on average $100 to attract a new customer. A customer who had had their credit card for five years generated about $100 profit per year, whilst a cardholder of ten years' standing accounted for some $300 per year (Clancy and Shulman, 1991). Ten years later in the UK, MBNA was offering an introductory interest rate of 1.9 per cent APR for the first six months on balance transfers from other credit cards. Existing customers paid 14.9 per cent APR on the balance of their MBNA account. Given that a number of credit cards regularly run similar offers, it is not surprising that an increasing number of customers are transferring their credit balance periodically to take advantage of introductory rates. Given the economics of customer retention in this sector, a strategy that rewarded long-term customers would seem far more logical.

Develop supporting systems

Gronroos (1994) argues that in order to practice RM, the task of the marketer should be approached from a process management perspective. In order to maintain relationships, the organisation must implement systems for managing communications, product quality and service recovery. These are discussed in the next section of this chapter.

Ending relationships

A planned approach to ending relationships

The ending of a relationship should ideally be a conscious decision. Whilst many businesses work hard to establish, develop and maintain relationships, less attention appears to be given to relationship dissolution. For example, Colgate and Stewart's study of personal banking services in New Zealand found that the personal bankers managed on average 500 customers – far too many with which to maintain satisfactory relationships. However, in the absence of any data regarding the profitability of each customer, the personal bankers were unable to focus their efforts on the most valuable relationships. Instead, they tended to take a reactive stance, giving attention as demanded by each customer (Colgate and Stewart, 1998).

Ending complex relationships

In business-to-business relationships resource ties and the complexity of commercial links between the buyer and supplier usually mean that the process of dissolution must be more carefully considered (Hakansson and Snehota, 1995). This situation also exists in some high value, complex consumer products, such as financial or legal services, where the bonds between customer and supplier may be many and varied. In organisations which operate purely in low value, high volume sectors, failure to manage the process properly in such situations can inflict serious damage on the disengaging organisation. Too abrupt a dissolution may lead the ex-partner to engage in negative word of mouth, and be viewed unfavourably by the disengaging organisation's other partners or customers. On the other hand, too gentle an exit may extend the relationship unnecessarily, and create additional costs that do not directly benefit the disengaging organisation. Alajoutsijarvi *et al.* (2000) identify ten exit strategies, as illustrated in Figure 5.3.

Direct exit strategies

Direct exit strategies are those in which the disengaging organisation clearly signals its dissatisfaction with the relationship. Where the former is uninterested in the impact of dissolution on the partner, this may be presented as a fait accompli. If the disengaging organisation has already taken the decision to withdraw, but is concerned about the effects of the

	Partner-centred	Self-centred
Direct	Mutual discussion Negotiated separation	Fait accompli Ultimatum Blame attribution
Indirect	Disguised withdrawal Fading	Signalling Cost escalation Withdrawal

Figure 5.3

Relationship exit
strategies

Adapted from Alajoutsijarvi, K., Moller, K. and Tahtinen, J. (2000) 'Beautiful exit: how to leave your business partner', *European Journal of Marketing*, 34, 11/12, 1274.

action on other customers or partners, it may engage in blame attribution to establish that the decision was caused by the shortcomings of the partner, thus abdicating responsibility for the decision. For organisations more concerned about their partners, a negotiated separation allows both parties the opportunity to rationalise the event, and plan for the effects that this will have on their businesses. The revocable exit is appropriate when the relationship is salvageable – the parties discuss the state of the relationship with a view to finding a solution. In the case of a mutual discussion, agreement is possible without serious compromise on either side. In an ultimatum strategy, the views of the two parties will be so far apart that one party will have to compromise its own interests or lose the partner.

Indirect exit strategies

Indirect strategies are subtler, but usually take longer, and leave the partner uncertain as to the state of the relationship. Disguised exits involve a conscious attempt to conceal the intention to end the relationship. By cost escalation or otherwise signalling dissatisfaction by making greater demands on the partner (e.g. more frequent deliveries, more stringent quality requirements etc.), the disengaging organisation alters the terms of the relationship in such as way as to be unacceptable to the partner. This transfers the initiative, and, therefore, the responsibility for making the decision to exit onto the partner. The disguised withdrawal strategy involves letting the partner down gently, by scaling down the business conducted with the partner over a period of time, without revealing the ultimate intention to exit. This allows the partner to adapt to the loss of business over time, and soften the impact of final dissolution. Tacit strategies involve the least effort on the part of the disengaging organisation. Business is simply discontinued without explanation, either gradually in the fading strategy or abruptly in withdrawal. The former is classified as partner orientated, since it allows them to adjust gradually to the end of the relationship.

Choice of strategy

Alajoutsijarvi *et al.* (2000) identified examples of the various exit strategies in four relationships between businesses. They noted that different strategies were appropriate in different circumstances, but from their findings, the following key factors can be identified:

- Power of the partner: in a market were there are few alternative partners, or the partner to be 'dropped' enjoys an influential position, partner-centred strategies are more appropriate. The possibility that the disengaging organisation may need to reactivate the relationship, or that the ex-partner will damage other relationships, means that the disengaging organisation should be sensitive to its partner's interests.
- The mechanics of the relationship: when the relationship involves strong personal bonds between individuals in the two organisations, partner-centred strategies are more appropriate, to avoid damaging staff morale and retention.
- The relationship network: where the details of the dissolution are likely to be widely known throughout the disengaging organisation's relationship network, the disengaging organisation should behave in line with the relational norms of the network. For example, a network that values trustworthy, partner-centred behaviour will react badly to self-centred strategies, whereas one that values direct action and economy of effort may react badly to partner-centred strategies.

Implications for relationship maintenance

Alajoutsijarvi *et al.* (2000) note that the organisations in the study tended to move from one strategy to another, signalling dissatisfaction through an indirect strategy, before moving on to a more direct approach. In the same way, Stewart (1998) found that in the consumer banking sector, customers rarely took an abrupt and unilateral decision to close their accounts. Exit usually occurred only after they had made a deliberate effort to signal their dissatisfaction or negotiate a solution to their problem. If the bank responded positively at this stage, it was likely that the relationship could be saved. Few could be salvaged once the customer had taken direct action to withdraw. In other words, an organisation will normally be given early warning of a customer's intention to withdraw, if it remains sensitive to indirect withdrawal strategies. This, and other aspects of relationship recovery are discussed in more detail in Chapter seven.

The limitations of strategy

Strategy belongs more properly to the planning stage of RM rather than to implementation, since a strategy is essentially an intention rather than an action. Whilst a strategy provides the guidance needed to make decisions about resource allocation, and provides motivation and direction for staff, it offers little in terms of concrete results. Throughout the discussion of strategies, reference has repeatedly been made to the systems and structures that must be set up in order to implement a given stratcgy. These will now be examined in more detail.

Structures

The functions of organisational structure

In defence of structure

For the purpose of this section, structure is defined as the allocation of authority, responsibility and resources within an organisation. For reasons that will become clear as the section progresses, the subject of organisational structure is somewhat unfashionable amongst the academic community. The trend in industry at present is towards flatter and more fluid structures, eroding the distinction between different levels and functional areas of the organisation. It may, therefore, be worth reviewing some of the positive effects of a clearly defined organisational structure. Many practitioners understand the task of managing a business unit through concepts of structure; a corporate structure diagram provides a useful overview of the key functions performed by the business, and the ways in which individuals interact. According to Jacques (1990), organisational structure or hierarchy has the following functions:

- Separating out jobs which have different levels of complexity or involve different types of mental activity;
- Ensuring that people are accountable for what they do (and don't do);
- Adding value to work as it progresses through the organisation;
- Providing a vehicle for performance evaluation and staff appraisal.

This list could be extended, however, by the inclusion of the functions discussed below.

Motivation and direction of staff

By assigning leadership and authority to individuals, the structure provides a vehicle by which instructions can be passed down through the organisation, and a control mechanism that ensures that these instructions are carried out. Such control may be exercised through coercion and the use of penalties, or positive motivation and the use of rewards. In addition, the fact that structures clearly assign leadership roles helps staff to know whom they should look to for instruction, guidance and advice. The presence of hierarchy also motivates staff by offering the opportunity of career progression.

Flow of information

A clear structure can enhance the flow of information through the business. Staff on the ground have a clear point of reference (i.e. the manager/supervisor) from which to receive information from senior management and feed back comments, ideas or views. It also helps senior management to influence the flow of information – if the dissemination network is clearly defined, in theory, senior management can control what information is transmitted to specific parts of the organisation.

Understanding organisational roles

Perhaps the most powerful function of the organisational structure is in helping individuals within the organisation to understand their roles and responsibilities and how they fit with, and are separate from, others in the organisation. If this did not happen, the business could not function.

Disadvantages of corporate structures

Despite these powerful advantages, the trend at present is towards flatter, less rigid structures, cutting out layers of management and defining organisational boundaries and responsibilities less rigidly. Often, the primary motivation for such downsizing is the reduction of the overheads caused by superfluous layers of management. Gattorna and Walters (1996) note, however, that the traditional hierarchy may obstruct the implementation of customer service programmes. What, then, are the problems created by too rigid or elaborate a structure?

Promote internal focus

The fact that structures provide a means by which individuals or departments can obtain greater power or rewards than others in the organisation can encourage staff to view the organisation itself as their competitive arena, and to ignore the external environment. Managerial attention becomes focused on the struggle between departments for resources and prestige, whilst individuals pursue personal goals rather than those of the organisation. Meanwhile, the business becomes further and further out of step with its customers and its competitors.

Obstruct information flow

The creation of formal lines of communication can actually obstruct the flow of information throughout the organisation. Doyle (1994) argues that flattening the structure is a necessary stage in the development of a customer-orientated organisation, since an extensive hierarchy creates communication barriers between the customer and senior management. Similarly, the segregation of groups of staff into different departments, each with its own objectives or performance targets, inhibits inter-functional coordination. Perhaps the most obstructive distinction, from the marketer's point of view, is the distinction between customer-facing staff and those without a direct role in customer service. This creates the impression that the responsibility for satisfying customers resides with a defined group of staff, leaving the others free to focus on the work of the organisation – such an attitude makes it difficult for customer orientation to permeate the entire business.

Reduce flexibility

The existence of strictly defined procedures, lines of communication and responsibilities militates against responsiveness to customer needs. Research by Miles and Snow (1978), for example, suggests that organisations that focus on configuring internal structures for maximum efficiency – called defender organisations – are only effective in stable environments. The organisations that performed better in dynamic environments tended to have flatter, more flexible structures, with decentralised control. Called 'prospectors' by Miles and Snow (1978), these organisations are better able to adapt to changing conditions and new opportunities.

Inhibit inter-functional coordination

The sum effect of the disadvantages outlined above is to reduce the effectiveness and efficiency with which the parts of the business work together to meet the needs of the customer. Without such coordination, the RM programme will not be successful.

Promoting inter-functional coordination

The marketer must therefore pay particular attention to issues or structure when implementing RM programmes. The following give examples of strategies and tactics that can be employed. It should be recognised that whilst a fundamental rethink of the organisational structure is usually the ideal course of action, in practice few marketers have the freedom to effect such changes.

Flatter structures

Commonly known as downsizing, organisational renewal or reforming, the elimination of layers of middle management was a popular managerial pastime in the 1990s. A study of a major American trade association showed that 90 per cent of its members downsized between 1989 and 1994 (Cravens and Piercy, 1994). Although the benefits of such a strategy should be clear from the preceding discussion, a note of caution should be sounded. Ford, for example, was unable to recreate the success of its Taurus car, since no one was left after the downsizing who could remember how it was designed (Griffiths *et al.*, 2001). It is not just knowledge that may be lost through injudicious downsizing. Customers may defect in reaction to the redundancy of individuals with whom they had strong personal links, either because of active canvassing on the part of the members of staff concerned, or in retaliation to what they see as an unethical business practice.

Decentralisation

Christopher *et al.* (1991) recommend that the authority over the marketing function be decentralised, to facilitate close and fast support to customers. By devolving the authority needed to satisfy customers to those staff with direct customer contact, the business can respond immediately to changing customer needs, customising the service product on an individual basis. Batman and Soybali (1999) found, for example, that German tour operating companies owed much of their success to a decentralised structure. The empowerment of customer-facing staff to make key decisions not only improved service responsiveness and flexibility, but also improved staff motivation and productivity.

Organising business teams and functions around customers

According to Cravens and Piercy (1994), the 1990s trend for downsizing was accompanied by the reorganisation of the business into key processes, such as sales generation or customer service, and multifunctional teams became the primary business unit. Integrating staff from various functions in this way achieves greater coordination between what have hitherto been seen as separate elements of the organisation. In RM programmes, these teams should be organised around individual accounts or groups of customers (Christopher *et al.*, 1991). Where the number of separate customers means that teams must manage a number of customer relationships, care should be taken not to overload the team with accounts (Colgate and Stewart, 1998).

Customer champions

Organising teams or individual responsibilities around customers has benefits beyond the promotion of inter-functional coordination. By assigning responsibility for a customer or group of customers to a specific individual or team, the business creates a customer champion, responsible for representing the interest of the customer within the organisation. This is one of the founding principles of Key Account Management, discussed in more detail in Chapter nine.

The network view of the organisation

With the developments in the management of corporate structure outlined above, many theorists (e.g. Gummesson, 1996) believe that the traditional concept of structure should be abandoned, and organisations should be viewed as a network. The network is flexible, so that the business can be reconfigured to respond to changing environmental conditions or to exploit opportunities. Perhaps most importantly, the network extends beyond a single organisation, creating what Gummesson (1996) termed an 'imaginary organisation'. The need for this type of organisation is partly due to the trend towards downsizing, with suppliers being asked to perform tasks that were previously handled by internal staff (Griffiths *et al.*, 2001).

Research into the nature and operations of typical networks can be valuable in helping an organisation to manage relationships in supplier markets or with other marketing channel partners. In a dynamic marketing environment, it is easier to respond to change by reconfiguring the network than by restructuring a large internal resources base. Cravens and Piercy (1994) identify four types of network, as illustrated in Figure 5.4.

The hollow network

This form of network is found in highly unstable marketing environments. The core organisation has limited internal capabilities, but uses other organisations to perform functions in response to individual transactions. The network is transaction based – the core organisation forges temporary links with other organisations as and when needed, but does not maintain these in the long term. Cravens and Piercy (1994) give the example of The Registry Inc, which recruits software engineers, programmers etc. to perform contract services for corporate clients. The business uses a database of 50,000 technical specialists to recruit teams for each contract.

The flexible network

In contrast, the core organisation of a flexible network maintains longer-term relationships with other network members, but each member is more adaptable in the face of new demands or changing conditions. Thus the

Figure 5.4

Alternative types of network

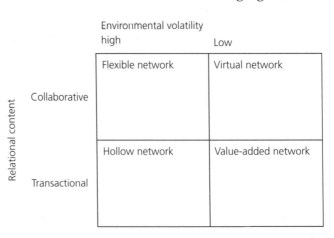

Source: Cravens, D. and Piercy, N. (1994) 'Relationship marketing and collaborative networks in service organisations', *International Journal of Service Industry Management*, 5, 5, 39–53.

network is able to thrive in a dynamic environment with limited changes to the structure of the network.

The value added network

Here, the organisations come together because of the way in which their core competencies complement one another in the creation of customer value. The core organisation is usually responsible for product innovation and design, using a range of suppliers and distributors on a transactional basis. This configuration is better suited to stable markets, where the core organisation is confident that the choice of suppliers and intermediaries will remain wide.

The virtual network

Still operating in a stable environment, the members of the virtual network seek to create competitive advantage through closer collaboration and the creation of joint systems. This form of network lacks the adaptability of the flexible organisation, instead focusing on the incremental development of collaborative systems. It is therefore more suitable to a stable environment.

Limitations of structural perspective

Thinking about the business in terms of its structure provides a useful snapshot of the organisation, its functions and relationships at a given point in time. It does not, however, help to develop an understanding of how the business will be managed on a day-to-day basis, or how the process of managing relationships will be tackled. Issues of structure are therefore less fundamental to the implementation of RM programmes than to those of systems – the topic of the next section.

Systems

The importance of systems

The importance of organisational systems to RM cannot be overstated – Gronroos (1996) argues that one of the three key strategic implications of RM is the adoption of a process perspective. The development of a customer's trust in a supplier requires the reliable fulfilment of promises over time. The successful implementation of RM therefore requires that careful attention be paid to the design and maintenance of systems and processes. This section examines the principles and practices of Total Quality Management (TQM) and Business Process Re-engineering (BPR), both of which have been identified by numerous authors as essential ingredients of RM. Because TQM is so important a part of RM, many of the principles, processes and techniques mentioned here are described in more detail in other chapters.

Total quality management

There is no commonly agreed definition of total quality management (TQM), a phrase which has been used to describe a wide range of business activities. Different TQM theorists have brought different perspectives and tools to bear on the problems of managing quality. Nevertheless, a number of common components which have clear interrelationships with RM principles can be identified.

Quality

Not surprisingly, the starting point of TQM systems is the development of quality specifications for the product or service in question, specifications which must be developed with reference to the customer. Manufacturing quality is commonly defined as 'fitness for use' (Juran and Gryna, 1988), hence the creation of a quality product can only be achieved by exploring the uses to which the product is put by the customer. Although this allows for some subjectivity in customers' judgements about quality, the definition of quality as fitness for use does assume that quality is an attribute of the product itself – something that can be created through the design and production process. This view of quality is described as *mechanistic quality*. As discussed in Chapter three, the concept of *humanistic quality* holds that quality is a subjective judgement made by the consumer of the product – it exists in the perceptions of the customer rather than being an attribute of the product itself (Holbrook and Corfman, 1985). The humanistic view of quality is generally applied to service products, the intangibility and variability of which mean that perceptions of quality are likely to differ widely between customers. However, given that tangible goods commonly include intangible elements, such as experience benefits or symbolic benefits, the concept also applies in the manufacturing context.

The humanistic view of quality causes difficulties in the development of quality specifications. Service marketers have addressed this problem either through specifications based on outcome quality or process quality. Outcome definitions, such as Parasuraman *et al.*'s (1985) five dimensions of quality, focus on specifying the perceptions that the service should create. The five dimensions of responsiveness, assurance, tangibles, empathy and reliability provide benchmarks that can be used to create targets and form the basis for the monitoring of customer perceptions. Process specifications involve mapping the sequence of events that make up the service experience, and identifying the critical incidents or 'moments of truth' (Carlzon, 1987). The service product can then be specified in terms of these events. The development of both outcome and process specifications is discussed in detail in Chapter seven.

Reliability

Having defined the product, the next stage of the TQM process is to develop processes that ensure that production consistently meets the quality specification. The quality specification is used to determine the format of production processes or service delivery and support systems necessary to meet customer requirements. Efficiency is often stressed – efficiency should be a secondary consideration to that of effectiveness in meeting quality specifications, since there is little point in improving the efficiency of ineffective processes. Nevertheless, the more efficiently an organisation meets these requirements, the greater its capacity for offering additional services or serving additional customers.

Continuous improvement

Meeting quality specifications in itself is not enough to ensure that customers perceive that a product is of high quality. As discussed in Chapter three, customers base their quality judgements on their expectations of product performance. These expectations are based on their experience of the product. Hence a performance standard that initially exceeds customer expectations quickly becomes expected. In order to continue to exceed customer expectations, therefore, the organisation must develop mechanisms for continuously improving the quality of its products in the eyes of the customer. This philosophy of continuous improvement is also called Kaizen.

Mechanistic approaches to TQM

Just as service quality can be viewed from a mechanistic or humanistic perspective, so too can the creation of organisational conditions necessary to create such quality. Mechanistic approaches view the organisation as a machine, comprising a number of different components (departments) that work together to create the final product. By improving communications between departments and aligning departmental targets and monitoring systems, the work of the various organisational components is synchronised. Mechanistic approaches put particular emphasis on the analysis of business processes, the creation of systems, teams and performance measures. Martins and Toledo (2000) for example, recommend that a total quality management program should contain:

- Guiding principles
- Targets and strategies
- Performance measures and check points
- Supporting processes
- Actions, deadlines and responsibilities.

Mechanistic approaches also include the adoption of behaviour systems such as the Deming wheel or the quality cycle (see Figure 5.5). Such models

Figure 5.5

The quality cycle

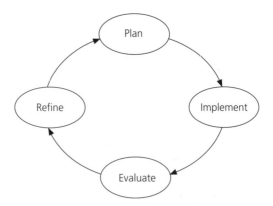

provide a template which staff at all levels of the organisation are trained to apply to their daily tasks. The intention is that consistent behaviour will lead to consistent results. The concepts of internal marketing (see Chapter six), and the establishment of service level agreements between departments are used by the mechanistic school to promote inter-functional coordination.

Humanistic approaches to TQM

Humanistic approaches regard the key challenge of TQM to be the creation of a quality culture in which staff use their own initiative and judgement to deliver a quality product, rather than adhering slavishly to predetermined quality specifications. For example, the leading TQM exponent Edward Deming (1986) proposes the movement is founded on three principles, two of which relate to staff rather than systems:

- Empowered employees
- Continuous improvement
- Quality improvement teams.

Humanistic approaches put greater emphasis on mechanisms which involve staff in the determination of quality specifications and continuous improvement. They therefore advocate methods such as employee suggestion schemes, quality circles, staff meetings, management by walking about and the devolution of authority to customer-facing staff. Less importance is placed on the monitoring of staff performance; indeed, Deming argues that staff that are subject to formal monitoring will not perform as well as those who feel that they are trusted to fulfil their duties without close supervision. Similarly, inter-functional coordination is still of prime importance, but this is achieved through communication, job rotation and the creation of cross-functional teams rather than formal devices such as the specification of service level agreements.

It should be stressed here that the humanistic and mechanistic approaches are not mutually exclusive; Deming's work, for example, includes elements of both. However, certain elements of the respective approaches do conflict. The organisation's approach to the monitoring of employee performance is one such element. The mechanistic approach demands that performance standards are carefully defined and monitored by senior management, whilst the humanistic approach delegates this responsibility to the staff on the ground. Methods for dealing with this conflict are discussed in depth in Chapter seven. It is worth noting here, however, that the subjective nature of service quality means that service products lend themselves more easily to the humanistic approach to quality management.

Business process re-engineering

Although BPR is treated as a different concept to TQM, it is effectively an extension of the same set of principles. Whereas TQM implements mechanisms by which the efforts of the various organisational components are coordinated to meet a customer-driven quality specification, BPR advocates that the organisation be totally redesigned around this specification, creating a structure based on business processes rather than functional areas. BPR therefore offers a more radical solution to the quality problem.

The BPR movement is led by Michael Hammer, but as with TQM, has spawned a variety of approaches and methodologies. According to Valiris and Glykas (1999), the common elements of all such approaches consist of a five-stage process (see Figure 5.6).

TQM, BPR and customer/supplier relationships

The application of TQM and BPR to RM goes beyond the provision of a means by which the organisation may fulfil its promises. Gummesson's concept of the imaginary corporation (Gummesson, 1996) advocates that

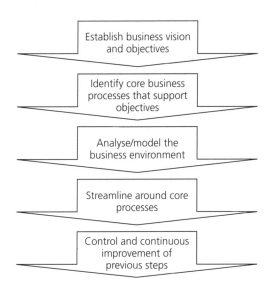

Figure 5.6

Key steps in business process re-engineering (BPR)

Establish business vision and objectives

Identify core business processes that support objectives

Analyse/model the business environment

Streamline around core processes

Control and continuous improvement of previous steps

Based on Valiris and Glykas (1999)

the relationship marketer should see their own organisation as part of a larger value system of suppliers and intermediaries, all of which collaborate to deliver value to the end consumer. The techniques of TQM and BPR should therefore be used to analyse, redesign and control the activities of the entire value chain, from initial supplier to the provider of after-sales service. Research by Dean and Terziovski (2001) supports the efficacy of such an approach. The research examined the management practices of 141 small to medium-sized service organisations in Australia. It found that the involvement of suppliers and customers in system change and development led to significant improvements in relationship quality and business performance.

Summary

Chapter five began by outlining the McKinsey Seven S framework, which sets out the key areas that need to be considered in implementing organisational change. The chapter addressed strategy, structure and systems, termed 'hard' management issues because they can be defined and influenced by senior management more easily than the other four areas. Strategies for initiating, developing, maintaining and ending relationships were outlined. It was stressed, however, that a flexible approach to strategy is integral to RM, since strategy is developed in collaboration with the customers, rather than being imposed on them by the supplier. The supplier's structure is an important element in enabling this flexibility. The chapter, therefore, went on to consider ways in which flatter structures could be developed around individual customers or groups of customers, and networks could be developed to create robust organisational structures that are sufficiently responsive to changing customer requirements. Finally, the systems that these structures supported were considered. An organisation's systems were presented as one of the most important elements in managing relationships, since they govern the nature of the customer's experience over time, and hence have a profound effect on ongoing customer satisfaction and trust. The chapter referred to principles and practices of Total Quality Management (TQM) and Business Process Re-engineering (BPR) in advising how systems could be developed that would enhance the quality and reliability of an organisation's total product offer, as well as facilitate continuous improvement.

Case Study   *Vodafone*

On May 2002, Vodafone announced annual losses for 2001/2 of £13.5 billion, the largest in British corporate history. Although the bulk of this deficit can be attributed to the reduction in the estimated value of key assets, some commentators argue that Vodafone faces a bleak future, paying the price for its failure to pay attention to existing customers. According to its harshest critics, the giant of the 1990s has become a gasping dinosaur in the new millennium.

The label of 'giant' does not exaggerate the extent of Vodafone's operations, with more than 101 million customers world wide across 28 countries, making it the world's largest mobile telecommunications company. In the UK alone, it has well over 13 million corporate and individual customers, operating analogue and digital mobile phone networks and services, radio paging, and voice messaging services. It also services national public data networks and operates over 300 retail outlets.

The fact that the company first started operating only 17 years ago makes such achievements all the more impressive. Racal-Vodafone gained the first licence to operate cellular phones in the UK in 1982, and launched the network in 1985. Six years later Racal and Vodafone split, and the Vodafone group was officially born. Since then, the company has grown swiftly through a series of deals, merging with America's Airtouch Communications in 1999, and, perhaps most famously, acquiring the German company Mannesmann in 2000.

It is this strategy of growth through acquisition, however, that feeds the growing doubts about the stability of Vodafone's foundations. In the past, the dizzying speed of market growth, and customers' seemingly insatiable thirst for new technology have made for an environment which tolerates mediocrity. It looks as though those days are past. Eighty per cent of Vodafone's growth last year came from

acquisitions or by increases in holdings of key companies abroad, not from 'true' customer acquisition. With market penetration at over 70 per cent in Europe and the US, and the lack of innovative applications hamstringing the potential of the mobile Internet, it seems that the company will have to look to its existing customers and products to provide future growth (Capell, 2002). Judging by Vodafone's customer defection rates, and failure to gain a significant increase in revenue per customer, this is something the telecoms giant is poorly equipped to do (*Marketing*, 2002a).

It seems that Vodafone has understood the need to shift the focus onto retention. According to its UK Marketing Director, Lance Batchelor:

> Eighty per cent of the battle is satisfying and leveraging existing customers, with the other twenty per cent of the emphasis acquiring customers (Marketing, 2002b: 18).

The way to achieve this, says Batchelor, is the development of vehicles for direct contact between customers and employees, at all levels of the organisation. Hence the creation of 'Club Vodafone' – an internal marketing communications exercise aiming to raise awareness of the company's various products, promote the brand internally and encourage staff to promote the brand more actively to external customers (*Marketing*, 2002c).

There is evidence that Club Vodafone is building on firm foundations. In the late 1990s, the company implemented an extensive internal coaching programme within its Radio Networks Division, designed to support a move to multi-skilled, process orientated teams. The combination of systems, structural and cultural change led to real improvements in operational flexibility and responsiveness (Eaton and Brown, 2002). The company also has a clear set of business principles, which set out its duties to shareholders, customers, employees and other stakeholders, and a Corporate Responsibility Programme that reports on the adherence to these principles (www.vodafone.com/), 4 September 2002). The company's efforts to market the brand internally can therefore draw on established corporate values.

In terms of Vodafone's strategy for external marketing, however, the direction looks less clear. Despite Batchelor's apparent commitment to retention, the company's strategy statement concentrates on growth rather than consolidation: 'Vodafone aims to be the world's leading wireless telecommunications and information provider, generating more customers, more services and more value than any of its competitors' (www.vodafone.com, 4 September 2002).

Similarly, Vodafone's *Future Vision* focuses not on the development of stronger links with customers, but on growth fuelled by globalisation and the development of communications technology (www.vodafone.com, 4 September 2002). Certainly, the strategy to date has been directed to the establishment of a 'global footprint', whereby Vodafone customers can access services all over the world. Presently, this benefit appeals only to a minority of business customers, amounting to no more than 5 per cent of all mobile phone users (*The Economist US*, 2002). Vodafone's vision, and apparently its strategy, are based on the assumption that this lifestyle will soon become the norm. Perhaps more worryingly, the company's *Future Vision* predicts that the number of customers will continue to double every two or three years (www.vodafone.com, 4 September 2002). The question is, will their *Future Vision* blind them to the need for building customer relationships today?

References

Capell, K. (2002) 'Vodafone's Gent may be making the wrong call...', *Business Week*, 15 July, 3791, 30.

Eaton, J. and Brown, D. (2002) 'Coaching for a change in Vodafone', *Career Development International*, 7, 5, 284–287

Economist, The (US) (2002) 'Written down but not out; Vodafone' 1 June.

Marketing (2002a) 'Opinion: customer focus is an invaluable rainy day policy', 16 May: 16.

Marketing (2002b) 'Navigating telecoms', Lance Batchelor, UK Marketing Director, Vodafone, 27 June: 18.

Marketing (2002c) 'Branding briefs: Vodafone produces internal communications pack', 15 August: 9.

Discussion questions

1. Identify the rationale for pursuing a RM strategy in the mobile telecom's market.

2. What advantages and disadvantages would a RM strategy offer over Vodafone's current strategy of expansion through acquisition?

3. Based on the evidence given in the case study, would Vodafone's systems and structures support a RM strategy?

4. What changes would have to be made, if any, to pursue RM more actively?

References

Alajoutsijarvi, K., Moller, K. and Tahtinen, J. (2000) 'Beautiful exit: how to leave your business partner', *European Journal of Marketing*, 34, 11/12, 1270–1290.

Batman, O. and Soybali, H. (1999) 'An examination of the organisational characteristics of selected German travel companies in Turkey', *International Journal of Contemporary Hospitality Management*, 11, 43–50.

Berry, L. and Yadav, M. (1996) 'Capture and communicate value in the pricing of services', *Sloan Management Review*, Summer, 37, 4, 41–52.

Carlzon, J. (1987) *Moments of Truth*, New York: Harper and Row.

Christopher, M., Payne, A. and Ballantyne, D. (1991) *Relationship Marketing – Bringing quality, customer service and marketing together*, Oxford: Butterworth-Heinemann.

Clancy, K. and Shulman, R. (1991) *The Marketing Revolution*, New York: HarperCollins Publishers.

Colgate, M. and Stewart, K. (1998) 'The challenge of relationships in services – a New Zealand study', *International Journal of Service Industry Management*, 9, 5, 454–468.

Cravens, D. and Piercy, N. (1994) 'Relationship marketing and collaborative networks in service organisations', *International Journal of Service Industry Management*, 5, 5, 39–53.

Dean, A. and Terziovski, M. (2001) 'Quality practices and customer/supplier management in Australian service organisations', *Total Quality Management*, 12, 5, 611–621.

Deming, E. (1986) *Out of the Crisis*, Cambridge: Cambridge University Press.

Dibb, S., Simkin, L., Pride, W. and Ferrell, O. (2000) *Marketing Concepts and Strategies*, Boston: Houghton-Mifflin.

Donaldson, B. and O'Toole, T. (2000) 'Classifying relationship structures: relationship strength in industrial markets', *Journal of Business and Industrial Marketing*, 15, 7, 491–506.

Doyle, P. (1994) *Marketing Management and Strategy*, Harlow: Prentice Hall.

Gattorna, J.L. and Walters, D.W. (1996) *Managing the Supply Chain: A Strategic Perspective*, Basingstoke: Macmillan Business.

Griffiths, J., Elson, B. and Amos, D. (2001) 'A customer-supplier model to improve customer focus in turbulent environments', *Managing Service Quality*, 11, 1, 57–66.

Gronroos, C. (1996) 'Relationship marketing: strategic and tactical implications', *Management Decision*, 34, 3, 5–14.

Grossman, R.P. (1998) 'Developing and managing effective consumer relationships', *Journal of Product and Brand Management*, 7, 1, 27–40.

Hakansson, H. and Snehota, I. (1995) 'Analyzing business relationships' in H. Hakansson, and I. Snehota, (eds) *Developing Relationships in Business Networks*, London: Routledge.

Holbrook, M. and Corfman, K. (1985) 'Quality and value in the consumption experience: Phaldrus rides again' in J. Jacoby and J. Olsen (eds) *Perceived Quality*, Lexington, Massachusetts: Lexington Books.

Jacques, E. (1990) 'In praise of hierarchy', *Harvard Business Review*, 68, 1, 127–133.

Johnson, J. (1999) 'Raising relationships. (Using predictive modelling to connect with customers)', *Bank Marketing*, 31, 6, 30(7).

Juran, J. and Gryna, F. (eds) (1988) *Juran's Quality Control Handbook*, 4th edn, New York: McGraw-Hill.

Lindgreen, A. and Crawford, I. (1999) 'Implementing, monitoring and measuring a programme of relationship marketing', *Marketing Intelligence and Planning*, 17, 5, 231–239.

Martins, R. and Toledo, J. (2000) 'Total Quality Management programs: a framework proposal', *Work Study*, 49, 4, 145–151.

Miles, R. and Snow, C. (1978) *Organisational Strategy, Structure and Process*, New York: McGraw-Hill.

Munsen, C., Rosenblatt, M. and Rosenblatt, Z. (1999) 'The use and abuse of power in supply chains', *Business Horizons*, 42, 1, 55–60.

Parasuraman, A., Zeithaml, V. and Berry, L. (1985) 'A conceptual model of service quality and its implications for future research', *Journal of Marketing*, 49, September, 41–50.

Sharma, N. and Patterson, P. (2000) 'Switching costs, alternative attractiveness and experience as moderators of relationship commitment in professional, consumer services', *International Journal of Service Industry Management*, 11, 5, 470–490.

Sheth, J. and Parvatiyar, A. (1995) 'Relationship marketing in consumer markets: antecedents and consequences', *Journal of the Academy of Marketing Science*, 23, 255–271.

Stewart, K. (1998) 'An exploration of customer exit in retail banking', *International Journal of Bank Marketing*, 16, 1, 6–29.

Valiris, G. and Glykas, M. (1999) 'Critical review of existing BPR methodologies: the need for a holistic approach', *Business Process Management*, 5, 1, 65–86.

Waterman, R., Peters, T. and Phillips, J. (1980) 'Structure is not organisation', *Business Horizons*, June, 14–26.

6 Implementing RM programmes
Shared values, staff, skills and style

Learning objectives

After reading this chapter, you should be able to:

- Explain the meaning of the term internal marketing, and the distinction between transaction and relational approaches to internal marketing.

- Outline the importance of shared values to the implementation of RM, and suggest some methods by which these might be developed and communicated.

- Identify different categories of internal relationship, and explain the management implications of these differences.

- Apply RM principles to the development of employee reward and training mechanisms.

Introduction

As discussed in Chapter five, issues relating to systems, structure and strategy are often termed 'hard' issues, since these components of the organisation are relatively easy to define, design and manipulate. The 'softer' issues of staff, skills, style and shared values are less clearly defined, and less amenable to direct manipulation. Nevertheless, their impact on the performance of the organisation is as great, if not greater than that of the hard components. In the previous chapter it was noted, for example, that no total quality management system will work if it does not have the support and commitment of the staff which operate it. This chapter therefore considers the impact of shared values, style, staff and skills, and suggests ways in which senior management can seek to influence these factors. Given the nature of these issues, it is harder to separate conceptual and practical issues into the four distinct classifications – no apology is made, for example, for the fact that issues discussed under staff might just as well be classified as style or skills issues. Much of the literature deals with such matters under the blanket term of 'internal marketing'. The chapter, therefore, begins with a look at developments in this area, which set out some key principles that should inform the management of the organisation and its staff. It then turns to more practical considerations under the remaining headings of the Seven S framework.

Internal marketing

Employees as customers

It has long been recognised that marketing cannot be exclusively concerned with issues external to the organisation. The implementation of any change, such as the move to a RM approach, must be supported by corresponding changes within the organisation, not only in terms of systems and structures but also in the attitudes and abilities of staff. More than twenty years ago, Leonard Berry first coined the term internal marketing, which he defined as 'the means of applying the philosophy and practice of marketing to people who serve external customers so that (i) the best possible people can be employed and retained and (ii) they will do the best possible work' (Berry, 1980).

The focus of Berry's conception of internal marketing was on employee recruitment and motivation, with a view of the employee as the customer and the job as the product. Although he developed the concept as part of an attempt to identify the differences between services marketing and its manufacturing counterpart, his approach to the development of internal marketing practice was informed by traditional approaches to marketing. Hence his assertion that 'The processes one thinks of as marketing – for example, market research, market segmentation, product modification and communications programming – are just as relevant to internal marketing as to external marketing' (Berry, 1983 in Payne *et al.*, 1995: 72)

Internal marketing as a change management tool

Although Berry's contribution in developing this area of marketing theory is significant, others have criticised his approach to the subject as being too narrow, and have built on his initial work. The literature on internal marketing is now broad, complex and often contradictory, stimulating debates that mirror those on external marketing.

Based on an extensive review of the literature, Rafiq and Ahmed (2000) identify five elements of internal marketing:

- Employee motivation and satisfaction: as seen in the work of Berry discussed above, many writers see internal marketing as a vehicle for staff acquisition, motivation and retention, which, it is argued, leads to greater productivity and external service quality.

- Customer orientation and customer satisfaction: Berry and his supporters saw the creation of employee satisfaction as an end in itself, albeit one with positive consequences for external customers. In contrast, Gronroos (1985) presents internal marketing as a vehicle for the explicit promotion of customer-orientated behaviour.

- Inter–functional coordination and integration: these are key elements of the marketing orientation as defined by Narver and Slater (1990). Hence Winter (1985), for example, recommends the use of internal marketing as a tool for aligning the efforts of the various functions within an organisation.

- A marketing-like approach to the above: clearly, there are other tools and techniques developed in other business areas that can achieve the functions identified above. Internal marketing must, therefore, look to marketing principles and practices in order to design and implement its programmes.

- Implementation of specific corporate or functional strategies: authors such as Piercy (2002) present internal marketing as a crucial stage in the implementation of strategic change. In this context, internal marketing is used as tool to generate understanding and support for strategic change, removing barriers such as complacency, the misallocation of resources and internal politics.

Internal marketing as a social process

Varey and Lewis (1999) argue for a broader definition of internal marketing. They suggest that the authors identified above tend to present internal marketing as 'simply persuasion of staff to a management determined situation' (Varey and Lewis, 1999: 929), and as a tool that is secondary to the prime business objective of customer and competitor responsiveness. They also point out that the marketing practices that are brought to internal marketing are limited to those of marketing mix management – Piercy, for example, develops a model of internal marketing based exclusively on the 4Ps (Piercy 1995).

Varey and Lewis' exhortations for the acceptance of a new paradigm for internal marketing mirror the debate surrounding RM. Indeed, the writers call for use of the term 'internal relationship marketing', which they define as 'an integrative process within a system for fostering positive working relationships in a developmental way in a climate of cooperation and achievement' (Varey and Lewis, 1999: 941).

The practice of internal RM involves the blurring of the internal–external boundary of the organisation through inter alia:

- Customer involvement in product design, production and service;
- Close partnership between suppliers and customers;
- Acceptance that relationships are enterprise assets;
- Open exchange of ideas of mutual gain;
- The systematic collection and dissemination of customer information (detailing and negotiating requirements, expectations, needs, attitudes and satisfaction).

Perhaps the most important feature of Varey and Lewis' approach is that internal marketing is not seen as a means of effecting change, but as an end in itself – the establishment of internal relationship marketing will create the conditions in which the organisation can move forward in partnership with its internal and external stakeholders, towards goals that can only emerge once these conditions are in place.

Internal RM as knowledge renewal

Ballantyne (2000) argues that the common denominator in all approaches to IM is knowledge renewal – that is, the generation and circulation of new knowledge – and states that there is a clear distinction between internal transaction marketing and internal relationship marketing. In this model, transaction marketing is concerned with the capture of knowledge, through measurement, control and research methods and knowledge codi-fication, in the form of new product information, policy, strategy etc. In contrast, internal relationship marketing is concerned with knowledge generation, through cross-functional teams and creative approaches to problem solving, and knowledge circulation through team-based learning programmes, feedback systems and skills development workshops. Trust is a prerequisite of internal relationship marketing – both between the organ-isation's various employees and between employees and the management. Without it, Ballantyne argues, the interaction, dialogue and motivation towards a common goal cannot occur.

Internal marketing – implementation tool or business philosophy?

The literature reviewed above points to two distinct approaches to internal marketing. In one, internal marketing is used by senior management as an enabling device for the implementation of a given initiative, such as RM. In the latter, internal marketing requires a radical rethink of the organisation, its systems and structures. Strategy is not preset by senior management, but emerges from dialogue between the various internal and external stakeholders. Although these tend to be portrayed in the literature as alter-natives, it is likely that they define the two ends of a spectrum (see Figure 6.1). Just as Chapter two identified a spectrum of external relationship marketing, an equivalent can be identified for internal marketing. Clearly, the latter approach is better suited to relationship marketing in its 'purest'

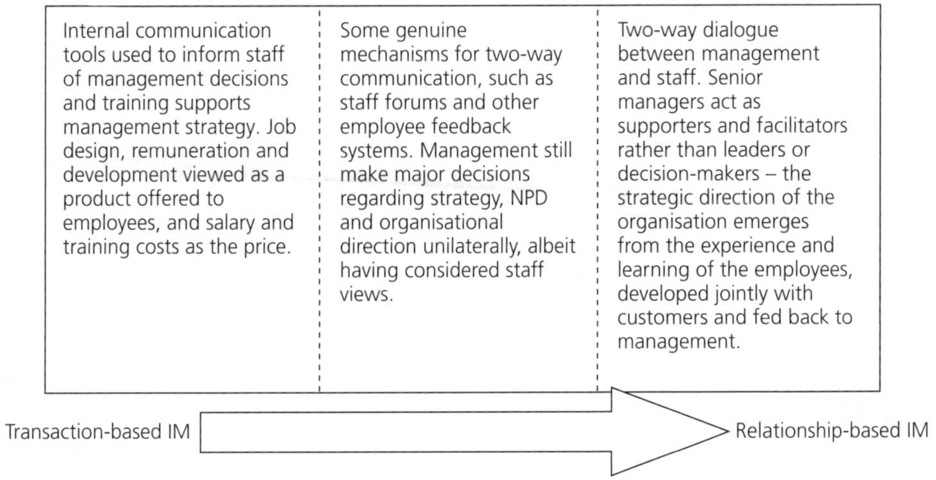

Internal communication tools used to inform staff of management decisions and training supports management strategy. Job design, remuneration and development viewed as a product offered to employees, and salary and training costs as the price.
Some genuine mechanisms for two-way communication, such as staff forums and other employee feedback systems. Management still make major decisions regarding strategy, NPD and organisational direction unilaterally, albeit having considered staff views.
Two-way dialogue between management and staff. Senior managers act as supporters and facilitators rather than leaders or decision-makers – the strategic direction of the organisation emerges from the experience and learning of the employees, developed jointly with customers and fed back to management.
Transaction-based IM
Relationship-based IM

Figure 6.1

The internal marketing transaction–relationship continuum

form, in which the boundaries between employees and customers should be all but gone. As noted in Chapter two, however, such an approach is not possible for all types of organisation. Even where this form of RM is appropriate, it may take many years to develop. Hence it is envisaged that even the most strictly transactional approach to internal marketing has its value, though often only as a stepping-stone to a more relational mode of operation. The rest of this chapter will therefore outline techniques that can be used at various points along the spectrum.

Shared values and culture

The importance of shared values

Christopher *et al.* define shared values as 'Those ideas of what is right and desirable (in corporate and/or individual behaviour) which are typical of the organisation and common to most of its members' (Christopher *et al.*, 1991: 164).

The presence of a set of shared values that permeate all levels of the organisation is essential for the development of a culture conducive to RM. In particular these shared values must include a commitment to quality and customer service (Christopher *et al.*, 1991).

Ethics and RM

It has been noted in previous chapters that ethics can be critical to the implementation of RM programmes. Given the effect of notions of fairness on customer satisfaction, and therefore on loyalty, it is proposed that the shared values should also define the ethical boundaries within which the organisation seeks to operate. These issues are discussed in detail in Chapter eight.

The mission statement

Purpose and value

This is the starting point for the creation of a RM-orientated culture. The mission statement should, in its most basic form, set out the long-term aim of the organisation. Wilson and Gillighan (1997) suggest that the mission can be derived from the answer to two simple questions: what business are we in, and what business should we be in? Mission statements often go beyond this requirement, however, attempting to define the way in which the ultimate goal of the business will be achieved. Asda's mission statement illustrates such an approach: 'To be Britain's best value fresh food and clothing superstore, by satisfying the weekly shopping needs of ordinary working people and their families who demand value' (www.asda.co.uk, 2002).

The statement not only defines the organisation's ultimate goal (to be Britain's best value food and clothing store), but also the target market (ordinary working people and their families) and the competitive positioning (value). The mission statement is supplemented with a statement of three values, intended to offer further guidance on the means by which the mission would be fulfilled:

- Respect for the individual
- Service to the customer
- Strive for excellence (www.asda.co.uk 2003).

In a study of 83 Canadian and North American companies, Bart, Bontis and Tapgar (2001) found that those mission statements which specified organisational means as well as ends had a greater effect on the performance of the business. They concluded:

> Through clearer specification of mission means – especially those that recognize an organisation's distinctive competence... – large diversified firms may finally have at their disposal the common denominator that enables them to create true 'unity of purpose' (Bart *et al.*, 2001).

Bart *et al.* further concluded that the relationship between the contents of the mission and financial performance is complex and indirect. Company performance is closely associated with employee behaviour, which is affected in turn by the degree of alignment between the stated mission and the organisation's systems. Whether, therefore, the mission statement promotes an integrated business, or is the product of one, is difficult to determine. It seems likely that both are true to some extent. On the one hand, a clear, meaningful mission statement provides guidance to employees, increasing their satisfaction, motivation and effectiveness. Conversely, a business that has clearly defined goals, value systems, and a strong cultural identity is likely both to perform well and to articulate a relevant and comprehensive mission statement. In any case, it will help the implementation of RM to develop a mission statement that reflects the values and goals of the organisation, and the importance it places on relationships as a means to achieving these goals.

Implementing the mission statement

The mission statement is unlikely to have a significant effect on employee behaviour without the commitment of staff throughout the organisation, particularly senior management. Bart *et al.* (2001) found a strong correlation between employees' perceptions of organisational commitment to the mission, and the alignment of their behaviour with the mission contents.

Marketing communications and shared values

The importance of communication

Marketing communications are clearly central to RM. Duncan and Moriarty (1998), for example, argue that trust and commitment are products of communication, concluding that 'Relationships…are impossible without communication'. It is tempting to view marketing communications as a systems issue rather than one of shared values. It should become clear, however, that the key to successful RM communications is the integration of the various messages transmitted *and* received by the organisation. It is the shared values that provide the basis for such integration, providing a set of guiding principles that temper the collective voice of the organisation. Before looking at how this can be done, however, we will look at the range of elements that comprise marketing communications.

Audience diversity

The traditional view of marketing communications is that separate mechanisms are used for communicating with internal and external customers respectively. The implication of RM is that the distinction between internal and external customers is virtually irrelevant. Communication systems should therefore encompass internal and external audiences, as defined in the Six Markets model of RM (see Chapter two). External audiences stretch far beyond the organisation's customers, including such groups as suppliers, intermediaries, shareholders, the press, the government, industry and professional bodies or trade associations, society as a whole and anyone who has a valid interest in what the organisation says, does or makes. Such audiences are commonly referred to as stakeholders.

Medium and message diversity

Stakeholders glean messages about the organisation from a number of sources. Marketing communications has traditionally focused on planned promotional activity such as advertising, public relations and direct marketing. Clearly, these channels are important, but research suggests that, in the early stages of a relationship at least, stakeholders put more trust in messages from personal or independent sources (Murray, 1991). Since RM focuses on customer retention, its communication strategies must also encompass the messages that customers gain from the consumption experience itself, since these will be decisive in determining repeat purchases. Gronroos (2000) identifies five types of message source:

1. *Planned messages* are the traditional communication media, such as advertising, telesales, mail-shots and personal selling.

2. *Product messages* are gained from the tangible aspects of the product, such as product design, durability, fitness for use and reliability.

3. *Unplanned messages* refers to independent and personal sources, such as word of mouth, news stories and product reviews.

4. *Service messages* are taken from the intangible elements of the product, such as interaction with sales staff, delivery or invoicing processes and complaints handling.

5. *Absence of communication* sends important messages about the care (or lack of it) with which the organisation treats its customers. Examples include failure to notify the customer of delivery delays or respond to a complaint.

The importance of integrated communications

Gronroos identifies two separate processes: the planned communication process is the deliberate delivery of planned messages and receipt of responses, whilst the interaction process consists of the customer giving and receiving messages through the consumption experience. He concludes, 'Only the integration of the planned communication and the interaction processes into one strategy that is systematically implemented creates relationship marketing' (Gronroos, 2000: 10).

Planned communication is crucial in recruiting new customers, developing relationships with existing customers and reinforcing the positive attitudes of existing customers' towards the organisation. It must be remembered, however, that these planned messages create expectations, against which the customer will judge the quality of the organisation's products. Failure to meet these expectations will destroy the customers' trust in the supplier. Hence, it is vital that the planned communication strategy be treated as an extension of internal policies, processes and values, as illustrated in Figure 6.2.

Establishing corporate values

This should be the foundation of any RM communication programme. There is little point in trying to develop the organisation's profile if it cannot withstand the critical gaze of the public eye. Establishing corporate values is more about internal processes than external. Quality assurance processes, a corporate code of ethics, and internal marketing all help to ensure that the organisation develops a consistent voice when dealing with

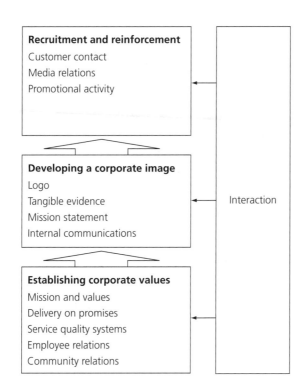

Figure 6.2

Relationship
communications

stakeholders. This provides the foundations on which a trusting relationship can be built.

Developing a corporate image

Corporate image is really an extension of the branding process. From the
RM manager's point of view, it helps ensure that any positive messages are
correctly attributed to the organisation, in the same way as a brand image
ensures that satisfied customers re-buy the correct product. From the stakeholders' point of view, it provides a vehicle for conceptualising the organisation. The use of consistent imagery in all of the organisation's messages,
therefore, consolidates the relationship by presenting a recognisable face,
which the customer will associate with the organisation's voice. Once
again, the key issue here is consistency. As relationships develop and an
increasing number of contacts develop between the supplier and customer,
it is essential that the various messages transmitted by the organisation do
not contradict one another.

Communicating a corporate image

Having created a consistent image, the organisation is ready to invite the
scrutiny of its wider stakeholders. Tools such as press notices, publicity
stunts, sponsorship, advertising and exhibitions ensure that the organisation attracts the attention of interested publics. In ongoing relationships,
there will usually be a substantial element of direct contact between the
customer and supplier, both formal and informal.

Interaction

The development of a consistent communication strategy has been presented here as a linear process. In fact there is a close and ongoing relationship between all three levels of communication, and at any stage the relationship can be destroyed by problems (such as the use of overly aggressive sales techniques) from within or without. Part of the RM manager's job is to prevent actions or events that will harm the relationship with customers or other stakeholders through proactive communications. Obviously, this will not always be possible, for example in the event of product failures, so provision must be made for damage limitation – reactive communications.

Staff and internal service quality

There is a significant body of evidence to suggest that internal service quality affects external service quality (e.g. Zeithaml and Bitner, 1996). Internal service quality can be defined as the degree to which the experience of working for the organisation creates employee satisfaction. External service quality is defined as the extent to which the service consumption experience creates customer satisfaction. As discussed in Chapter three, judgements of quality are subjective, based on a comparison of expectations and perceptions. In a study of customers and employees at 28 US banks, Schneider and Bowen (1993) found that employee perceptions of the service climate and the organisation's human resource management practices were positively correlated with customer perceptions of service quality.

The virtuous circle

Various authors have put forward the view that employee retention is essential for profitability. The two most comprehensive models are proposed by Reichheld *et al.* (2000) in the notion of the 'virtuous circle' and Heskett *et al.* (1994) with their model of the 'service–profit chain'. The two models are very similar, so the virtuous circle will be examined in more detail.

Reichheld *et al.* (2000) argue that profitability can be enhanced by relying on employees' natural predisposition to offer good service. The emphasis of their approach is on mechanisms which motivate the employees to achieve as highly as possible, and support mechanisms such as training programmes, which enable them to do their job to the best of their ability. He argues that this creates a 'virtuous circle' (Figure 6.3) in the following way:

- Profitable growth arises from loyal customers. It is far more cost effective to retain an existing customer than to attract a new one. Organisations that retain their customers do not have to constantly

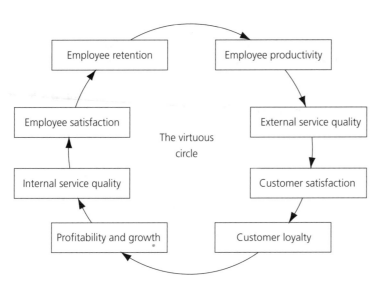

Figure 6.3

The virtuous circle

Based on Reichheld *et al.* (2000)

spend on promotional campaigns to replace lost custom. Even more importantly, loyal customers will recommend the business to friends and family etc., thus creating further growth.

- Customer loyalty arises from customer satisfaction. Customers will only remain with a provider that meets or exceeds their expectations.

- Customer satisfaction arises from high product value. Whether it is a service or a physical good, customers will be satisfied with a product which offers significant benefit in return for a cost which they consider reasonable.

- High product value is derived from satisfied, motivated staff who know their job well. Consider an employee starting a new job, whether it is on a production line or the front desk of a high street bank. Initially he will not perform particularly well. As he remains in the job, gradually learning the way things are done, both his productivity and the quality of his work will rise. This is particularly true in service organisations, but also applies to skilled or semi-skilled production jobs. The key to offering a good value product is therefore to develop good relationships with employees, so that staff are retained.

- Employee retention arises from satisfied staff. They will only seek new positions if they feel that they can get a better return for their efforts elsewhere.

- Employee satisfaction is caused by internal service quality. As illustrated in the section on internal marketing, employers offer their staff benefits such as pay, status, and promotion prospects in return for their effort. The better the benefits offered by the employer, the higher the satisfaction of the employee.

It should be noted that Reichheld *et al.* (2000) argue from a perspective that would be classed as transactional internal marketing under the internal marketing continuum discussed at the start of this chapter. It should also be stressed that recent research has found that satisfaction does not in itself guarantee customer retention. As discussed in Chapter three, trust and commitment are key pre-requisites of loyalty. It would seem likely that this applies equally to internal customers.

The implications of the virtuous circle approach

Advocates of the virtuous circle argue that organisations must focus on internal service quality in order to promote growth. Monitoring and control mechanisms, rather than focusing on profits, growth or customer satisfaction, are far better directed at employee satisfaction. In this way, the business will direct its attention to the cause of success rather than the effects. This has obvious implications for the design of monitoring and control mechanisms, which are discussed in more detail in the next chapter. In this chapter, however, the key implication of the virtuous circle model is the assumption that the RM manager must seek to create an environment within which members of staff are motivated and empowered to deliver good customer service.

Internal service quality

Hallowell *et al.* (1996) identify eight components of internal service quality, as illustrated in Figure 6.4. The elements can be defined as follows:

- *Tools* are the resources and information needed to serve customers.
- *Policies and procedures* are the systems that support the service process (e.g. procurement, maintenance or reporting). These should actively facilitate good customer service, for example by maintaining a pleasant service environment, or encouraging staff retention.
- *Teamwork* is the extent to which different individuals and business units cooperate when necessary to serve the best interests of the customer.
- *Management support* is the extent to which the actions of senior management help the employee's ability to serve.
- *Goal alignment* refers to the extent to which the goals of customer-facing staff match those of the management at all levels of the business.
- *Training* refers to the need for relevant, effective and timely job-related training.
- *Communication* may be horizontal communication necessary for inter-functional coordination, or vertical communication necessary for continuous improvement and a consistent culture.

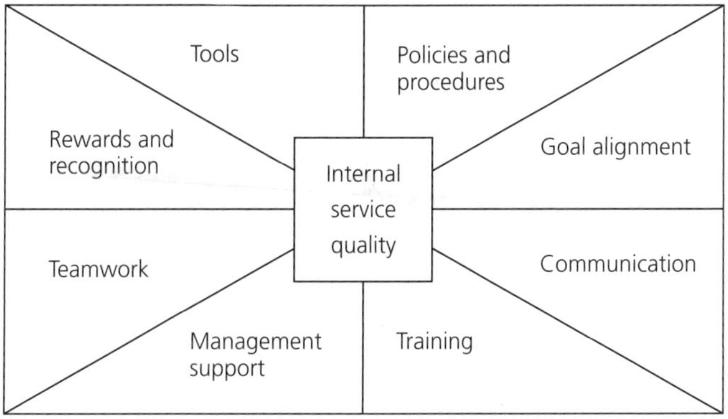

Based on Hallowell *et al.* (1996)

Figure 6.4

The eight components of internal service quality

- *Rewards and recognition* are the extent to which the employees are recognised and/or rewarded for delivering good customer service.

Managing these eight components effectively can enhance internal service quality and so improve external service quality, and therefore create satisfaction – one of the preconditions of a successful relationship.

Degree of customisation and the nature of the management task

The approach that the organisation takes towards the management of the eight components of internal quality described above should be informed by an understanding of the nature of the service. Lashley (1998), for example, recommends that the service be analysed according to the extent to which the service is customised to the individual needs of each consumer, and the degree of control that managers wish to exercise over employees. He also distinguishes between internal and external control. External control is imposed on the employee, through monitoring and reward schemes such as performance-related pay. Internal control, as the term suggests, comes from within the employees themselves. This form of control requires the employee to take ownership of the responsibility for meeting corporate objectives and service quality standards, regulating his own behaviour without direct intervention on the part of the organisation's management. Lovelock (1983) suggests that the scope for service personnel to exercise discretion in tailoring the service should also be considered. Both authors argue that the focus of management task will differ according to the relationship between these two key variables, as Figure 6.5 illustrates.

The service production line

This form of service is epitomised by McDonald's, where employees deliver a standardised service to a consistent standard. Here the emphasis on personal initiative is low, since processes conform to detailed preset specifications. The emphasis of human resource management here is on training the service providers to ensure that they understand the process, providing the necessary equipment to perform the service and monitoring and rewarding conformance to the specified service. Since the role of the service staff calls for relatively little initiative, the main focus is on staff training, and external monitoring and control.

The menu service

Here the range of choice available to the customer amounts effectively to a customised product. However, the customer controls the design of the product by selecting standardised modules from a set range, like items from a menu. The service staff need to be able to deliver a range of products or product elements at the customer's request. However, they have no authority to alter the nature of that product to better suit the customer, or to make the final choice as to which product is offered to the customer. Abbey National, for example, offer a range of savings and current accounts with varying rates of interest and facilities attached, as well as a credit card, mortgages, unsecured loans etc. The service staff need to be able to deliver whatever product is requested, whether it is a simple deposit or an enquiry about internet banking registration, but they do not determine the terms of the accounts or the range of products offered. Here the role of the service provider involves a degree of complexity, since he must understand the various products and the associated procedures. Nevertheless, the emphasis is still on external monitoring and control, since the specification of the product and its delivery will be determined by senior management. Similarly, staff development will focus on training in the delivery of the preset product range, rather than the broader education of the individual.

Figure 6.5		Degree of customisation	
Four types of service		Low	High
	Low	**Service production line** e.g. public transport fast food cinema	**Menu service** e.g. personal banking satellite TV *à la carte* restaurant
	High	**Performance service** e.g. large-scale education theatre performances health care (e.g. ante natal) courses	**Professional service** e.g. legal advice/ representation consultancy plumber

(Level of provider discretion)

Reprinted with permission of *Journal of Marketing*, published by the American Marketing Association, Lovelock, C. (1983), vol. 47, 3, page 15.

The performance service

The performance service involves a high level of discretion on the part of the service provider, but that provider will deliver the same service to all customers. In ante natal programmes offered by health authorities, for example, the programme will be the same for all participants – there is no scope for individually tailored sessions. Nevertheless, the tone and content of the sessions are determined to a large degree by the health visitor delivering the course. This element of discretion is a key consideration in the management of the service, since the provider contributes as much to the service design as the organisation's management. This reduces the level of external control that may be applied, since management are not in a position to specify performance standards with such clarity. Instead, control mechanisms will rely on the education of the individual in the values and standards of the organisation. Training and development will be broader in nature, focusing on the development of general skills, knowledge and confidence, rather than training the employee in specific routines. Because the organisation's management delegate much of the responsibility for creating customer satisfaction to the customer-facing employee, more careful attention will be paid to the recruitment of suitably qualified and experienced staff. Nevertheless, due to the standardised nature of the product, some degree of external control is possible.

The professional service

Professional services such as legal advice, medical care and consultancy combine a high degree of complexity with a high level of discretion on the part of the service provider. A solicitor, for example, must decide which service a customer needs before giving advice or representation. For this reason, external control is very difficult to apply to professional services, and the softer, less direct internal control mechanisms must be used. Because management must rely so heavily on the employee's ability to regulate his or her own behaviour, the recruitment process will often be lengthy, with detailed specification of the employer's requirements in terms of skills, knowledge and personality.

Implications for RM

Models such as the service–profit chain and the virtuous circle fail to distinguish between types of service, recommending themselves as a model for all service organisations. The classification discussed above, however, suggests that employee retention assumes a different level of importance in different types of service situation. There are obvious parallels between the customer–supplier and the management–employee relationship. The greater the perceived risk of the employment decision, the more extensive the information search (i.e. the selection process) conducted by the employer. Hence, in the case of high discretion services, employee retention takes on even greater importance. Given the risks associated with the recruitment of new staff, and the costs of the behaviour that these risks stimulate, employers will (and should) place a very high priority on the retention of staff. The relationship between employer and employee depends on trust and commitment, which are only built up over time.

In the case of a production line or menu service, however, the level of external control reduces the need for such trust. The responsibility for service quality rests with the monitoring and control systems, rather than the individual member of staff. Because of the relative simplicity of the service product, new staff can be trained more quickly and cheaply. Managers will, therefore, perceive a lower level of risk in the recruitment of new members of staff.

Hence, the management of employee relationships parallels that of external relationships. Just as the organisation will manage a portfolio of customer relationships, each receiving a different level of priority, so too will relationships with staff differ in strategic importance. Given that few businesses can meet all the needs of all of their employees all of the time, an understanding of internal relationship priorities is essential when considering trade-offs in investment in different staff groups.

Empowerment

Despite the fact that different levels of priority will, by necessity, be placed on the relationships with different members of staff, the aim of the organisation should be to minimise staff turnover at all levels. Various authors have suggested that the empowerment of customer-facing staff is a vehicle by which this can be achieved. Empowerment is a poorly defined term, used to describe initiatives from training programmes to quality circles. In a RM sense, it can be defined as providing systems, resources, authority or knowledge that enable staff to take ownership of relationship quality. Ashness and Lashley (1995) studied attempts to empower the service staff in Harvester restaurants by creating autonomous work groups. The restaurant business not only removed two layers of management, but also introduced the following initiatives:

- The articulation of corporate values, based on a commitment to customer service and to the empowerment of front-line staff;
- A flatter structure in which the responsibilities of all staff were clearly defined;
- New recruitment and training practices designed to enhance the skills and capabilities of staff;
- The introduction of communication, induction, rewards and appraisal systems.

Ashness and Lashley studied the effect of these initiatives on the staff of two restaurants. They found that the measures had increased the autonomy of the work teams, which had a greater responsibility for (and authority over) certain aspects of the service delivery. Although the design of the tangible service elements (the menu, decor etc.) was strictly controlled by the centre, restaurant staff had considerable discretion over the intangible elements, and over systems for the day-to-day running of the restaurant. Staff reported increased commitment to the organisation, and a positive effect on staff retention, though it was noted that staff turnover did appear higher at other Harvester restaurants (Ashness and Lashley, 1995).

Style

The impact of style

Style has been defined by Christopher *et al.* as 'The way managers collectively act with respect to use of time, attention and symbolic actions' (Christopher *et al.*, 1991: 164).

Clearly, issues of style are closely related to those of staff and shared values – management style is a product of the corporate culture, and an integral part of the human resource management polices and practices. Gronroos (1981), for example, identifies the adoption of a supportive management style as a key element of strategic internal marketing. The way in which managers behave will have a significant impact on the behaviour of staff for the following reasons:

- *Power*: obviously, because of their authority to recommend that staff under their management be rewarded or penalised for their behaviour, managers will have significant power to influence the behaviour of those members of staff;
- *Leadership*: staff will look to managers to provide guidance, support and model behaviour, because of their authority, and (usually) greater experience;
- *Communication*: managers provide a vehicle by which messages can be passed between senior management and the staff on the ground.

Clearly, it is important that managers at all levels of the organisation have a significant impact on the success of a RM strategy, and the initiatives discussed in this chapter must encompass this group of staff. Indeed, Christopher *et al.* (1991) suggest that managers should be at the vanguard of organisational change.

Exercising influence through reward systems

The reward systems of an organisation determine the way in which managers exert influence on staff. They therefore play a key role in the development and implementation of management style. Research by Allen and Kilmann (2001) indicates that reward practices can have a significant effect on the implementation of TQM. The study looked at the reward systems used by 100 organisations, and compared these to organisational performance. The various rewards encountered could be divided into monetary and non-monetary categories. The study found that the appropriate use of rewards was closely associated with better performance.

Non-monetary rewards

Allen and Kilmann (2001) suggest that non-monetary reward systems are better used in the early stages of the introduction of TQM, when senior management are seeking to establish a quality culture throughout the company. Such practices provide for positive reinforcement of appropriate behaviour, without involving a fundamental shift in the organisation's systems and structures. Non-monetary rewards that were associated with high quality performance include:

- *Rewards in kind*: gift certificates, merchandise or similar tangible rewards;
- *Celebrations*: special events, parties or dinners;
- *Praise*: verbal or written expressions of recognition;
- *Staff development*: training, education or experience that will increase the individual's employability;
- *Advancement*: promotion criteria based on quality achievements.

For example, Asda gives staff reward points for meeting various performance targets. Reward points can be exchanged for store credit, or saved towards a larger purchase from a special range of merchandise. The hi-fi retailer Richer Sounds rewards top-performing staff with the use of the company limousine.

Monetary rewards

Although there is evidence that non-monetary rewards work well in the introductory stages of TQM, Allen and Kilmann (2001) argue that, in order to become embedded into the culture of the organisation, appropriate behaviour must ultimately be rewarded financially. This involves assimilating quality-based rewards into the performance targets, appraisal systems and pay structures of the business. Such fundamental changes could not be contemplated during the introductory stages of TQM, but must be made in order to consolidate any changes. Monetary reward systems that were associated with high quality performance in Allen and Kilmann's 2001 study were:

- *Profit sharing*: workers are awarded a proportion of corporate profits;
- *Gainsharing*: bonuses are paid to employees on the basis of gains in productivity or profitability;
- *Employment security*: staff are rewarded by agreements to safeguard jobs;
- *Compensatory time*: staff are given the option to take overtime pay as time off rather than money;
- *Individual reward systems*: rewards are based on individual attainment rather than departmental or other unit performance;
- *Quantity-based performance appraisals*: staff are rewarded according to quantity-based targets rather than quality based goals.

RM reward systems

In summary, then, a wide variety of rewards may be used to influence the behaviour of employees on a daily basis, and hence the culture or style of the organisation. It should be stressed, however, that the choice of which behaviour to reward is more fundamental to the success of RM than that of how to reward it. Too many organisations reward customer getting rather than customer keeping (Reichheld *et al.*, 2000), an approach which is clearly not conducive to the development of a RM culture.

Individual or team-based rewards?

Accepted TQM principles suggest that rewards should be team-based rather than individual, thus fostering a sense of teamwork and collective effort towards common goals. Similarly, accepted theory dictates that goals or objectives should focus on quality rather than quantity. Allen and Kilmann (2001) note that despite this, the practice of individual rewards and quantitative goals were both positively correlated with high quality performance. They attribute this contradiction to the wider cultural characteristics of Western society, in which individual effort (and reward) is highly prized, and quantitative measures are seen as being more objective (and so fairer) than qualitative ones. They therefore suggest a balanced use of both of the different types of measures and reward systems.

Skills

The importance of skills

Skills factors encompass the capabilities, or distinctive competencies, of the organisation. Many of the issues discussed in this and the previous chapter could be included under this heading; for example, the establishment of a TQM system would in itself constitute a valuable organisational skill. Once again, the interrelationship between the seven elements of the McKinsey framework is apparent; variations in one element must impact on the others. To avoid repetition, however, this section will address issues of skills development, by looking at the training necessary to underpin RM. An appropriate training programme will serve two key functions in RM. First, it will motivate and empower staff, serving as a vehicle for enhancing internal relationships, and thereby indirectly benefiting external ones. Second, it will have a direct effect on the maintenance of relationships with external customers, by increasing the effectiveness of the organisation's staff and so increasing service quality.

Training and quality

It has long been recognised that TQM systems must be underpinned by appropriate training. This principle has been formally integrated into the ISO9000: 2000 quality management systems standard, which requires the demonstration of a systematic approach to training within the organisation. Nevertheless, care must be taken in planning and delivering such training. Christopher *et al.* (1991) warn of the dangers of jumping directly into intensive, large scale 'quality training', which can be a waste of time and resources. A great many such initiatives fail because the organisation neglects to put in place the communication, management or reward systems discussed earlier in the chapter. Such developments are needed to consolidate the development of quality skills, ensuring that staff actually put their newly developed skills into practice. Even so, the planning and implementation of training programmes need careful thought.

The training process

The training process is illustrated in Figure 6.6, together with some of the methods associated with each stage of the process. It is worth noting that this process is derived from TQM principles, which stress the cycle of reviewing, planning, implementation and monitoring/evaluation in all business activities. The process is also implicit in the criteria for the award of ISO9000: 2000, which requires the qualifying organisation to demonstrate effective systems for the assessment of both the need for, and the effectiveness of, training programmes.

The training needs assessment

Also called the skills audit, the purpose of the needs assessment is to identify the purpose and nature of training. Although the importance of this stage seems clear, the pressure on training to deliver quick solutions means that it is often overlooked (Zemke, 1998), or amounts to little more than the

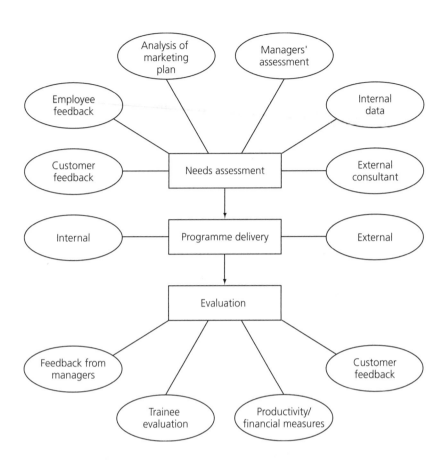

Figure 6.6

The Training Process

judgement of a few senior managers as to what is required (Matthews *et al.*, 2001). Nevertheless, many of the approaches recommended by human resource management textbooks are too slow and complex to be of practical use. Conducting a regular 'needs survey' tends to result in token, habitual responses rather than a meaningful analysis of skills gaps (Zemke, 1998). The organisation should, therefore, strike a compromise between obtaining a thorough, objective evaluation of any skills gaps, and the need to maintain momentum and deploy resources wisely. The skills audit should draw on several sources of information, in order to provide a balanced picture.

External consultant

The employment of an external consultant to conduct the needs assessment is a way to gain an impartial view of the organisation's skills gaps. If properly selected, the consultant will bring to the task expertise and experience beyond that of the business. On the negative side, the employment of an outside expert may be misinterpreted by employees, leading to defensiveness and non-cooperation. Since the consultant will be unfamiliar with the organisation's culture and strategy, there is greater scope for misunderstandings to arise regarding the nature of the skills requirements than if the audit was conducted by internal staff.

Internal data

Businesses routinely collect information that can offer useful insights into training needs. Zemke (1998) suggests that the following sources can offer insights into skills gaps:

- Error data;
- Customer complaints;
- Grievance records;
- Exit interview records.

Using existing internal data has the advantage of being cheap and quick. As with all secondary data, however, it is unlikely to meet the precise information needs of the skills audit. Since the data will have been collected for other purposes, it must be interpreted with care.

Managers' assessments

In a survey of 450 European companies, Matthews *et al.* found that the most widely used and highly rated sources of information on training needs were the judgement of senior managers and the opinion of supervisors (Matthews *et al.*, 2001). This could be seen as a positive tendency, demonstrating the commitment of managers to TQM and skills development. Alternatively, a top-down approach could be viewed as dictatorial and be resisted by employees. Certainly, the majority of writers on TQM stress the importance of staff involvement in all processes, including training, to promote a sense of ownership over the systems and initiatives of the organisation. Matthews *et al.* conclude that much depends on the culture of the organisation. The balance of methods will also play a part; management input can lend structure and direction to feedback from customers or employees, but should not be seen as a replacement of these two key sources.

Analysis of RM plans

The information offered by the sources discussed so far is largely reactive in nature, identifying training needs though shortfalls or problems experienced in the implementation of RM plans. Careful analysis of the organisation's future plans can help to anticipate future needs. Here senior managers have an important role to play in determining the skills that will be required to meet the changing requirements of the business's strategic customers, both present and future. At the same time, the attention paid to current shortcomings should not suffer in the attempt to forecast future events.

Employee feedback

Involving staff in the process of identifying training needs will not only provide useful insights into the types of training required, but also help to ensure that any training delivered is well received. It should be noted, however, that these benefits will only occur if the staff perceive that senior management listen and act on such feedback. The collection of staff opinion raises expectation regarding the relevance of the training – management must be careful to communicate exactly how the comments of staff have been taken on board in the development of any training programmes. Failure to do this will lead to disenchantment with, and resistance to, the training.

Customer feedback

In the European survey mentioned above, customer feedback was one of the least frequently used sources of information in assessing training needs, and was rated as being of relatively low importance by respondents. From the RM perspective, however, this is arguably the most important source of information. Soliciting customer feedback works in the same way as with employees. As well as providing a useful external perspective on skills shortfalls, it also demonstrates a commitment to customer satisfaction, and adds to the dialogue and trust between the two parties. As with employees, however, the organisation must be careful to meet the expectations that it creates by soliciting the customer's feedback.

Delivering the programme

Remarkably little is written about the delivery of training programmes, presumably because this deals with operational rather than strategic issues. The key decision to be taken by the manager is whether to rely on in-house or on the job training, or whether to draw on outside expertise, taking the employees out of the working environment to undergo training.

Internal training

Conducting training on the job, perhaps through a workplace mentor or supervisor, has a number of advantages. Employees learn new skills as and when needed, through application to their daily duties. For an organisation in which a culture of continuous improvement and customer service are already established, internal training can be an effective vehicle for the transmission of corporate values to new staff, since both trainer and trainee are immersed in the organisational culture and routines. Similarly, if the training involves the development of skills or knowledge specific to the organisation, established employees are best placed to offer such training. For example, for the American health food store Wild Oats Inc. the delivery of effective customer service requires staff to be knowledgeable about the store's product range. Service staff are expected to answer queries on the ingredients, health benefits and preparation guidelines for its various products. Training is therefore delivered in-house by managers, who are familiar with the latest product lines (Sunoo, 2001). For the RM-orientated organisation, internal staff can offer insights on the particular requirements of customers, as well as communicating the values and missions of the organisation.

External delivery

For the business that sees training as a vehicle for organisational change, internal training is unlikely to bring the influx of new ideas or practices required. The use of external training programmes allows the trainee to reflect on their current working practice away from the culture that has created such practice. It therefore tends to facilitate a more critical view of current systems, culture or habits, and a greater openness to change. The employment of external training staff also increases the receptivity of trainees to new ideas and practices, not only because of the broader experience that trainers bring to the programme, but also because the trainees are more likely to perceive external trainers as independent of management influence. In many cases, the use of external training or education will be dictated by necessity – in the case of professional service training, for example, it is unlikely that internal staff will have the necessary expertise to offer training.

Evaluating the effectiveness of training

Considering the level of investment businesses regularly make in staff training there is surprisingly little evidence of the systematic monitoring of training effectiveness. As Matthews *et al.* observe, 'investment in training appears to be an act of faith' (2001: 490). The academic literature recommends that a number of different measures of training effectiveness be employed. For example, Kirkpatrick (1998) identifies four assessment levels:

- *Reaction*: trainees' initial assessment of the training;
- *Learning*: trainees' evaluation of the learning gained;
- *Behaviour*: managers', supervisors' or other independent view of the change in the trainee's behaviour as a result of the training;
- *Results*: measurement of the employee's performance (e.g. customer satisfaction or employee productivity).

Information about each of these levels of effectiveness can come from the sources described below.

Trainee evaluation

The ubiquitous evaluation form, usually filled out as the trainees pack their bags to leave the session, has been widely criticised as an objective measure of training effectiveness. For example, Sadri and Snyder (1995) note that trainees' perceptions of training programmes change over time, so that gathering feedback directly after the course distorts the results of the evaluation.

Nevertheless, considering the role of training in promoting staff retention, the perceptions of trainees are important. According to the Price-Waterhouse–Cranfield surveys of European HRM, training for new employees is the most popular incentive offered to new recruits, and a vital tool in staff retention (Matthews *et al.*, 2001). In order to fulfil these functions, training must be viewed positively by the participants. It is suggested, however, that trainees be asked to evaluate the effectiveness of training some time after the event. This allows more careful reflection on the training experience, as well as allowing trainees to attempt to apply the training in the workplace.

Productivity/financial measures

A variety of methods can be used to assess the tangible impact of training programmes, such as changes in productivity or financial performance. Obviously, in order to be of use, such measures must be taken before and after the delivery of the training, and the evaluation should take account of any other variables that might have distorted the results. If carefully conducted, however, impact measures can be used to perform a cost benefit analysis of the training. It is important to stress, however, that the practical difficulties of implementing such a system mean that it is not widely used in industry (Matthews *et al.*, 2001). It could also be argued that measurement of training effectiveness strictly on a financial basis does not take account of the less direct benefits to organisational culture and employee motivation.

Feedback from managers

Qualitative feedback from trainees' managers or supervisors can provide a perspective on changes to behaviour, learning and the functional effectiveness of the employee. Although this feedback may suffer from subjectivity, it can be a useful qualifier of feedback from other sources. It is also relatively cheap and simple to administer, particularly in organisations with a hierarchical culture, where the mechanisms for employee appraisal by managers are already in place.

Customer feedback

The benefits of customer evaluation are the same as those of customers' contribution to the training needs assessment. Such feedback provides a valuable external view of the impact of training and the changes in trainee behaviour. It also has the added benefit of cementing the relationship between the customer and supplier, demonstrating the supplier's responsiveness to customer needs.

Skills: implications for RM

The preceding framework provides guidance on the development of new skills and competences. As with reward systems, the question of *how?* is less important than that of *what?* – a training needs assessment conducted by internal staff is likely to identify training requirements that perpetuate the organisational mindset. Instead, the RM manager should question whether existing skills and practices support the adoption of a relational approach. Estienne (1997) notes that traditional training in conflict resolution emphasises the identification and confrontation of differences, whilst the relational approach emphasises the maintenance of rapport. It is vital that subtle distinctions such as this are reflected in staff development programmes, so that employees at all levels are able to contribute to the retention of customers.

Summary

This chapter dealt with the 'soft' issues of RM implementation. Issues relating to the management, development and motivation of employees are often addressed under the heading of internal marketing. A review of the literature reveals a number of approaches. Some take a transactional, marketing mix-based approach, in which the employee is seen as the customer and the job and its benefits take the form of the product. This approach to IM commonly takes the form of internal communications and training programmes, in which a management-determined strategy was sold to passive employees. At the other end of the spectrum, some recommend internal RM, in which networks of employees and customers generate and exchange knowledge in an organisational environment characterised by trust, openness and dialogue. In this scenario, senior managers, employees and customers all make significant contributions to the formulation and dissemination of organisational policy. It was noted that transactional internal marketing, whilst being limited in its compatibility with RM in its purest form, could play an important role in initiating the move to a RM strategy, which, in the early stages at least, would require a strong lead from senior management.

Having considered the general principles of internal RM and internal marketing, the chapter looked at some practical tools. Internal RM must be supported by a strong set of shared values, which define not only the goal of the organisation but also the ethical and commercial values to which it will hold in pursuit of those goals. The implementation of RM, therefore, should be supported by values that reflect a commitment to the development and maintenance of trust and commitment between the organisation and its various markets, customers or stakeholders. The formulation of a mission statement is an important part of the development and dissemination of shared values, but it was stressed that an organisation communicates, explicitly and implicitly, on a number of different levels, and the shared values must permeate all of these levels.

Sections on staff, skills and style looked at practical tools that could be used to motivate and empower employees to support RM. A focus on staff retention will safeguard investments made in staff training and development. Organisations are therefore advised to focus on the creation of internal service quality. The role of reward systems in shaping staff behaviour was also examined, and a framework was proposed for the assessment and development of individual skills. Staff development and reward systems are seen as powerful drivers of organisational culture, so the importance of reflecting RM values in these systems cannot be over-emphasised.

Case Study   *Internal marketing the Asda way*

Even before its takeover by Walmart, Asda had established a clear reputation for offering a range of good quality products at low cost. In a market where price competition is hard and margins slim the success of a value, positioning depends on Asda's ability to control its operating costs, in particular the problem of 'shrinkage' through theft, breakage and obsolescence.

The Asda staff manual sets out the procedures by which colleagues are encouraged to minimise waste and maximise customer value. Staff are introduced to the manual during a two-day induction programme, during which they are educated about the Asda philosophy, and their personal responsibility for the success of the organisation (see appendix A). The manual is not discarded after induction, however. It takes the form of a ring-binder file, into which additional pages can be inserted. As well as containing useful information about pay scales, holiday entitlements and other company rules and regulations, the manual is used as a career diary. During regular appraisals, managers sign a form to verify that the employee is competent in various roles throughout the store – so develops a job ladder; a permanent record of the individual's career development. This also serves to encourage both the employee and the manager to consider regular changes of role within the store. Needless to say, development is rewarded both financially and through the allocation of greater responsibility.

It doesn't stop there. Daily routines stress the importance of communication between employees throughout the company. Each department holds a weekly 'huddle' – time out from the normal routine when the department can get together (on the company's time) to discuss operational issues. Colleague circles, monthly store meetings and listening groups provide further opportunities for exchanging ideas. In case any slip through the net, Asda staff can complete a 'Tell Archie' form, sending their business idea direct to the Chief Executive himself.

It's not all warm and furry, however. Each department is allocated waste targets – whilst attainment of these targets is rewarded with store vouchers, continual failure to meet them draws unwelcome attention from the store manager. Stores are regularly visited by a team of mystery shoppers, who rate the quality of service, cleanliness, product availability and other aspects of store provision against a complex points system.

It is difficult to know the truth of how these mechanisms work in practice – many an organisation boasts superb staff manuals, which in reality never make it out of the locker or desk drawer. Judging by Asda's success in controlling its operating costs, however, it would seem that theirs does work.

Appendix A:

Asda's Mission and Values (www.Asda.co.uk 31 January 2003)

Every company needs a mission and purpose – it helps you to remain focused and gives everyone a welcome sense of direction. We're no exception.

Our Mission Statement is:

To be Britain's best value retailer exceeding local customer needs… Always

Our mission tells us that we want to focus on British shoppers and a commitment to providing a level of service that is not just good, but exceeds the needs our customers. We also need to recognise that the community that each store serves has different needs and that we play a big part in the community. At the heart of our mission is to be the best value retailer. This is supported through our commitment to an everyday low price philosophy. This means that our prices are not a sale or promotional price, customers can trust that we will always have the lowest prices.

Our Purpose is:

To make goods and services more affordable for everyone

Our purpose shows our commitment to everyday low prices without compromising on quality. We are constantly striving to find ways of selling the same products for less each year. Also we're always on the lookout for new products and services which we can sell and pass on better savings to our customers. Finally it reaffirms what our customers demand – Value. We must always make this our top priority.

But just as important as your destination are the ground rules you adopt on the way there – in other words, the values you cherish as an organisation and which guide your day-to-day decisions.

Values are just words on a piece of paper unless you live them through your behaviour at work. Below are the three ASDA Values, and some examples of the behaviours we expect from people to show that they're living the value in their work. Sam Walton established and operated Wal-Mart on a foundation of three simple, yet very important values, which he called the Basic Beliefs. These summarise how we work at ASDA too. We all have personal values, things we hold dear and expect from others. If your personal values match closely with our three basic beliefs then you're likely to fit in well and enjoy your job.

Read the ASDA Values below – is this what you believe in? If so, get in touch.

Respect for the Individual
- 'Our people make the difference' Every colleague is vital to our success. Our objective is to have an environment that fully taps the potential of all colleagues…our future is in everyone's hands.
- Everyone is referred to by their first name and we always wear name badges.
- We treat others with respect and offer to help our colleagues out. Listening and respecting others' ideas and opinions.
- Communicating just about everything we can with our colleagues is central to our success.
- Ask for help if you need it. Own problems, don't leave them for someone else.
- Treat others as you would like to be treated yourself.

Service to the Customer
- The customer is the person who pays everyone's wages and who decides whether a business is going to succeed or fail.
- Think like the customer.
- Smile, smile, smile and greet anyone who passes you.
- We're in the business to sell. Know what our customers want and the quality they demand. Offer better value than any of our competitors.
- Take a customer to a product rather than just pointing.
- No excuses, satisfaction guaranteed. Respond to all requests quickly and exceed customers' expectations in everything that you do.
- Have a passion for product knowledge and keeping it up to date.

Strive for excellence
- Excellence means going beyond the normal job.
- Each day we should strive to be better than the last.
- New ideas and goals make us reach further than ever before. We try to find new and innovative ways to push out boundaries and constantly improve.
- We hate waste. By eliminating waste and controlling our expenses, we can reduce our prices to the customers.
- Be successful: listen, learn, put forward your ideas and grow as an individual.

Discussion questions

1. Outline the mechanisms by which ASDA seeks to influence the behaviour of its employees.

2. Where does ASDA's approach to internal marketing (IM) lie on the continuum between transaction-based IM and IRM?

3. To what extent do you think that the mechanisms outlined in the case supports the development of long-term relationships with customers?

4. Suggest improvements to ASDA's IM systems.

References

Allen, R. and Kilmann, R. (2001) 'Aligning reward practices in support of total quality management', *Business Horizons*, 44, 3, 77–84.

Ashness, D. and Lashley, C. (1995) 'Empowering the workers at Harvester Restaurants', *Personnel Review*, 24, 8, 17–32.

Ballantyne, D. (2000) 'Internal relationship marketing: a strategy for knowledge renewal'. *International Journal of Bank Marketing*, 18, 6, 274–286.

Bart Bontis, N. and Taggar, S. (2001) 'A model of the impact of mission statements on firm performance', *Management Decision*, 30, 1, 19–35.

Berry, L. (1980) 'Services marketing is different', *Business*, May–June, 25–26.

Berry, L. (1983) in Payne, A., Christopher, M., Clark, M. and Peck, H. (1995) *Relationship Marketing for Competitive Advantage: Winning and Keeping Customers*, Oxford: Butterworth-Heinemann, 64–74.

Christopher, M., Payne, A. and Ballantyne, D. (1991) *Relationship Marketing: Bringing Quality, Customer Service and Marketing Together*, Oxford: Butterworth-Heinemann.

Duncan, T. and Moriarty, S. (1998) 'A communication-based model for managing relationships', *Journal of Marketing*, 62, 2, 1–13.

Estienne, M. (1997) 'The art of cross-cultural management: an alternative approach to training and development', *Journal of European Industrial Training*, 21, 1, 14–18.

Gronroos, C. (1981) 'Internal marketing – an integral part of marketing theory', *Proceedings of the American Marketing Association Service Marketing Conference*, 236–268.

Gronroos, C. (1985) 'Internal marketing – theory and practice', *American Marketing Association's Conference Proceedings*, 41–7.

Gronroos, C. (2000) 'Creating relationship dialogue: communication, interaction and value', *The Marketing Review*, 1, 1, 5–15.

Hallowell, R., Schlesinger, L. and Zornitsky, J. (1996) 'Internal service quality, customer and job satisfaction: linkages and implications for management', *Human Resource Planning* June, 19, 2, 20–31.

Heskett, J., Jones, T., Loveman, G., Sasser, W. and Schlesinger, L. (1994) 'Putting the service profit chain to work', *Harvard Business Review*, March–April, 164–174.

Kirkpatrick, D. (1998) *Evaluating Training Programmes*, 2nd edn, San Francisco: Berrett-Koehler.

Lashley, C. (1998) 'Matching the management of human resources to service operations', *International Journal of Contemporary Hospitality Management*, 10, 1, 24–43.

Lovelock, C. (1983) 'Classifying services to gain strategic marketing insights', *Journal of Services Marketing*, 47, Summer, 9–20.

Matthews, B., Akiko, U., Kekale, T., Reka, M., Pereira, Z. and Silva G. (2001) 'Quality training: needs and evaluation – findings from a European survey', *Total Quality Management*, 12, 4, 483–490.

Murray, K. (1991) 'A test of services marketing theory: consumer information acquisition activities', *Journal of Marketing*, 55, 10–25.

Narver, C. and Slater, S. (1990) 'The effect of a market orientation on business profitability', *Journal of Marketing*, 54, 4, 20–35.

Payne, A., Christopher, M., Clark, M. and Peck, H. (1995) *Relationship Marketing for Competitive Advantage: Winning and Keeping Customers*, Oxford: Butterworth-Heinemann.

Piercy, N. (1995) 'Customer satisfaction and the internal market', *Journal of Marketing Practice* 1, 1, 22–44.

Piercy, N. (2002) *Market-led Strategic Change a Guide to Transforming the Process of Going to Market*, Oxford: Butterworth-Heinemann.

Rafiq, M. and Ahmed, P. (2000) 'Advances in the internal marketing concept: definition, synthesis and extension', *Journal of Services Marketing*, 14, 6/7, 449–463.

Reichheld, F., Markey Jr, R. and Hopton, C. (2000) 'The loyalty effect – the relationship between loyalty and profits', *European Business Journal*, 12, 3, 134–139.

Sadri, G. and Snyder, P. (1995) 'Methodological issues in assessing training effectiveness', *Journal of Management Psychology*, 10, 4, 30–33.

Schneider, B. and Bowen, D. (1993) 'The service organisation: human resource management is crucial', *Organisational Dynamics*, Spring, 39–52.

Sunoo, B. (2001) 'Results-orientated customer service training', *Workforce*, 80, 5, 84–91.

Varey, R. and Lewis, B. (1999) 'A broadened conception of internal marketing', *European Journal of Marketing*, 33, 9/10, 926–944.

Wilson, R. and Gillighan, C. (1997) *Strategic Marketing Management*, 2nd edn, Oxford, Butterworth-Heinemann.

Winter, J. (1985) 'Getting your house in order with international marketing – a marketing pre-requisite', *Health Marketing Quarterly* 3, 1, 69–77.

Zeithaml, V. and Bitner, M. (1996) *Services Marketing* New York: McGraw-Hill.

Zemke, R. (1998) 'How to do a needs assessment when you think you don't have time', *Training*, 35, 3, 38–41.

7 Monitoring and controlling relationships

Learning objectives

After reading this chapter, you should be able to:

- Outline the general approaches to monitoring and control, and comment on the strengths and weaknesses of each approach.

- Identify specific techniques for monitoring relationships.

- Evaluate the role of service recovery in RM management.

- Outline the principles and techniques for controlling RM activities.

Introduction

The preceding chapters have looked at the theoretical approach to managing relationships, and examined issues of implementation. This chapter is concerned with the methods for monitoring and controlling the state of the relationship, both at the strategic and tactical levels. Although these issues form a separate chapter for ease of presentation, monitoring and control mechanisms are an integral part of both planning and implementation. Monitoring systems provide the information that informs the planning process, while control mechanisms ensure implementation of the plan. As noted at the start of Chapter four, this relationship is often presented as part of the classical planning cycle, in which the organisation moves periodically through discrete stages of planning, implementation and evaluation and so back to planning. More recent theories of strategic planning propose that the three stages occur simultaneously, with managers constantly updating plans and implementation strategies in response to monitoring feedback. In Chapter four, it was argued that this model of 'emergent strategy' is better suited to the RM paradigm, in which strategy develops from interaction between the various parties to the relationship. This chapter therefore sets out the means by which this interaction can take place, and the mechanisms by which an organisation can act on the information gained. It begins by looking at questions concerning the general approach that should be taken to monitoring and controlling RM, before describing a selection of commonly used techniques. The advantages and disadvantages of various measures are evaluated.

Approaches to monitoring and control

Hard versus soft monitoring and control

Hard monitoring and control mechanisms rely on quantitative measures of activity or achievement, and reward or punishment systems that are directly linked to those measures. Hard monitoring/control mechanisms are appropriate in circumstances where an employee's output or performance levels are easily defined and measured, and are critical to the success of an organisation. Budgetary control is a form of hard monitoring and control with which nearly all managers are obliged to work. For obvious reasons, it is critical that managers do not spend organisational resources too freely, and spending is easily measured in monetary terms. Budget overspends are usually penalised in some way, if only with the displeasure of senior management. Hard mechanisms are based on the principle that employees must be closely monitored, and constantly offered incentives in order to optimise their performance.

Soft monitoring and control mechanisms, as the name suggests, are less clearly defined. They are based on the principle that properly selected and trained employees do not need constant attention from senior management in order to perform well, and indeed will perform better if not directly monitored or controlled. Soft mechanisms are particularly appropriate when employee achievements are difficult to define, or where variations in activity or output are not critical. Customer service is an area in which soft monitoring mechanisms are often advocated. Although customer satisfaction can be monitored and linked to employee reward schemes, this often creates an adversarial relationship between customers and service staff. Better results can often be achieved by relying on employees' natural predisposition to offer good service. The emphasis of this approach is on mechanisms which motivate the employees to achieve as highly as possible, and support mechanisms such as training programmes, which enable them to do their job to the best of their ability.

Performance versus diagnostic monitoring

A further distinction should be made between monitoring mechanisms that provide an indication of corporate performance, and those that serve as a diagnostic tool. Performance indicators such as profitability and customer satisfaction measure the effects of a company's actions, providing feedback on its success or failure. As such, they are useful to senior management, shareholders and other stakeholders in providing reassurance that the company is successful, or warning that a change of strategy is needed. Those within the company who are responsible for managing success or reacting to failure will benefit from diagnostic monitoring, such as service quality measurement and cost benefit analysis. These measures look in more depth at actions of the company and their effect on the customer and allow managers to learn from failures and identify the causes of success.

A comprehensive monitoring system must include both diagnostic and performance monitoring mechanisms. The latter provide a strategic snapshot for senior managers, as well as summary information for interested stakeholders, whilst the former provide the information necessary to remedy problems and effect continuous improvement.

The balanced scorecard approach

There is a tendency for businesses to confine their monitoring mechanisms to financial measures of performance. Financial measures have much to recommend them – ultimately, the business will stand or fall by the amount of money it makes, and performance is easily defined and analysed in financial terms. The problem with financial measures, however, is that they tend to indicate the effects of business success rather than the causes. A company may be dismayed by falling profits or productivity levels, but quite unable to determine what action must be taken to remedy the situation. For this reason, it is widely accepted that organisations should use both financial and operational performance measures (e.g. Shaw and Reed, 1999; Gummesson, 1999).

The balanced scorecard approach advocated by Kaplan and Norton (1992) offers guidance on the development of corporate performance measures. It advocates the establishment of a range of performance indicators which are grouped into four different perspectives:

- *Financial* – could include measures of sales, profitability or cash flow;
- *Customer* – could include measures of customer loyalty, satisfaction levels, the balance of existing and new business or cooperative projects;
- *Internal business* – focuses on operational effectiveness, measuring factors characteristics such as production costs, cycle times, reliability and defects. It also refers to the human resources and competencies developed by the organisation;
- *Innovation and learning* – deals with the organisation's capacity for continuous improvement, measuring improvements to customer value and production processes.

RM-orientated scorecard measures

Use of the balanced scorecard not only ensures that a range of strengths and weaknesses can be identified and managed, but also prevents the organisation from becoming fixated on a single aspect of its business such as production efficiency or new product development. It is important, however, to avoid choosing performance indicators indiscriminately. The scorecard should be developed with a clear strategic mission in mind, and informed by shared values as to the way in which the corporation seeks to compete. For the RM-focused organisation, the scorecard should reflect the relational perspective. Examples of key indicators are given in Table 7.1.

Different levels of monitoring

The balanced scorecard approach is a technique for monitoring corporate level performance. As such, it portrays a broad picture of the organisational performance, and conveys relatively little in the way of diagnostic information. Such information is appropriate to corporate-level monitoring. Senior managers are concerned with establishing that the organisation is generally healthy, and identifying the areas of strength or weakness, but the diagnosis and rectification of specific problems is likely to be delegated to the managers charged with the management of specific relationships.

Table 7.1	Perspective	Dimension	Indicators
The balanced scorecard – some illustrative examples of RM-orientated measures	Financial	Profitability	ROCE
			Margins
		Turnover	Sales by value or volume
			Market share
			Growth
	Customer	Retention	Income from existing customers vs income from new
			Average length of customer relationships
		Satisfaction	Satisfaction levels
			No. of complaints/compliments
		Communication	Average no. of contacts with customer
			Average level of feedback from customer
	Internal business	Keeping promises	No. of defects
			No. of complaints
			No. of returns
		Efficiency	Waste reduction targets
			Costs
		Staff satisfaction	Satisfaction levels
			Staff retention/turnover
	Innovation and learning	Customer input	Customer involvement in R&D projects
		Innovativeness	No. of new products/improvements made

Adapted from Kaplan and Norton (1992)

Relationship-level monitoring must, therefore, provide more detailed information about the contribution of individual relationships, or groups of relationships, to the overall performance of the organisation. In terms of financial monitoring, for example, corporate-level monitoring should give information about the general profitability of the organisation, through measures such as return on capital employed (ROCE) and profit margins. At the relationship level, the manager must have access to information about the profitability of each customer, or in high volume, low value markets, each segment or type of customer. This information should be sufficiently detailed to identify and rectify specific problems – for example by recognising and prioritising those customers that offer particularly profitable relationships. Information that is relevant to corporate performance may then be filtered up to the next level (see Figure 7.1). The next section deals with the measures that can be used for relationship-level monitoring.

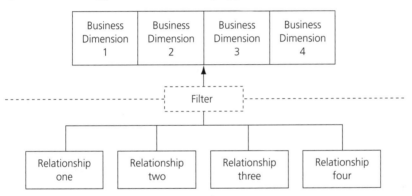

Corporate level: tracking performance and identifying general areas of strength and weakness

Relationship level: identifying, diagnosing and rectifying customer-specific problems

Figure 7.1

Two levels of RM monitoring

Measures of relationship success

Relationship-level monitoring

As illustrated in Figure 7.2, relationship-level monitoring centres on three main areas:

- Relationship facilitators: those factors that contribute to the development of the strong, long-term relationship. As discussed in Chapter three, quality, trust and satisfaction are all prerequisites of customer loyalty, and so serve as valuable measures of RM performance.
- Relationship features: those factors that describe the nature of the relationship itself, as is evident in the behaviour of the customer towards the supplier. These measures include various indicators of customer loyalty, fidelity and commitment.

● Relationship returns: the monetary rewards accruing to the supplier from the relationship. The most satisfied, trusting and loyal customer, may not provide the best returns. Hence it is necessary to take various measures of the relationship's financial performance.

Figure 7.2

Relationship-level
monitoring

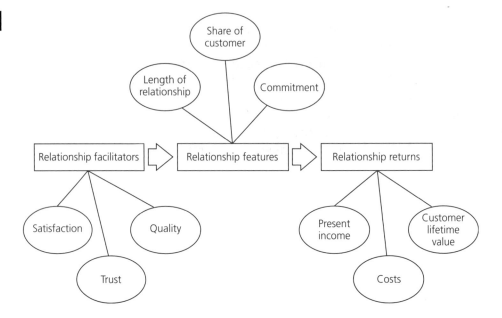

Specific measures of each element are discussed below. It should be stressed that not all of them will be appropriate to all organisations, and that RM managers must be careful not to overload themselves with exhaustive monitoring data, or upset their customers with incessant requests for detailed feedback. In order to gain a balanced picture of relationship performance, however, one or two measures from each element should be taken.

Relationship facilitators: three levels of attitude monitoring

The monitoring process may focus on any one of three levels of customer attitude. The cognitive level deals with rational thoughts and judgements – the information that is known to the customer about the service provider. Here, the focus is on the measurement of service quality and costs, which is the customer's rational judgement about the benefits received from the relationship, and the cost of maintaining it. The affective level deals with the customer's emotions towards the supplier or product, measured through satisfaction. Finally, the conative level focuses on the customer's actual behaviour.

Monitoring the customer at all three levels of attitude is important, since it gives the supplier a holistic picture of the customer, and hence a sound basis for predicting future behaviour. Generally, customers will seek to

reduce inconsistencies between attitudes at the affective, cognitive or conative levels of attitude (known as dissonance). Heider (1946) found, for
example, that a customer's liking for a salesman would affect his attitude
towards the products recommended by that salesman. Similarly, Festinger
(1957) found that customers with strong attitudes towards a product or
supplier engage in dissonance-reducing behaviour, for example by actively
ignoring information that conflicts with their established attitudes. At the
same time, if a customer's attitude at one level is changed, that customer is
more likely to bring their attitudes at other levels into line with this new
attitude. If, for example, a customer develops a liking for the salesperson of
a competitor, he will look for rational arguments as to why they should
switch to that supplier. Measurement at all three levels can provide an early
warning system, indicating attitude changes before they result in disloyal
behaviour and the customer defects.

Satisfaction

Customer satisfaction

As discussed in Chapter three, satisfaction is an emotional state arising
from the favourable disconfirmation of expectations. The link between
satisfaction and loyalty has received a great deal of attention from theorists.
Heskett *et al.* (1994) claim that satisfaction is one of the most important
prerequisites of loyalty, whilst Liljander and Strandvik (1995) offer
empirical evidence that satisfaction is a reliable predictor of a consumer's
intentions to re-buy. The measurement of customer satisfaction levels is
commonly used to monitor relationship quality (see for example,
Gummesson, 1999). Satisfaction is a relatively short-lived and subjective
state, and customers often find it difficult to make reliable judgements
about their own satisfaction levels, particularly in retrospect. To combat
this, organisations should take a structured approach to measuring satisfaction. For example, Hewlett Packard measures satisfaction with a six-minute
telephone survey in which several different questions test satisfaction on
each of nine dimensions, including communication skills, competence of
staff, reliability and responsiveness. Satisfaction ratings are given on a scale
of 1–100. An average rating for each dimension can then be derived from
the various questions (Shaw and Reed, 1999).

Employee satisfaction

Given the importance of employees in the implementation of RM
programmes, there is a strong case for measuring employee satisfaction. In
their model of the virtuous circle Reichheld *et al.* (2000) claim that the relationship between satisfaction and loyalty works in the same way for internal customers as for external – staff satisfaction leads to staff loyalty and
retention, lowering training costs and increasing experience, skills, motivation and productivity. Similarly, in their model of the service–profit chain,

Heskett *et al.* (1994) recommend measuring staff satisfaction with internal service quality (see Chapter six for a full discussion of these models).

The virtuous circle approach, however, considers staff satisfaction arising from the internal service quality created by the organization; with pay, recognition, reward systems and other terms and conditions of employment. The implementation of RM implies the additional need to monitor staff satisfaction with the state of customer relationships. Given that relationship success depends on interpersonal bonds between the individual members of staff and customers, the emotions of employees concerning the relationship are of critical importance. The relationship is unlikely to endure if employees in the supplier organisation do not derive satisfaction from it.

Drawbacks of satisfaction monitoring

Satisfaction is frequently used to measure relationship quality: according to Shaw and Reed (1999), 73 per cent of senior managers cite satisfaction as a key business performance indicator. However, the practice has a growing number of critics. Reichheld *et al.* (2000) cite evidence from the automobile industry that throws doubt on the link between satisfaction and loyalty. Having linked customer satisfaction scores to dealer incentives and bonuses, car manufacturers have found that average satisfaction scores have risen to 90 per cent, whilst repurchase rates have remained constant at 50 per cent. Reichheld *et al.* attributes this to dealers 'playing the system' by putting emotional pressure on customers to return high satisfaction scores, and the fact that satisfaction is an inherently unstable state. Hence 60–80 per cent of customers who defected to a competitor said they were satisfied or very satisfied on the survey just prior to their defection.

It seems, therefore, that satisfaction surveys are a poor quantitative measure of relationship performance. As discussed in Chapter three, the role of expectations in determining satisfaction means that customer satisfaction levels may change without any influence from the supplier. Add to this the practical difficulties in conducting reliable and valid satisfaction surveys, and the practice becomes even less useful. Nevertheless, such surveys can provide useful qualitative feedback, identifying problems or major shifts in customer expectations.

Complaints data and satisfaction monitoring

It should be stressed that satisfaction monitoring need not take the form of formal, quantitative surveys. Useful indications of customer satisfaction can be gained by monitoring customer complaints, particularly at the individual relationship level. The various uses of complaints data are discussed later in the chapter.

Service quality

The measurement of service quality creates similar benefits and difficulties to that of satisfaction. According to accepted theory, satisfaction arises from a positive judgement of service quality received and costs incurred (see Chapter three). The rationale for quality measurement is therefore that it focuses on the cause of satisfaction rather than the result, and therefore has greater diagnostic power. Two main models of service quality exist.

SERVQUAL

The SERVQUAL instrument is a questionnaire designed by Parasuraman, Zeithaml and Berry (1988). Its design is based on two principles:

- Customers' judgements of service quality are made by comparing perceptions with expectations.
- These judgements are made on five quality dimensions of reliability, assurance, tangibles, empathy and responsiveness (see Chapter three for definitions).

The questionnaire uses a Likert scale to gain customer ratings of both expected service and perceived service on each of these dimensions. Quality scores are then derived by subtracting expected quality ratings from perceived quality ratings. Scores may also be weighted to reflect the importance that customers place on each item.

SERVPERF

This competing model, offered by Cronin and Taylor (1992), disputes the two key principles underpinning SERVQUAL. Cronin and Taylor offer empirical evidence that the inclusion of expectations in the measurement of service quality is at best unnecessary, and at worst that it detracts from the reliability of quality ratings. Furthermore, the five dimensions of quality overlap. They advocate measuring perceptions of quality alone, and also recommend that each industry develops its own understanding of the quality dimensions as perceived by its customers.

Which to use?

Both measurement tools have their strengths and weaknesses, and the debate rumbles on in the academic literature. There is a good argument that the measurement of expectations increases the diagnostic power of service quality measurement, by capturing the standards against which the customer is judging the supplier, as well as the perception of how the supplier performs (Parasuraman *et al.*, 1994). However, the work of several researchers indicates that expectations are often poorly defined in customers' minds, and are not a reliable benchmark against which to measure quality (e.g. Teas 1993). Hence SERVPERF may provide a more reliable performance measure of service quality.

There is also general agreement that the five dimensions of quality defined by Parasuraman *et al.* differ from industry to industry (e.g. Teas, 1993; Carman, 1990; Shaw and Reed, 1999). Suppliers should, therefore, use focus groups to explore the dimensions on which their customers form quality expectations before embarking on a monitoring programme. This exercise should be repeated at regular intervals to ensure that the dimensions used remain relevant and comprehensive.

Relationship features: measuring loyalty

Critics of service quality and satisfaction monitoring generally advocate the monitoring of loyalty or repeat purchases (e.g. Reichheld *et al.*, 2000). Loyalty has two important advantages – it measures behaviour, or *conative attitudes*, and it can be derived from internal data.

Measuring behaviour

So far, the monitoring of attitude variables has been considered. It should be noted, however, that the measurement of attitudes such as satisfaction and perceived quality has not been found to be a reliable or accurate predictor of customer behaviour (Boulding *et al.* (1993). Although they can provide useful general information on relationship performance and the diagnosis of problems, many researchers argue that information on customers' past behaviour provides a firmer foundation for future planning (see for example Reichheld *et al.*, 2000; Shaw and Reed, 1999).

Internal records

Provided the supplier captures the data necessary to identify the customer at a later date, loyalty can be monitored without additional customer surveys. That is not to say that the monitoring of loyalty is either cheap or easy. Reichheld (1993) suggests that it is more difficult than implementing satisfaction surveys. However, the fact that loyalty monitoring can be built into sales data means that customers need not be troubled by requests to complete satisfaction or quality surveys.

Measures of loyalty

Loyalty can be measured in a number of different ways, the relevance of which will depend on the nature of the product and its market:

- *Length of relationship*: according to the theory of the relationship life cycle, relationships become more profitable as the relationship lengthens. It is also reasonable to assume that a customer who has remained loyal for a significant period of time will do so in the future. Loyalty measured in terms of time is therefore a good indicator of relationship value. However, it should be remembered that time is not a definitive indicator of either profitability or customer satisfaction – the customer may be exploiting, or being exploited by a one-sided relationship.

- *Share of customer*: this measure is used in direct consumer marketing as a measure of loyalty, assessing the extent to which the customer uses competitors' products alongside that of the supplier. Although useful as a performance indicator, this measure offers little diagnostic information.

- *Commitment*: commitment is an important indicator of loyalty. Suppliers can look for evidence of commitment in the volume of ongoing business a customer places with the organisation, and its willingness to invest in the relationship.

Relationship returns: measuring financial performance

Clearly, the financial benefits arising from a relationship will be of prime importance to the RM manager. The concern here is more with performance than with diagnosis – most of the financial measures serve as an indicator of the contribution made by a specific relationship to corporate financial objectives. Measures of relationship performance differ from traditional financial performance indicators in terms of their long-term focus, and their concern with indirect relationship benefits.

Long-term focus

Since the justification for RM centres on long-term gain, care should be taken in setting the timescale against which relationship returns are assessed. As discussed in Chapter four, building relationships often requires a significant investment in the early stages, which is recouped as the relationship matures. Care should therefore be taken to assess income and costs of a relationship over its entire life cycle, rather than at a particular point in time.

Indirect benefits

A number of the financial benefits of RM derive from indirect sources. Increases in income arise from cross-selling and referral business, whilst costs may be reduced by savings on promotional spending and the ability to plan and develop products and processes with greater certainty. Although many of these savings are very difficult to quantify, the organisation should seek to encompass as many as possible in its financial measures, in order to recognise the financial benefits of RM as fully as possible.

Measuring financial performance

A selection of the following measures may be used:

- *Profitability.* This is also described as Return on Relationship (ROR). Given that in some retail sectors, as many as 80 per cent of customers may be unprofitable (Shaw and Reed, 1999), it is worth measuring relationships in money terms, by monitoring net profit from each relationship. It should be stressed, however, that profitability is a performance indicator rather than a diagnostic tool.

- *Income.* Current income is clearly important, and must be monitored by the RM manager to ensure cash flow constraints are met. In terms of more overall performance, however, broader measures are more appropriate.

- *Cross-purchasing.* Income from cross-selling may be overlooked if different parts of the organisation monitor income from individual goods or services separately. Care should be taken to monitor all income from a particular customer as a whole.

- *Referral.* The tendency of loyal customers to generate new business through word-of-mouth is a frequently-cited benefit of RM. In order to assess the value of a particular relationship, therefore, the supplier should have a system for gauging the amount of business generated by its customers. Data collection should not only record if a new customer heard of the supplier through word-of-mouth, but also identify which customer is responsible for the referral. In practice, such a system is more likely to be feasible only in business-to-business markets.

- *Customer lifetime value.* The relationship between the income generated and costs incurred by servicing a particular customer will vary over the life of the relationship. Attempts should therefore be made to assess the total net income arising from a particular customer over the relationship life cycle.

- *Servicing cost.* On the other side of the profitability equation lie the costs of servicing a particular customer. Some customers are habitually more expensive to satisfy than others, for example because they have special requirements or require an unusually high level of service support. In the latter case, it is often difficult to trace the cost of staff time to an individual customer. Shaw and Reed (1999) recommend the use of Activity-Based Costing (ABC) to establish servicing costs. ABC is an accounting technique whereby staff keep a record of time spent on a particular activity, for example in dealing with a complaint from a particular customer. The time log can then be used to determine the cost of servicing a particular account.

Selecting relationship-level measures

As a general principle, an organisation should use as many measures as it can manage without overloading its managers with information. A single performance indicator or diagnostic measure rarely captures all the necessary information, whilst a range of measures will not only reduce the risk of shortcomings or opportunities going unnoticed, but also will help to set the results of one particular indicator in a broader context.

Complaints analysis and handling

The importance of complaints

The management of complaints impacts on both the monitoring and the control of relationship quality, working on two levels as illustrated in Figure 7.3. At the operational level, complaints handling is concerned with service recovery. This is a crucial element of RM management, since the inherent variability of value added services means that failures are bound to occur. Recovery is the practice of rectifying mistakes, either by rectifying the mistake, compensating the customer or merely apologising for the failure. Clearly, service recovery mechanisms are a vital part of a RM strategy, by facilitating customer retention. The next level, however, is an equally important part of a long-term relationship strategy. As discussed in Chapter five, a supplier must engage in continuous improvement in order to ensure that the service provided keeps pace with increasingly demanding customer expectations. Strategic complaints analysis provides information that can inform such improvement.

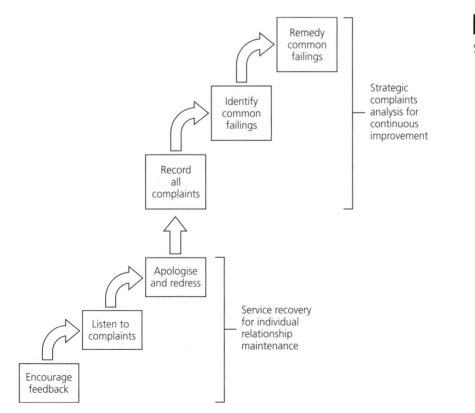

Figure 7.3

Service recovery

It should be noted here that although this section will refer exclusively to complaints, suppliers should also encourage positive comments. Information regarding the positive aspects of the customer's experience should be captured and analysed in the same way as the negative.

Service recovery

Promoting customer retention

It is in the interests of the supplier to invite complaints; a customer who complains is offering the supplier the opportunity to continue the relationship. Many customers, however, will simply defect after an unsatisfactory service encounter. As a rule, customers dislike complaining because it costs them time, effort and emotional stress. Stewart (1998) found, however, that retail banking customers normally made some form of effort to resolve a negative service incident by contacting their branch or a similar point of contact. The fact that banking customers tended to make such an effort rather than merely defecting was probably because of the high switching costs in the sector. It seems logical, therefore, to assume that customers who are committed to a relationship for more positive reasons would do likewise.

In Stewart's study, the most frequently stated cause of customer exit was the sense of frustration, anger, disappointment or other negative emotion caused by the bank's failure to respond positively to the complaint. In short, in relationships characterised by high commitment, it is failure of service recovery that leads to defection rather than the initial failure itself.

Principles of service recovery

Effective service recovery is based on four principles:

- *Make it easy to complain.* In order to overcome customers' natural disinclination to complain, procedures and channels for customer complaints should be as clear and as flexible as possible. Complaints-handling staff should be trained in the interpersonal skills necessary to set customers at ease.

- *Establish the grounds for complaint.* Customers will be more willing to complain if they are confident that they will be successful. The publication of a simple, comprehensive guarantee, a customer charter or a similar definition of acceptable service levels will provide such confidence.

- *Offer immediate redress where possible.* Until the complaint is resolved, the customer will experience negative emotions concerning the source of their grievance. The more quickly the complaint is resolved, the lower the negative impact on the customer's attitudes, and therefore the easier the customer will be to placate. Where possible, therefore, it is advisable to delegate authority and responsibility for resolving complaints to customer-facing staff, so that problems can be resolved as they arise.

- *Communicate*. Seiders and Berry (1998) note that customers' negative perceptions of a service failure are intensified if they feel that the failure could have been prevented. Often, all that is needed in order to diffuse customer dissatisfaction is an apology, together with an explanation of why the failure occurred, and the steps that have been/will be taken to ensure that it does not recur.

Strategic complaints analysis

Complaints are often used as a performance indicator, with a high level of complaints being taken to indicate poor performance. Train operating companies, for example, are fined by the Regulator if formal customer complaints rise above a certain level. In terms of monitoring, complaints are far more useful as a diagnostic tool, and as such should be welcomed. The complaints can be analysed both qualitatively and quantitatively, revealing useful information about both parties to the relationship.

Company weaknesses

The most obvious information provided by complaints analysis is the identification of weaknesses in production and service delivery processes. By categorising complaints, senior managers can quickly identify complaints that derive from a common failing.

Changing customer expectations

Because of the link between dissatisfaction and expectations, an increase in customer complaints may be caused by increased expectations rather than declining company performance. Provided that performance indicators are in place to establish that quality levels have not deteriorated, complaints can provide useful clues regarding trends in customer expectation.

Key product attributes

Customers will only complain about the performance aspects of goods and service that are important to them. Analysing complaints therefore indicates those dimensions of quality (or costs) about which customers are most sensitive.

Controlling service quality

The GAPS model for managing service quality

The GAPS model of service quality was developed by Parasuraman *et al.* (1988). As discussed earlier, they developed the SERVQUAL questionnaire to measure service quality by investigating perceptions and expectations in respect of five dimensions. The larger the gap by which perceptions fall short of expectations, the lower the quality of service.

Where large 'quality gaps' occurred, Parasuraman *et al.* investigated the possible causes. These studies led them to develop the GAPS model for managing service quality (see Figure 7.4). Any one of the four company gaps will lead to a mismatch between customer expectations and perceptions. For example, if companies do not correctly monitor what customers' expectations are, they have little hope of designing and implementing a service that meets those expectations (gap 1). At the other end of the model, if managers lead customers to have unrealistically high expectations by the promises they make in their advertising etc., customers will also be disappointed (gap 4). Service quality can therefore be managed by introducing systems to reduce each gap. Marketing information systems will ensure that managers remain aware of customer expectations (gap 1). They must then design a service specification that ensures that expectations regarding the five dimensions of quality are met (gap 2) and ensure, through monitoring, control, support and motivation that service providers actually deliver the service to the specified standard (gap 3). Finally, the organisation must be careful that it does not create unrealistically high customer expectations with its promotional messages (gap 4). Companies may use guarantees or service contracts as a way of specifying exactly what the customer has a right to expect of the supplier.

Figure 7.4

The GAPS model of service quality

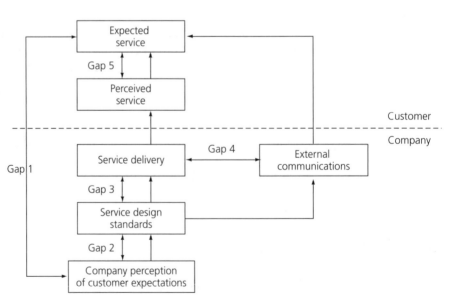

Reprinted with permission of *Journal of marketing*, published by the American Marketing Association, Parasuraman, A. Zeithaml, V. and Berry, L. (1988), vol. 52, issue 2, page 36.

Hard control techniques

The closure of gaps 2 and 3 clearly presents particular problems. The intangibility and heterogeneity of service products mean that it is difficult to define how the service should be delivered, and harder still to develop mechanisms that ensure that delivery is consistent. Hard control techniques attempt to define service delivery with sufficient clarity to allow for monitoring and control.

Service blueprinting

This technique involves the development of a flowchart that describes the service encounter from the customer's point of view. Blueprints map out not only the processes that are visible to the customer, but also the supporting processes that must take place. Timings or other performance standards can then be placed on each element of the process.

Critical incidents analysis

Critical incidents analysis is an adaptation of service blueprinting that focuses only on the events or interactions that are crucial in shaping the customer's perceptions of service quality. Carlzon (1988) described such events as 'moments of truth'; events by which the customer will judge the service provider. Concentrating only on these events simplifies the service specification. An understanding of the critical incidents for a given service can be identified using customer focus groups, developed into a process specification and used for the purposes of staff training and performance monitoring. Mystery shoppers are commonly used to monitor conformance to the specification.

Soft control techniques

The GAPS model provides a prescriptive and clearly defined framework for managing service, and hence relationship, quality. However, there is some debate about the practicality of implementing the GAPS model. The section on monitoring earlier in the chapter examined the difficulty in measuring expectations and perceptions which are fluid and poorly defined. Authors such as Reichheld (1993) and Heskett *et al.* (1994) have suggested that external service quality is too dynamic and subjective for organisations to gauge correctly, let alone design into organisational systems. Instead, senior managers should concentrate on internal service quality, ensuring that staff are competent, motivated and supported by a customer-centred culture. Under these conditions, senior management can delegate the authority and responsibility for the quality of service delivery to the staff on the ground, who are best placed to determine and respond to changing customer expectations. This argument is implicit in the virtuous circle (Reichheld *et al.*, 2000) and the service–profit chain models discussed in Chapter six. Using such systems, the role of management is to monitor internal service quality, through measures such as staff satisfaction and retention, and to control it by the means discussed in Chapter six.

Hard or soft control?

Naturally, the prudent organisation will use a combination of hard and soft measures and control mechanisms. It is worth noting, however, that the key value of RM strategies lies in the human elements of service quality – time and again studies of successful relationships stress the importance of personal relationships between individuals. It is impossible to design qualities of this kind into a relationship, just as it is virtually impossible to objectively monitor the strength of personal bonds in quantitative terms. Although hard monitoring and control has an important place in reassuring managers and other stakeholders regarding corporate performance, it is proposed here that soft monitoring and control techniques are more appropriate to a RM strategy.

Summary

This chapter dealt with the final stage of the planning process – that of monitoring and control. It began by reviewing the general approaches to monitoring, noting the distinction between hard and soft monitoring. Whilst hard measures have an important place in managing RM, the ephemeral nature of many RM success factors means that mechanisms for soft monitoring must not be neglected. The difference between performance and diagnostic monitoring was also discussed, and it was noted that the former is more appropriate to corporate-level monitoring, whilst the latter should form the larger part of individual relationship monitoring.

Having outlined the general principles involved, the chapter went on to identify specific measures by which different aspects of RM could be monitored. At the corporate level, monitoring should draw on the balanced scorecard approach advocated by Kaplan and Norton (1992). At the relationship level, various measures were recommended for monitoring the facilitators, features and financial returns on relationships.

Next, issues of relationship maintenance and complaints handling were considered. Complaints constitute valuable monitoring information which can be used to maintain relationships with individuals and also to inform continuous improvements and product or process innovation.

Finally, the chapter outlined several control issues, and reviewed Parasuraman, Zeithaml and Berry's (1988) GAPS model for controlling service quality. It ended by considering the difference between hard and soft control, and recommending the latter as being better suited to the philosophy and practice of RM.

Case Study *Richer and richer...*

Julian Richer opened his first hi-fi shop at the age of 19. The pokey premises at London Bridge, with its steady flow of commuter traffic, were perfect for his 'pile 'em high, sell 'em cheap' business approach. Few would have guessed that, nineteen years down the line, he would be the owner of 27 stores and the chairman of another 10 companies. The Richer Sounds stores remained true to their London Bridge roots, typically occupying the cheaper ends of towns. Nevertheless, in 1998, sales per square foot in these outlets were worth nearly 100 times more than those of PC World or Curry's. And the secret?

'Spend some serious time thinking about fun. How can you liven up the workplace? What goodies can you offer people in your organisation? How can you treat yourself better to create a happier atmosphere?' (Richer 1996).

Such goodies include £5 every month to each employee so that they can go down the pub to discuss ideas for improving the business, use of a limousine to the best performing stores, and free use of holiday homes in France and the UK, regardless of performance.

Gimmicky, perhaps? Not according to Richer's employees. Quite apart from the excellent productivity figures, Richer Sounds has an enviably low staff turnover, and a suggestion scheme that generates more output per employee than any other in the UK. Such loyalty does not imply stagnation. Richer's policy of promoting from within the organisation means that employees can grow with the company. For example, Richer Consulting, established in 1996, was staffed entirely by employees from store management most of who had worked for the company since leaving school.

Richer's management success manual, 'The Richer Way' had sold over 25,000 copies by 1998, and the list of Richer Consultancy's clients grows ever longer and more prestigious, including organisations such as Asda. As well as making a successful business, it seems likely that Richer will make a lasting contribution to the style of management in the UK.

References

Richer, J. (1996) 'Mr Motivator', *Director*, 49, 6, 40–41.

Discussion questions

1. Based on the evidence in the case study, Richer Sounds' approach to organisational control is predominantly 'soft'. What are the strengths and weaknesses of this approach?

2. Suggest 'hard' monitoring and control mechanisms that would remedy some of the weaknesses of the 'soft' approach.

3. To what extent could the control mechanisms applied to the management of retail relationships be applied to Richer Consulting's operations?

References

Boulding, W., Kalra, A., Staelin, R. and Zeithaml, V. (1993) 'A dynamic process model of service quality: from expectations to behavioural intentions', *Journal of Marketing Research* (February) 7–27.

Carlzon, J. (1988) *Moments of Truth*, New York: Harper and Row.

Carman, J.M. (1990) 'Consumer perceptions of service quality: an assessment of the SERVQUAL dimensions', *Journal of Retailing*, 66, Spring, 33–55.

Cronin, J. and Taylor, S. (1992) 'Measuring service quality: a re-examination and extension', *Journal of Marketing*, 56, July, 55–68.

Festinger, L. (1957) *A Theory of Cognitive Dissonance*, Evanston, IL: Row, Peterson.

Gummesson, E. (1999) *Total Relationship Marketing: Rethinking Marketing Management: From 4Ps to 30Rs*, Oxford: Butterworth-Heinemann.

Heider, F. (1946) 'Attitudes and cognitive organization', *Journal of Psychology*, 21, 107–12.

Heskett, J., Jones, T., Loveman, G., Sasser, W. and Schlesinger, L. (1994) 'Putting the service profit chain to work', *Harvard Business Review*, March–April, 164–174.

Kaplan, R. and Norton, D. (1992) 'The balanced scorecard approach – measures that drive performance', *Harvard Business Review*, January–February, 71–79.

Liljander, V. and Strandvik, T. (1995) 'The relationship between service quality, satisfaction and intentions', in D. Kunst and J. Lemmick (eds) *Managing Service Quality*, Vught, Paul Chapman.

Parasuraman, A., Zeithaml, V. and Berry, L. (1988) 'SERVQUAL: a multiple-item scale for measuring consumer perceptions of service quality', *Journal of Retailing*, 64, 1, 12–40.

Parasuraman, A., Zeithaml, V. and Berry, L. (1994) 'Reassessment of expectations as a comparison standard in measuring service quality: implications for future research', *Journal of Marketing*, 58, January, 111–124.

Reichheld, F. (1993) 'Loyalty-based management', *Harvard Business Review*, 71, 2, 64–71.

Reichheld, F., Markey Jr, R. and Hopton, C. (2000) 'The loyalty effect – the relationship between loyalty and profits', *European Business Journal*, 12, 3, 134–139.

Seiders, K. and Berry, L. (1998) 'Service fairness: what it is and why it matters', *Academy of Management Executives*, 12, 2, 8–20.

Shaw, R. and Reed, D. (1999) *Measuring and Valuing Customer Relationships – How to Develop the Measures that Drive Profitable CRM Strategies*, London: Business Intelligence Ltd.

Stewart, K. (1998) 'An exploration of customer exit in retail banking', *International Journal of Bank Marketing*, 16, 1, 6–29.

Teas, K. (1993) 'Expectations, performance evaluation, and consumers' perceptions of quality', *Journal of Marketing* 57, October, 18–34.

8 Ethical considerations in RM

Learning objectives

After reading this chapter, you should be able to:

● Discuss ethical criticisms of marketing in general.

● Define the concepts of consumerism and social responsibility, and explain the reasons for the rise to importance of these concepts.

● Define ethics and analyse different ethical schools of thought.

● Evaluate the role of ethics with specific reference to the characteristics of RM.

Introduction

RM literature largely ignores the role of ethics. Within the framework for RM presented in this book, ethics play a prominent role in RM and are the platform upon which planning, implementation and monitoring of RM strategies are constructed. Borrowing Gummesson's terminology, Kavali *et al.* (1999) state that the short-termism of traditional marketing encourages hit and run tactics, which seeks a short-term increase in sales resulting in conflicts between customers and companies. In contrast RM promotes the idea of customers as 'co-producers' and 'members' of various marketing programmes where long term interactions are the basis for creating value, and where the interaction takes place between equal and respectful parties.

This chapter begins with a discussion of general criticisms directed at marketing and how consumerism and the concept of social responsibility have emerged to protect consumer rights and to offer an alternative philosophy of marketing activity. The chapter proceeds to define ethics in marketing. This is followed by an examination of the relevance of ethics to

RM, with specific references to the characteristics of RM as outlined in Chapter two. The importance of ethical behaviour in conducting two-way dialogue, keeping of promises, long-term commitment and achievement of mutual benefits is stressed, if RM strategies are to be implemented successfully. Finally, some implications of the Data Protection Act (1998) for operators of RM strategies are discussed.

The background

Criticisms of marketing

Marketers have, over the years, been criticised for the way in which they sometimes operate. Accusations levelled at marketers include:

- Charging high prices (due to too many intermediaries taking a share of the profits, cost of heavy advertising and generally high mark ups);
- Deceptive practices relating to promotion, pricing and packaging;
- High pressure selling and marketing of shoddy or unsafe products;
- Planned obsolescence (Kotler *et al.*, 2001).

In recent years there have been more specific criticisms directed at marketers. These include:

- Insider dealings in shares;
- Mis-selling of personal pensions;
- Mis-selling of endowment mortgages;
- Excess payment to top directors or so-called 'fat cats';
- Alleged use of child labour in Asia and elsewhere by companies such as Nike and Adidas.

Intervention by government and consumer organisations

Consumer organisations, pressure groups and government (through legislation and quango organisations) continue to monitor the activities of marketers. This is because although there are those who speak in defence of marketing, complaints continue to be expressed. For example, in the summer of 2002 the government began to impose a big shake-up of the mortgage and savings industry in Britain, where the suppliers have often been accused of charging excessive fees and creating complex products which customers find difficult to understand. Continued vigilance is thought to be necessary as reports of unsatisfactory products and shoddy practices continue to be exposed in the media. Recent reports have ranged from the low hygiene standards adhered to by many food service suppliers to most of Britain's doctors failing to meet the required standards in their surgeries, which are often packed with long queues and frustrated patients (BBC News 24, 24 July 2002). There are also many reports about unwanted mobile messages sent to millions of people including children. Such messages have included the promotion of sex chat lines and other material generally considered as unsuitable for children.

Where consumers' interests have been seen to be seriously endangered, government has sought to protect them through legislation. For example:

- The Trade Descriptions Act (1968) – false or inaccurate descriptions of products are covered under this Act which requires that those selling a good or service be truthful regarding such areas as the size, quantity, fitness for purpose, use, manufacture and previous ownership.

- The Sale and Supply of Goods Act (1994) – requires that goods sold should be of satisfactory quality, unless defects are made clear to the customer prior to purchase. This Act puts the onus for providing redress on the seller rather than on the manufacturer.

- The Consumer Protection Act (1997) – this Act covers the safety standards which customers are entitled to expect, and gives legal rights to those who have been injured by products.

The EU also works towards the harmonisation of consumer laws amongst the member states and when necessary issues Directives to protect consumers' interests, for example, the EU Data Protection Directive (1995) which is concerned with the collection and processing of personal information (data) on people as consumers and individuals.

Consumerism, social responsibility and ethics

Concern with consumer protection assumed greater significance than previously during the 1980s when due to the political and economic climate prevalent at the time individual and corporate greed reached new heights. This was coupled with frequent reports on the damage to the earth's environment and its resources.

The origins of consumerism, however, are generally agreed to be traceable to the 1960s, if not before, when Ralph Nader in the USA criticised car manufacturers for low safety standards on their products. The concept has been defined as 'an organised movement of citizens and government agencies to improve the rights and power of buyers in relation to sellers' (Kotler *et al.*, 2001: 55).

The movement seeks to add to the traditional rights of buyers which are:

- Not to purchase a product that is offered for sale;
- To expect the product to be safe;
- To expect the product to perform as claimed by the seller.

Additions sought are the right:

- To be well informed about important aspects of the product offered for sale;
- To be protected against products and marketing practices which are questionable;
- To improve the 'quality of life' through influencing products and marketing practices (adapted from Kotler *et al.*, 2001).

The concept of social responsibility is partly a response to consumerism. It reflects consumers' wider interests in the effects of production and consumption both for the earth's environment and for consumers. It can be identified as an 'organisation's obligation to maximise its positive impact and minimise its negative impact on society' (Dibb *et al.*, 2001: 766). Ethical issues are a dimension of the concept of social responsibility.

Ethics

Ethics defined

Social responsibility is a contract with society, while 'ethics relate to carefully thought out rules of moral values that guide individual and group decision making' (Dibb *et al.*, 2001: 768). In marketing, ethics refer to the moral principles that guide marketing decisions.

Ethics are controversial, and a total consensus on many issues is impossible to obtain. There are, however, issues relating to social responsibility and ethics which, it may be suggested, many seem to agree upon at present. These include activities which result in heavy pollution of the air and water, depletion of earth's natural resources (e.g. forests) without attempts at renewal, animal testing of cosmetics, bribery, misleading advertising and promotion of harmful products.

Some organisations attempt to adhere to ethical standards of behaviour in order to gain competitive advantage over their rivals. This is exemplified by the Body Shop whose policy of not testing their products on animals and putting something back into the communities from whose land they draw their raw materials has help them expand and benefit from a loyal customer base. In contrast, many companies have over the years been the subject of repeated negative publicity which, some may argue, has damaged their image and profitability.

Nestlé is one such company which has been the subject of discussion in marketing literature. The main criticism of the company relates to the aggressive promotion of infant formula milk and, by implication, the promotion of bottle feeding around the world when medical evidence favours breastfeeding, particularly in countries where a safe water supply is not always available. Consequently, a number of consumer action groups have campaigned for the boycott of Nestlé's products. Additionally, in 1999 Nestlé's campaign to sell its water brand – Pure Life – in Pakistan was also condemned for creating fear about contamination of urban water supplies and urging people to buy their bottled water.

Approaches to ethical decision-making

Marketers often face questions about their marketing activities and the way in which these activities relate to their various stakeholders. Many of these questions need to be answered from an ethical perspective. Ethical theories can be divided into relativism, utilitarianism, universalism, the justice theory and the virtue theory (Schlegelmilch, 1998: 29–34):

- *Relativism* holds that each situation must be judged according to its own merits, and that universal standards cannot be applied to judge the morality of a decision. A relativist believes in 'when in Rome do as the Romans do'.

- *Utilitarianism* advocates that the moral merits of a decision lie in whether it serves the greatest number of people. Applied to a business setting, decisions would be made after a consideration of its effects on the various stakeholders and the final choice would be the decision that served the largest number of stakeholders.

- *Universalism/deontology* proposes that the ends, or successful results, do not justify a decision that is basically unethical. Those subscribing to this theory believe in the maxim 'do unto others as would have them do unto you'. An idealistic theory, universalism is difficult to apply in practice as, often, different stakeholders have conflicting interests, e.g. customers and shareholders.

- *The justice theory* stands in opposition to utilitarianism, and translated into practical terms implies that loss of individual liberty nullifies any gains in economic efficiency and prosperity.

- The *virtue theory* advocates acting in the true spirit of virtuousness, and going beyond mere duty and self-interest in doing so.

Marketers face not only the dilemma of acting in the interests of all of their stakeholders which may not always coincide, but also the possibility of their personal ethics clashing with the ethics of the organisation they work for. Organisations in Britain and the rest of Europe are increasingly following the American example and producing ethical statements and codes of conduct which, if nothing else, can act as a clarification and point of reference for all employees.

Ethics and RM

Whilst there is a widespread debate concerning the moral nature of business in general, ethical evaluation of business practices in the area of RM is not very common (Takala and Uusitalo, 1996). Surprisingly, given the characteristics and key concepts inherent in RM the literature makes scant reference to ethics. Even though in mass marketing it may be difficult to prove whether a company, such as Nestlé, would profit from a more ethical stance, RM clearly cannot develop without adherence to what customers may interpret as ethical conduct by suppliers. Based on the definition of RM by Gronroos which has been adopted by this book, it was made clear in Chapters two and three that RM relies on two-way communication and dialogue between a customer and the supplier to pinpoint customer needs and wants. This enables the customisation of products and communication by the supplier. Keeping of promises, generation of trust and long-term commitment by both parties were highlighted as essential in RM. The voluntary nature of the commitment as opposed to entrapment, equality of power and mutual achievement of objectives were also discussed. It was also highlighted that achievement of mutual objectives was central to RM. Hence, it is perhaps obvious that successful RM can only be operationalised from a platform of ethical behaviour by both parties involved. Behaviour that is perceived as unethical by customers could easily lead to lack of trust in the supplier and ruin the chances of developing a long-term relationship.

Although the relationship between customers and suppliers is the focus of attention in this chapter, the points raised and the issues discussed apply equally to all the stakeholders in a relationship, e.g. employees and intermediaries.

RM and ethical issues in communication

An area where ethical considerations pose major challenges for the creation of successful RM strategy is communication and two-way dialogue between customer and supplier. Improvements in technology including powerful computers, smart cards (cards with micro-chips embedded in them for the purposes of recording customer transactions as well as personal information), the growing utilisation of Internet-enabled communication and call centres make it possible for companies to collect substantial information on customers. Indeed, except in the case of very small organisations, technology-based collection of information is a prerequisite for the application of RM to retailing and consumer service markets (Long *et al.*, 1999). A US study reported that 97 per cent of the websites studied collected personal information. Of these only 62 per cent indicated to the customers that information was being collected. Additionally 57 per cent of the sites contained devices for tracking by third parties (Deitel *et al.*, 2001). No wonder many customers on both sides of the Atlantic are concerned with the security of information they provide on the Internet.

The main ethical issues regarding communication relate to:

- Frequency of information gathering/contact;
- The nature of the information gathered;

- Methods of gathering information;
- The purposes for which the information is used;
- Privacy of information.

It is important that the dyadic relationship between the customer and supplier is based on the exchange of up-to-date information between the parties. At the same time, to require customers to fill in questionnaires or verbally respond to a long line of questioning during each contact may be regarded by the customer as a nuisance. A right balance ought to be struck between the need for up-to-date information about the customer and the need to respect his time.

The type of information gathered must be strictly necessary for the conduct, and continuation, of the relationship between the customer and the organisation. Questions which are not necessary need not be asked.

Information gathering methods also need to be above board and customers must be informed as to what type of data is gathered and kept about them and by what methods these data are collected.

The purpose for which the information is gathered must be notified to the customer, and subsequently not used for other purposes and not shared with other organisations without the customer's consent. This consent must be clearly sought. The information held on the customer must be clearly available to him and the opportunity to make corrections must be given.

Customers provide information to suppliers with whom they are in a long-term relationship on the understanding that the information will be kept safe, private and not seen by those who do not need to see it. Such information may include sensitive personal demographic and financial information provided to a health worker, a lawyer, a financial adviser, etc. Not respecting customers' need for the privacy and security of the information which they provide would be tantamount to basing the relationship on rocky grounds with a short lifespan because trust, the key element that glues the parties in a relationship together, would be broken. Many reports of hacking into information on databases make customers feel uncomfortable about supplying information about themselves on the Internet.

Long et al. (1999: 4), postulate that 'As technology for collecting customer data has become more sophisticated, so marketing managers have witnessed an increasing concern among customers about the impact of these new marketing management techniques on their private rights'.

The situation is made more complex by the fact that customers have different privacy thresholds. This depends on the type of information being collected, how it is collected and who the collector is. Generally a higher level of involvement with the type of information collected and a perception of the trustworthiness of the collector are helpful in raising the threshold (Long et al., 1999).

Customers also have a duty not to divulge information about suppliers which they have acquired as a result of long-term relationships, to competitors or others in such a way as to cause a disadvantage to those suppliers.

RM and the ethics of keeping promises

As discussed in Chapters two and three, the keeping of promises helps create trust between the parties in a relationship and achieve the required long-term commitment. Indeed, in practice, trust is often taken to mean that the trusted party will keep their promise.

The keeping of promises is not obligatory from the utilitarian perspective if breaking a promise will be to the advantage of most people involved in the situation. This is in contrast to deontology which regards keeping of promises as an indisputable duty, even if it means going beyond the legal requirement (Takala and Uusitalo, 1996).

The breaking of promises may not just lead to the break-up of a relationship between customer and the supplier and a lost opportunity, but also to bad publicity and damage to efforts to create a trustworthy image. According to a report on BBC television (19 June 2002) Ryanair's one millionth customer was awarded over £43 000 by the High Court in Dublin after it abandoned its promise to give her free flights for life. Jane O'Keaf, 35 years old, was given the free flights prize in 1988.

Ryanair claimed the prize was a gift and that O'Keaf had no written contract with them. The judge, however, found Ryanair had breached its contract with the customer when it began to restrict the offer nine years later. One may wonder if the money which was perhaps saved by Ryanair was worth the negative publicity.

An additional point to consider with respect to promises is that sometimes they are not clear and the actual promise and the perceived promise may not coincide. Vague statements regarding quality, refunds, delivery times, etc., can only endanger the building of a long-term relationship and must be communicated as simply and clearly as possible. Complicated documents produced by suppliers, as well as requests by customers, should be discussed and explained in person, whenever possible, to make sure that the other party clearly understands the content. Finally, the pressure to keep promises and to tell the truth in communication with customers will be greatest when the supplier is facing adverse economic circumstances or exaggerated demands from other stakeholders, e.g. shareholders or employees. In such circumstances being honest and transparent with customers is the best option as at least some customers, if not all, may be sympathetic.

Unethical behaviour by stakeholders, other than customers, is not conducive to building long-term relationships with customers, and the company, as discussed in previous chapters, must use internal marketing to effect cultural change in the organisation. Connected and external stakeholders, where possible, ought to be selected from amongst organisations which share the same values and objectives.

Long-term commitment

In a long-term relationship, customers forgo opportunistic behaviour, and additionally may even be paying premium prices so as to gain certain benefits from their commitment to a supplier. Suppliers have a duty to help customers achieve the objectives for which they have invested in the relationship and the initial efforts to get customers to commit themselves should not be replaced with taking the customer for granted.

The methods used to gain and maintain customer loyalty have been discussed earlier in this book. It has been stressed that lock-in tactics and exit barriers are not genuine relationship-building tactics, and neither are exaggerated promises and over-persuasive communication. In light of the discussion in this chapter these activities may also be regarded as unethical.

Customers also have a duty to respect the time and other resources invested in the relationship by suppliers and should refrain from opportunistic behaviour, and consider exiting from the relationship only after their complaints or requests have not been attended to satisfactorily. The supplier ought to be given the opportunity to put matters right, just as the customer has the right to seek redress.

Mutual objectives

Parties engage in a long-term relationship and forsake opportunistic behaviour in order to achieve their respective objectives. For a customer this could typically comprise core service benefits as well the additional benefits categorised by Gwinner *et al.* (1998) as confidence, social, and special treatment benefits (see Chapter two). Suppliers typically expect to make a profit, to enjoy the loyalty of the customer and enjoy a more steady trade.

As stated earlier, marketers face the dilemma of balancing the objectives of, and the benefits sought by, their different stakeholders. A fair balance needs to be struck and transparency and honesty in matters such as accounting are required.

The legal implications of unethical RM

It was stated earlier that various laws exist to protect consumers' rights. One important piece of legislation which particularly relates to RM is the Data Protection Act (1998). This is because application of RM strategies in consumer markets requires the continuous utilisation of databases for collection and analysis of customer data, for profiling of customers and for communicating with them. Despite watering down of the Data Protection Act due to pressure from direct marketing organisations, the Act places important obligations on organisations which hold information on customers and others.

The Act which is based on the EU Data Protection Directive (1995) outlines eight principles of 'good information handling'. According to these, information (data) must be:

- Fairly and lawfully processed;
- Processed for limited purposes;
- Adequate, relevant and not excessive;
- Accurate;
- Not kept for longer than is necessary;
- Processed in accordance with the customer's rights;
- Secure;
- Not transferred to countries without adequate data protection.

There are several implications arising out of the above points. For example information about customer and employee health, race and religion must be handled delicately and obtained with the full consent of the data subject (customer, employee, etc.). Also, the information gathered may not be used for purposes other than those for which it is collected, making the practice of combining databases for the purpose of customer profiling and managing customer relationships (see Chapter ten) questionable. Addition of information, for profiling purposes, which may be of questionable relevance to customer files, e.g. hobbies, religion or sexual orientation, may also pose problems. Importantly, the Act requires that declarations as to what use the organisation would put the captured data must be visible at the point of collection. Many websites on the internet currently do not take this point into account.

Summary

Marketers have been criticised for their activities on numerous occasions. When these criticisms have been strong and widespread, government has intervened through legislation. There has been a growing trend towards consumerism in the last couple of decades, and some producers of goods and services have attempted to gain a competitive advantage by subscribing to ethical policies. Consumerism refers to the organised movement of citizens and government agencies to improve the rights and power of buyers in relation to sellers (Kotler *et al.*, 2001). Marketing ethics refer to moral codes of behaviour in conducting marketing activities.

RM relies heavily on the creation of trust and commitment between the customer and supplier – on the keeping of promises and the achievement of mutual objectives. It is essential that suppliers are seen to be acting ethically and honestly. Otherwise they cannot rely on the commitment and loyalty of customers. Gathering and using data, keeping of promises, a genuine commitment to the customer and striving for the achievement of mutual objectives are the areas which need special attention. Finally, the implications of the Data Protection Act (1998) regarding the kind of information gathered and how the information handled should be remembered when designing RM programmes were discussed. Customer privacy must be respected, and larger users of data should seek legal advice when setting up their systems and procedures.

Case Study   *British Airways*

Those wishing to find out prices or to book an airline ticket can log on to the British Airways website by merely typing in the words British Airways. On the first page of the site details of travel requirements can be typed in. At the bottom of the page there are four icons, one of which is: Privacy and legal. Clicking on this icon takes the viewer to a page containing the following information:

These pages outline our legal and other policies.

Privacy Policy

The use of personal data that you provide when you visit our web site.

How we use your Booking Data

What we do with the data you give us whilst making a booking.

Security Policy

How we ensure the security of your data.

Web site Terms and Conditions

These apply when you use our web site.

General Conditions of Carriage

These apply when you travel with British Airways.

Those wishing to find out more about the privacy policy can click on the Privacy Policy icon and open another page containing the following information.

Privacy Summary

We collect three types of information online:
About you – the information you type in
About how you use our site – because we can track this using something called 'cookies'
About your travel patterns – if you make bookings with us

The main ways we use this information:
To tailor how our site can help you
To fulfil your travel requirements and deliver what you have asked us for
To treat you more personally
To maintain your records
To send you appropriate marketing communications
For anonymous analysis about how our customers use the site

The main way we let other selected companies use this information:
To help fulfil your travel requirements and help deliver what you have asked us for

And, for your peace of mind:
For over 30 years we have been safeguarding customer information on our computers
You can stop us sending you marketing communications
You can stop us tracking how you use our site

How do we collect data about you and your use of this website?
How do we use your data – including marketing use and how to opt out of it?
Who can your data be disclosed to?
How may you amend data submitted by you?

What countries will your data pass through?	(http://www.britishairways.com/travel/home.
Why do you link to other websites?	jsp/home/public/en_gb, downloaded:
Confidentiality of your booking reference	25.7.2002)
How do we keep your data secure?	
Do we take statistical data?	Those still curious enough can click on *view our*
Can you make changes to this policy?	*full privacy policy* lines and get answers for any
	of the above questions.

Discussion questions

1. If someone is merely booking a ticket or enquiring about prices, how confident do you think they would feel that British Airways will not use their details for direct marketing?

2. Are you worried about receiving unsolicited mail? Why?

3. How do you think British Airways can make customers feel more comfortable about the privacy of information they provide on the airline's website?

References

Data Protection Act (1998) HMSO, available at http://www.Hmso.gov.uk/acts/acts 1998/19980029.htm last accessed 5 November 2002.

Deitel, H.M., Deitel, P.J. and Nieto, T.R. (2001) *e-Business and e-Commerce – How to Programme*, New Jersey: Prentice Hall.

Dibb, S., Simkin, L., Pride, W.M. and Ferrell, O.C. (2001) *Marketing Concepts and Strategies*, 4th European edn, Boston: Houghton Mifflin.

EU Data Protection Directive (1995) EURIM, available at: http://www.eurim.org/briefings/ brief12.htm last accessed 5 November 2002.

Gwinner, K.P., Gremler, D.D. and Bitner, M.J. (1998) 'Relational benefits in services industries: The customer's perspective', *Journal of the Academy of Marketing Science*, 26, 2, 101–114.

Kavali, S.G., Tzokas, N. and Saren, M.J. (1999) 'Relationship marketing as an ethical approach: philosophical and managerial considerations', *Management Decision*, 37, 7, 537–581.

Kotler, P., Armstrong, G., Saunders, J. and Wong, V. (2001) *Principles of Marketing*, 3rd European edn, Harlow: Pearson Education.

Long, G., Hogg, M.K, Hartley, M. and Angold, S.J. (1999) 'Relationship marketing and privacy: exploring the thresholds', *Journal of Marketing Practice*, 5, 1, 4–20.

Schlegelmilch, B. (1998) *Marketing Ethics: An International Perspective*, London: International Thomson Business Press.

Takala, T. and Uusitalo, O. (1996) 'An alternative view of relationship marketing: a framework for ethical analysis', *European Journal of Marketing*, 30, 2, 45–60.

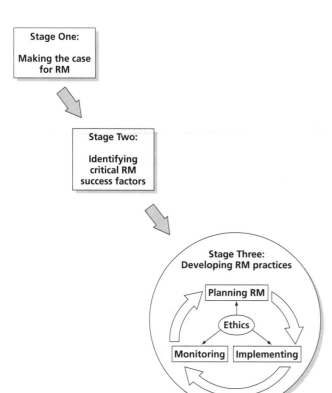

Key account management

Introduction

Key Account Management (KAM) is a common manifestation of RM in business-to-business markets. With its roots in selling, the theory and practice of KAM is narrower in scope than that of RM – it can be seen as the application of external RM principles in a business-to-business context, predominantly from a supplier's perspective. Nevertheless, the subject offers valuable insights into the practical considerations of implementing RM, and hence can in turn inform the development of the broader theory.

This chapter begins by defining KAM, its costs and benefits, before looking at the nature of the business-to-business relationships and the key stages in their development. Decision-making frameworks for identifying key accounts and developing KAM programmes are then considered. The chapter ends with a discussion of the contribution that KAM can make to the wider theory of RM, and whether KAM practices in turn can be informed by more general work on RM.

What is KAM?

KAM defined

KAM is a management practice aimed at optimising the relationship between a supplying organisation and a buying organisation. As is usual in the marketing literature, there is some debate over the precise meaning of the term. Further confusion is created by the fact that KAM is used interchangeably with National Account Management (NAM), Strategic Account Management (SAM), and Account Management (AM), although there appear to be no significant distinctions between the meanings of the four terms. Nevertheless, there is general consensus that KAM consists of three elements. Kempeners and van der Hart (1999) represent these elements well by defining [key] account management as follows:

> The process of building and maintaining relationships over an extended period, which cuts across multiple levels, functions and operating units in both the selling organisation and in carefully selected customers (accounts) that contribute to the company's objectives now or in the future.
>
> (Kempeners and van der Hart, 1999: 311)

As reflected in this definition, the practice of KAM is characterised by:

- The conscious selection of key accounts: the starting point of KAM is the identification of customers who will equate to strategic partners. All KAM programmes must therefore employ a mechanism for selecting these key accounts, based on the strategic objectives of the organisation;
- The development and maintenance of long-term relationships: having identified the key customers, the organisation must have strategies and systems in place to build and maintain a business relationship with that customer;
- The establishment of cross-functional processes for servicing accounts: this is a common feature of all definitions and examples of KAM. In order to enable the other two features of the KAM programme, the organisational structure and systems must enable multifunctional processes based around individual accounts.

KAM activities

Homburg *et al.* (2002) identify KAM by the activities that the suppliers undertake in order to build and maintain relationships. These include:

- Special pricing
- Customisation of products and services

- Development of special products or services
- Joint coordination of workflow
- Information sharing
- Taking over the customer's business processes.

McDonald (2000) focuses on the communication ties between the two companies, which move from the 'bow tie' formation shown in Figure 9.1 to a 'diamond' structure (Figure 9.2). Such a shift in structure can be both a response to and a stimulus for relationship development.

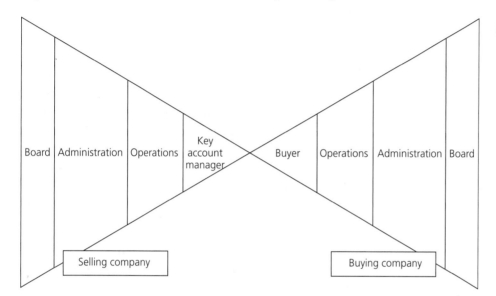

Figure 9.1

The bow tie structure evident in early KAM relationships

Source: McDonald, M. (2000) 'Key account management – a domain review', *The Marketing Review*, 1, 15–34. Reprinted with permission of Westburn Publishers Ltd.

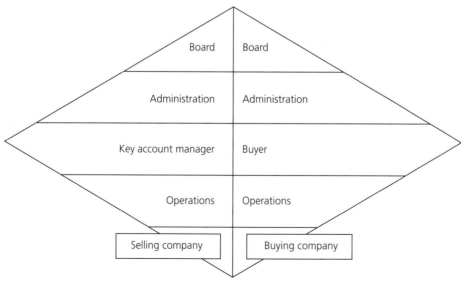

Figure 9.2

The diamond structure evident in mature KAM relationships

Source: McDonald, M. (2000) 'Key account management – a domain review', *The Marketing Review*, 1, 15–34. Reprinted with permission of Westburn Publishers Ltd.

The rationale for KAM

Before examining the mechanics of KAM and its implementation, it is worth considering the advantages (and penalties) of the practice. These are summarised in Figure 9.3. The supplier benefits from increased turnover, since the proper selection and development of accounts will lead to, amongst other things, the cultivation of the high volume, high value customers. At the same time, costs associated with the winning of new customers, such as marketing research and communications, are reduced. Ellram (1991) further notes that long-term relationships give the supplier the opportunity to plan its production and logistics with greater certainty, perfecting repetitive operations. Hence, both production and transaction costs may be reduced. The buyer in turn benefits from products and service that are specifically tailored to its needs, whilst receiving some of the benefit of the supplier's cost reductions in the form of price discounts.

It is the mutual benefits, however, that bring the greatest strategic advantages to the parties involved. Both parties enjoy reduced risk, alleviating the threat of both short-term crises in supply and demand, and long-term planning uncertainty. By pooling their resources, the two companies not only make efficiency gains, but are able to explore business opportunities that might require a prohibitively high investment were they operating individually. Resources here refer to intangible assets, such as brand image, skills, information and organisational competencies as well as to tangible assets. By sharing information, for example, the two parties may be able to develop products, processes or strategies that could not have been developed individually. Similarly, one party may be able to capitalise on the brand image of its partner by association to gain access to new markets or buyers. Finally, Ojasalo (2001) notes that the benefits of KAM may occur at the individual as well the organisational level, through the enhanced social interaction arising from the bonds that inevitably form between individuals in the two companies. Given the effect this has on employee satisfaction and motivation, this would have indirect benefits at the organisational level.

It should be stressed, however, that these benefits arise from the successful implementation of KAM, and represent the greatest benefits which can accrue. It will be seen that the development of KAM infrastructure involves a significant investment in terms of management time, staffing and training; an investment that will probably not create a return during the early stages of the relationship. The proper selection of key accounts, and the

Figure 9.3			
Benefits of key account management	**Supplier benefits** Increased turnover Reduced costs Increase profitability	**Mutual benefits** Risk reduction Shared resources Innovation and learning Social relations	**Buyer benefits** Customised products/services Price reduction

proper development and maintenance of these relationships, is critical to the long-term profitability of the KAM programme.

The key account development cycle

Stages in the key account development cycle

As with all relationships, key account relationships develop over time and require different treatment at different stages in this development. The literature offers two competing models of key account development, though the differences are nominal. The explanation offered below is a synthesis of the two.

Pre and early KAM

These stages are described by McDonald *et al.* (1997) as the 'scanning and attraction stages'. Here the supplier is concerned with the identification of potential key accounts, and gaining information by which the selection decision can be made. The move into early KAM is characterised by the willingness of the supplier to make adjustments to its standard offering. The types of information needed to select key accounts are discussed in the next section. Given the fact that customers in the pre or early KAM stages of development are of relatively low importance to the organisation, sales representatives play the central role in this process, with no special infrastructure or resources being devoted to the customer (Millman and Wilson, 1995). The focus of the relationship remains on the product, and on a set of relatively discrete (albeit repetitive) transactions.

Mid-KAM

Here the focus of the relationship begins to shift to process, as trust and commitment develop between the two parties. Hence the range of value added services offered by the supplier assume as great an importance in the eyes of the buyer as the product and its price. Both begin to view the relationship as long term, though the buyer will still maintain contact with alternative suppliers. The number of contact points between the two companies will increase, and the management of the account will tend to shift towards more senior levels of the organisations, as it takes on greater strategic importance.

Partnership and synergistic KAM

At this point in the relationship, the boundaries between the two companies reduce as the structural and social bonds between them strengthen. The sharing of sensitive information and joint problem-solving will be common practice, and both formal and informal contacts will occur regularly at all levels of both organisations. Synergistic KAM is described by McDonald *et al.* (1997) as 'quasi-integration' – a state in which the two organisations operate jointly.

Uncoupling KAM

Relationship disintegration may occur at any stage. McDonald *et al.* find that relationship breakdown is most frequently attributed to a breach of trust. Millman and Wilson (1995) stress, however, that relationship dissolution should not necessarily be viewed as a failure, since it may be in the interests of a party to end a relationship. Whether intentional or not, the uncoupling stage should be managed carefully to reduce the social and economic impact on the organisation.

Implications of the key account development cycle

Clearly the different stages of the cycle bring differing levels of investment and varying returns. The early and mid-KAM stages are particularly demanding for the supplier, requiring investment in activities such as information gathering, communications and the developing of value added services in an attempt to gain the confidence of the buyer. The major benefits of KAM, however, occur in the later stages. The supplier must, therefore, ensure that the balance of its relationship portfolio is maintained, so that the superior returns from mature relationships can fund the development of those in the early or mid-KAM stages. For a fuller discussion of this area, see Chapter four.

Identifying key accounts

The need for selection criteria

Given the cost/benefit implications of the key account development cycle, the need for the careful selection of potential key accounts is critical. Millman and Wilson (1995) describe the example of a business relationship between two multinational companies agreeing to develop jointly an advanced pigmentation system. Whilst the selling company saw the project as the start of a long-term, strategic relationship, the buyer viewed it as a one-off project. The buyer terminated the arrangement after two years, leaving the seller shocked and bitter, with no resulting sales gain to soften the blow. If a selling company is to profit from KAM, it must minimise the likelihood of such strategic failures. Although research in the field of KAM is limited, it has been found that companies that explicitly define and identify key accounts are more successful in targeting resources, and show a more sophisticated understanding of their customers (Millman and Wilson, 1999). The remainder of this section reviews various criteria for the selection of key accounts suggested by research into KAM.

Relationship history

Obviously, this criterion presumes that KAM is being implemented against a background of established accounts, and cannot be easily applied to new prospects. The literature commonly points to longevity as an indicator of the strategic importance of an account, constituting evidence of commitment and trust, both of which are important ingredients of strategic relationships (McDonald, 2000). Ojasalo (2001) points out, however, that longevity is no guarantee of profitability.

Volume

Theorists are virtually unanimous in identifying sales volume as a key determinant in the selection of key accounts (Krapfel *et al.*, 1991; McDonald *et al.*, 1997; Campbell and Cunningham, 1983). Research suggests that practitioners also find this criterion simple to apply, since it is easily quantified and readily accepted by key players within the organisation. When promoting the importance of the account internally, key account managers found that sales turnover was well-recognised throughout the business (McDonald *et al.*, 1997). It should be stressed that potential sales volume is as important as current – the same research found that achieving links with fast-growing companies or companies in developing markets was also a prime strategic consideration.

Profitability

Ojasalo (2001) points out that high sales volume does not always lead to profitability, and that to be of value, the total revenue from an account must exceed its servicing costs within a given time frame. The quantification of profitability, however, is not straightforward. The majority of costs associated with the servicing of key accounts involve services, management time, and the resolution of day-to-day problems. Intangible activities such as these are difficult to cost, particularly in organisations where a single team or manager handles more than one account. Similarly the benefits accruing from a relationship may be equally nebulous and difficult to quantify – gains in areas such as innovation, learning and reputation are hard to assess in anything but qualitative terms. Hence Millman and Wilson (1999) found that assessments of the net value of business relationships tended to rely on the subjective judgement of those involved in their operationalisation.

Status

Ojalaso (2001) identifies the fact that organisations often derive benefit from association with a reputable partner. Research by McDonald *et al.* (1997) found that some selling companies actively targeted national or multinational or 'blue chip' companies, since the prestige associated with these organisations facilitated the winning of further customers. It was also noted that companies with a good reputation were more likely to focus on long-term value-creating activities rather than short-term cost issues, and hence were more receptive to KAM initiatives.

Ease of replacement

This criterion is relevant to the decision to develop rather than to initiate a key account relationship, since it applies to existing customers only. Krapfel *et al.* (1991) recommend that by calculating the cost of replacing an exiting customer or supplier, an organisation can obtain a useful quantitative measure of the relationship's value.

Resources synergies

Campbell and Cunningham (1983) identify this as a separate criterion, whilst Millman and Wilson (1999) subsume it within broader considerations of strategic fit. The selling organisation will be able to service the account more effectively if it is able to leverage any resources or competences that distinguish it from its competitors. Hence, it should look for partners amongst organisations that would benefit particularly from its unique strengths. Similarly, it should ensure that these partners command resources that may in turn benefit the selling organisation.

Strategic compatibility

Millman and Wilson's (1999) notion of strategic fit also encompasses the alignment of organisational goals, modus operandi, culture and relational norms. Similarly, McDonald *et al.* (1997) note that not all organisations seem willing or able to maintain long-term relationships, so receptivity to a KAM programme is an important consideration. More practical considerations such as compatibility between present and intended product and market arenas, and even such mundane issues as the physical location, should not be ignored.

Criteria for selecting a key supplier

The literature tends to view KAM from the perspective of the supplier, and most of the criteria outlined above have been formulated with the supplier in mind. Many apply equally well to the buying company that is considering the development of strategic relationships with its supplier – the volume criterion, for example, becomes a question of whether the supplier can reliably fulfil current and future orders in the volume needed by the buyer. Similarly, issues of strategic compatibility or resource fit are mutual concerns. In addition, McDonald *et al.*'s research identified that the buying company is likely to weigh the following factors in its choice of strategic partner:

- Product quality: whether goods or service, the quality of the product and the relevance of value added service will be of prime importance to the buying organisation.

- Ease of doing business: aggravation and problem-solving are significant costs to the buying organisation, and purchasing officers look very favourably on those suppliers that minimise these costs.

- People quality: purchasing officers take account of the personality and skills of key contacts in the selling company, valuing such qualities as honesty, integrity and, above all, 'a spirit of understanding' (McDonald *et al.*, 1997: 748).

By understanding the criteria that the customer will apply in selecting suppliers, the supplier will be in a better position to design a KAM system that suits their needs.

Servicing key accounts: KAM activities

Adding value for key accounts

Having identified the key accounts, the next stage in the KAM process is to identify the means by which the relationship can be developed (Cann, 1998). This can in part be addressed by the installation of special resources dedicated to the servicing of the account, as discussed in the next section. However, before investing in such resources, the organisation must have a clear idea of the activities to which they will be applied. There is a clear, though tacit, consensus in the literature that such activities involve adding value rather than cutting prices. Homburg *et al.* (2002) refer in passing to 'special pricing' and Ojasalo (2001) implies the use of discounting by listing cost savings as one of the benefits to buyers of key account relationships. Otherwise, the KAM literature is silent regarding the potential of pricing as a tactic in relationship development, focusing instead on the means by which added value can be generated – McDonald *et al.* (1997) even found that suppliers actively targeted non-price-sensitive accounts so that the investment made in the account could be recouped through premium pricing.

Figure 9.4 summarises the key activities or tactics that may be employed. These are arranged as a hierarchy of measures. Although the position of each element in the hierarchy is not definitive, it serves as a rough indicator of those elements that are basic prerequisites of any strategic relationship, and those which characterise highly developed partnerships.

Quality improvement

This is perhaps the fundamental element of KAM, and the prerequisite of a strategic relationship most commonly cited by buyers (McDonald *et al.*, 1997; Millman and Wilson, 1995). In the words of Millman and Wilson, 'The desire to serve key customers better must be matched by the capability to do so' (1999: 332). Given the long-term focus of strategic relationships, product excellence at any one moment is less important than the capability to continuously develop product offerings in response to market conditions, buyer requirements and competitor activity. Since in all but the earliest stages of the relationship the supplier's total offering is likely to involve a significant service element, even suppliers of manufactured goods must be able to reassure buyers of the quality of their processes and people, as well its manufacturing capability (McDonald *et al.*, 1997). Hence the focus from the outset is on internal process quality rather than product quality.

Figure 9.4

Adding value to key accounts

Customisation

Again, this can be seen as a prerequisite of any relationship. In order to initiate any degree of exclusivity in the relationship, the supplier must be able to offer the buyer something that its competitors cannot. Customisation may derive from the physical modification of tangible goods, or from the development of tailored services or transaction routines.

Conflict resolution and problem-solving

Selnes (1998) found that the flexibility of the supplier in accepting responsibility for resolving the buyer's problems was a key determinant of a buyer's trust in their supplier, which in turn was a key antecedent of motivation to enhance the relationship. Responsiveness is often considered to be a dimension of service quality, since the ability of the supplier to resolve differences, or the difficulties of the buyer will determine the latter's satisfaction with repeated transactions over time (Parasuraman, Zeithaml and Berry, 1988). It is listed separately here because it represents an important step from away from a focus on specific, product-related transactions, and towards the development of a total offering based on joint processes.

Information sharing

Millman and Wilson (1995) found that mature relationships are characterised by the free exchange of commercially sensitive information between the two parties. Selnes (1998) states that the sharing of information can stimulate relationship enhancement in two ways. First, information is a valuable resource which can greatly enhance the operations planning of the buyer. Second, willingness to yield potentially sensitive information is taken by the buyer as an expression of trust – an important antecedent of relationship development.

Resource sharing

Perhaps the pinnacle of key account relationship building is the ability of the two parties to share resources for mutual advantage. Whether through temporary joint ventures, or the development of permanent systems or structures, the sharing of resources is both a result of, and a stimulus for, very close bonds between organisations.

Communication

Communication occupies a special place in the servicing of key accounts, since it underpins all of the other tactics, and is universally cited as being of central importance to the initiation, development and maintenance of key accounts. The two major models of KAM development identify the various stages by the nature and extent of the communication channels existing between the two companies (McDonald, 2000). A key tactic for relationship development is therefore the development of communication channels between buyer and supplier.

Research by Schultz and Evans (2002) suggests that the nature of communication is important:

- *Informality*: customers are concerned about efficient interaction, and find informal methods less cumbersome than formal channels. Perhaps more importantly, informal communication is strongly linked to trust, suggesting that it is perceived to be more open and frank than carefully managed interaction;

- *Bidirectionality*: in order to add value to the relationship, communication must be two-way, with suppliers both listening to and acting on feedback from the customer, and keeping them informed.

- *Frequency*: in keeping with customers' preference for informal modes of communication, frequent, short episodes of interaction make customers feel they are being 'kept in touch with';

- *Strategic content*: the content of communication is just as important as the mode and frequency. Customers respond better to communication which they feel to be of strategic importance and react badly to being bombarded with trivial detail.

Servicing key accounts: developing a KAM infrastructure

Identifying the type of KAM system

Having identified the key accounts, the next stage in the development of KAM is the design of the system through which they will be serviced. Shapiro and Moriarty (1984) describe five major types of key account programme:

- *No programme*: no formal system or infrastructure is developed;
- *Part-time programme*: people with other roles take on the additional responsibility of managing the account;
- *Full-time programme (unit level)*: the system is operated by fully dedicated staff, but decentralised at business unit or division level;
- *Corporate-level programme*: the system is run centrally by dedicated staff;
- *National account division*: a separate operating unit is dedicated to the account.

From a study of some 400 German and US suppliers, Homburg *et al.* (2002) identified eight distinct types of KAM system:

- *Top-management KAM* involves highly formalised KAM programmes. As the label suggests, such programmes exhibit the highest degree of top management involvement, and are usually located at the organisation's headquarters. Most have dedicated sales managers responsible for key accounts, and make extensive use of key account teams. Collaborative activities, such as the coordination of the manufacturing schedules, are of high intensity, and the supplier is proactive in developing such activities. Despite this positive picture, access to functional resources, such as marketing resources, is low.
- *Middle-management KAM* is also highly formalised, but attracts less involvement from senior management. The intensity of collaborative activities and the proactivity of the supplier are only of medium level. Key account managers tend to be locally based, and enjoy less prominent positions in the corporate hierarchy than their counterparts in top-management KAM systems. Access to functional resources is low.
- *Operating-level KAM* is also relatively formalised, involving standardised procedures, and contributing significant value to the key accounts. Senior management involvement, however, is lower still, and a still

greater proportion of account managers are based at local level. Access to functional resources is low.

- *Cross-functional, dominant KAM* offers the most positive picture against all criteria. Access to resources is high, and senior management involvement is significant. Processes and structures are well developed, and key account managers enjoy a prominent role. Proactivity and intensity of collaboration are both high. Of all the organisations surveyed, those employing this form of KAM system spend the greatest proportion of their time on external activities.

- *Unstructured KAM* systems are characterised by a lack of formality and standardisation, and a reactive stance to collaborative activity. With little top-management involvement, account managers in this group spend the lowest proportion of their time on external activities.

- *Isolated KAM* is a system in which KAM activities are instigated by local sales effort but lacks support from the central business units. Although the involvement of senior management is moderate, access to functional resources is limited, and selling centre *esprit de corps* is low.

- *Country-club KAM* systems exhibit a high degree of involvement from top management, but little else. Structures and processes are poorly developed, and teams are hardly ever formed. Special activities are neither intense nor proactive. The authors suggest that this form of KAM amounts to little more than representation by senior managers.

- *No KAM* operators may pay lip-service to a KAM system, often by awarding sales or general managers the title account coordinator or similar. However, no special activities of any significance are undertaken for their key customers.

Homburg *et al.* (2002) took a number of measures of the success of the various companies, both at the account level (i.e. how well the particular relationships were performing) and the organisational level (how well the business as a whole was performing). Perhaps predictably, the no KAM and isolated KAM approaches performed the worst, whilst cross-functional, dominant KAM companies performed particularly well against organisation-level outcomes. Top-management KAM systems were found to be associated with the most profitable companies, suggesting that greater gains from other approaches are offset by higher costs.

This research offers valuable insights into the range of KAM systems that may be applied. It is also possible that rather than being alternatives the various systems are stages in the development of a KAM system. The key conclusion arising from the research is the desirability that senior management be actively involved in the design and implementation of KAM systems, rather than delegating the task to local sales managers.

The role of the account manager

The role of the key account manager will vary considerably depending on the nature of the organisation, its environment and the KAM system in force. Millman and Wilson (1995) tentatively suggest a list of functions which are commonly associated with such posts:

- Maintaining the sales/profitability of key accounts;
- Customising the seller's total offering to key accounts;
- Facilitating inter-level or inter-functional processes that add value to the total offering;
- Promoting the KAM concept within the organisation;
- Promoting the interests of the account within the organisation.

Based on the research by Homburg *et al.* described above, and work by other authors (e.g. Millman and Wilson, 1996; McDonald *et al.*, 1997; Schultz and Evans, 2002), it is clear that the key account manager plays a crucial role in the implementation of KAM. Decisions on the responsibility, authority and resources allocated to key account managers will be critical in determining the effectiveness of the programme. Kempeners and van der Hart (1999) suggest the following checklist:

- Full or part-time system: should account managers be dedicated full time to the servicing of key accounts, or should they also have other responsibilities?
- The position of account managers in the system: should they be integrated into the sales department or should a new organisational layer be created? Should they be physically located at head office, or locally? Should different levels of key account management be created?
- Allocation of responsibility: how many accounts should each manager control?
- Allocation of authority: what resources should the account manager control? Should these be held centrally, or dedicated entirely to the account manager?

These questions have significant implications for the organisation's structure, since the KAM framework will have to be integrated with existing structures and processes. Homburg *et al.*'s (2002) research indicates that, if medium-term profitability is the chief focus, a centralised, highly developed key account executive function is not always the optimum solution, due to the cost of installing and maintaining such a system. It is possible, however, that the superior returns of such a system will pay dividends in the longer term.

Skills of the key account manager

Given the importance of the key account manager, a significant amount of research has been conducted into the skills necessary to perform this function. According to Millman and Wilson, the demands of the role require:

> High calibre people who are not only sufficiently 'rounded' to be able to diagnose/analyse complex commercial and technical situations; but also equipped to cope with highly politicized interaction, together with personal tensions and ambiguities inherent in the boundary-spanning role.
>
> (Millman and Wilson, 1995: 17)

Shultz and Evans (2002) also single out communication skills as the key competence required of key account representatives, particularly the ability to share information of a strategic nature, rather than communicating predominantly on tactical issues. McDonald *et al.*'s (1997) research adds the following requirements:

- Integrity;
- Product service knowledge;
- Understanding the buying company's business and business environment;
- Selling/negotiating skills.

Possession of these skills and competences is understandably rare, and organisations seeking to implement KAM must be prepared to invest heavily in the selection, retention and development of suitable candidates.

The key account team

The use of key account teams to support the manager varies considerably between different examples of KAM systems, with account managers in some companies having no support from teams (Kempeners and van der Hart, 1999; Homburg et al., 2002). Homburg et al. (2002) found that the companies that performed best at the operational or account level made extensive use of teams. Schultz and Evans (2002) recommend the use of key account teams. Not only do they enable frequent contact with the customer, but they also help the flow of information in the selling organisation, so that relevant information about the customer and the account is transferred to all points of customer contact.

According to Kempener and van der Hart, key account team decisions relate to the constitution and control of teams:

- Constitution of account teams: the role of the account team is to support cross-functional activities. To be of value, therefore, the teams should comprise members from all functions that have a hand in servicing the account. Team members may be full or part-time, and certain members (or indeed entire teams) may be involved only on an *ad hoc* basis, to solve a particular problem.

- Control of account teams: the most formalised control structure involves the key account manager with line-management responsibility for a dedicated, full-time team. Where part-time or ad hoc members are involved, however, line management responsibility may be shared, or rest wholly with a manager in a functional department.

Clearly there are significant trade-offs here between efficiency and effectiveness, as demonstrated in Homburg *et al.*'s (2002) finding that the most formalised and successful systems were not necessarily the most profitable. Moreover, the development of a permanent structure would be inappropriate in the early stages of a relationship – it is implicit in the notion of the account development cycle that supplier investments increase as trust develops between the two parties, and the chance of exit reduces (McDonald, 2000; Millman and Wilson, 1996). As with the various options for designing the role of the key account manager, so the different account team structures might be used by the same organisation at different stages of the account's development.

The relevance of KAM to RM

A specific application of RM

Theories of KAM have been developed in high value, low volume, business-to-business markets, usually as an extension of theories of personal selling. This naturally sets limits on the applicability of KAM to RM practices in other types of market, in particular to mass markets. Nevertheless, the KAM literature illustrates some important general principles of RM.

The need for senior management support

Both the empirical research and theoretical work provide strong evidence to suggest that KAM strategies will not work without the active support of senior management. This reinforces the general principle that RM requires a fundamental change in the values, goals and resource priorities of the organisation, and will not be successful if viewed as a tactical issue. In the early stages at least, RM initiatives must be championed by influential members of the organisation's management if they are to succeed.

The need for cross-functional coordination

KAM programmes appear to work better when they are supported by teams arranged around customers rather than functional areas. The development of KAM relationships involves a move away from the focus on rigid structures producing standardised offerings, and towards a more flexible, network structure which can adapt to changing customer requirements, calling on new members and resources as circumstances require. This mirrors the consensus in the more general literature that RM is best supported by a network structure based on process rather than functional areas (see Chapter five, Structure and Chapter six, Internal Marketing (IM).

The importance of communication

Finally, the KAM literature underlines the central role of communication in building and maintaining the trust on which relationships depend. Whether dealing with customers, employees, channel members or referral markets, the management of relationships hinges on the development of open dialogue between the parties involved. This is as true for mass consumer markets as for business-to-business sectors.

Summary

This chapter examined the application of relationship marketing principles in a business-to-business context. Much of contemporary relationship marketing theory developed from research into relationships between buying and selling organisations, so the scrutiny of current practices provides useful insights into the implementation of RM. KAM was defined as the deliberate selection and cultivation of strategically important clients, effected through the establishment of cross-functional, customer centred activities. The benefits and pitfalls of KAM were outlined, as well as the key activities that characterised the practice of KAM.

It was noted that the KAM literature accepted the existence of a relationship development cycle, and hence that strategic relationships should be managed on a portfolio rather than an individual basis. The key stages of strategic relationship development were outlined, and their implications for profits and costs were discussed.

The remainder of the chapter looked at the practical challenges of establishing KAM in an organisation, and derived a number of lessons for RM generally. The chief of these was the importance of senior management commitment, without which any RM initiative would be likely to fail.

Case Study *NCR Corporation*

Creating and delivering quality standards in customer satisfaction

The implementation of a web-based, continuous customer satisfaction measurement and tracking system has enabled NCR to monitor customer feedback and develop appropriate relationship management strategies and tactics.

NCR: from cash registers to information technology

NCR Corporation, based in Dayton, Ohio, started off in life as the National Cash Register company, famous throughout the US and Europe for producing high quality mechanical cash registers, a product line which began in 1882. Some models can still be found working in corner shops today! Office accounting machines were introduced in the 1920s using the expertise it developed in money handling and data processing, the computerisation of which began in the 1950s. NCR gradually moved during the 1970s into the manufacture and maintenance of automatic teller machines (ATMs), sophisticated devices which are often referred to as hole-in-the-wall cash dispensing machines but which, in reality, are sophisticated electronic devices running off a complex computer network. NCR still produces digital electronic cash registers and scanning equipment in the form of electronic point-of-sale (EPOS) terminals for supermarkets and small cash tills for corner shops (mom and pop stores as they are known in the US).

The result is that NCR has made the transition to become, effectively, an information technology products and services organisation. Its product range includes media products such as paper and ink, data gathering and analysis tools for distribution channels and data warehousing management for large organisations such as Wal Mart and the US Postal Service. The company was purchased by AT&T in 1991 in a hostile takeover bid. The acquisition was a failure, particularly in cultural terms, so in 1996 NCR was 'spun off' from AT&T. Led by Lars Nyberg who became the new CEO, NCR has transformed itself into a successful $6.5 billion global organisation.

As with all corporate success stories there are many factors involved – people, culture, organisational processes and maturity, vision, excellent marketing and, of course, a dose of luck and good timing. But a key part of the success is NCR's commitment to stakeholder satisfaction measurement, using the results of continuous survey-based customer relationship measures to guide the development of strategy and company processes.

Managing the survey methodology

NCR obtains survey feedback from customers in almost 60 countries on a twice yearly basis across key segments including retail, telecommunications, transport and financial services. The results, covering customers who account for 80 per cent of NCR's revenues, produce metrics, or measurements, which are used by the various business units for performance improvement through goals and objectives. A range of survey techniques are used including telephone interviewing, personal interviews and questionnaires. A web-based customer market information system resides in a powerful database which also includes data on key customer decision-makers and their purchasing profile. NCRs sales and marketing executives can access the database to find out satisfaction results and match them to customer spending patterns.

A key feature of the data collection process is that results are immediately made available online. Details include customer comments, individual and group reports. Customer comments and feedback at account level are made available within ten days of a survey, compared with ten weeks before the web-based system was introduced.

NCR executives can thus address customer problems rapidly and use the continuous survey feedback to modify relationship marketing strategies. Dissatisfied customers can be identified quickly and an account manager delegated to deal with the problem before it is too late and the customer moves to another supplier. NCR set benchmarks for satisfaction levels which, if not met, result in immediate remedial action. Follow-up meetings involve the planning of sales and marketing activities designed to seek more information about apparent problems and to implement remedial action. A tracking system ensures that problems are identified and followed-up.

Integrating survey results into ongoing relationship programmes

By implementing this online customer survey system, NCR has developed a way of tracking quality and satisfaction levels across its global customer base. It has created a new dimension on the purpose of the customer relationship survey and management programmes. Instead of being a passive, historic measure of customer satisfaction, it has become a live tool or methodology for enabling executives to react rapidly to evolving problems. This results not just in a first aid set of remedial actions but leads directly to changes in sales and marketing strategies for relationship management.

Nevertheless, the NCR case does not just illustrate the usefulness of integrating customer feedback into a management culture which can make effective use of technology. What is more important is that NCR has developed a culture where management and processes are focused on the customer. In so many large organisations today, marketing and so-called relationship management programmes are driven by internal culture, processes and procedures. Without fundamental changes to corporate culture however, long-term customer loyalty – and hence customer value – cannot be developed.

Case study by Mike Wilman

Discussion questions

1. Classify NCR's approach to KAM according to the typology suggested by Homburg *et al.* (2002).
2. Critically appraise the systems and structures that NCR have in place for managing key accounts.
3. Suggest the organisational changes needed if NCR is to enhance its strategic use of key account management.

References

Campbell, M. and Cunningham, M. (1983) 'Customer analysis for strategic development in industrial markets', *Strategic Management Journal*, 4, 4, 369–481.

Cann, C. (1998) 'Eight steps to building a business-to-business relationship', *Journal of Business and Industrial Marketing*, 13, 4/5, 393–405.

Ellram, L.E. (1991) 'Supply chain management', *International Journal of Physical Distribution and Logistics Management*, 21, 1, 13–22.

Homburg, C., Workman Jr. J. and Jensen, O. (2002), 'A configurational perspective on key account management', *Journal of Marketing*, 66, 2, 38–61.

Kempeners, M. and van der Hart, H. (1999) 'Designing account management organisations', *Journal of Business and Industrial Marketing*, 14, 4, 310–355.

Krapfel, Jr. R., Salmond, D. and Spekman, R. (1991) 'A strategic approach to managing buyer–seller relationships', *European Journal of Marketing*, 25, 9, 22–48.

McDonald, M. (2000) 'Key account management – a domain review', *The Marketing Review*, 1, 15–34.

McDonald, M., Millman, T. and Rogers, B. (1997) 'Key account management: theory, practice and challenges', *Journal of Marketing Management*, 13, 8, 737–757.

Millman, T. and Wilson, K. (1996) 'Processual issues in key account management: underpinning the customer-facing organisation', *Journal of Business and Industrial Marketing*, 14, 4, 328–337.

Ojasalo, J. (2001) 'Key account management at company and individual levels in business-to-business relationships', *Journal of Business and Industrial Marketing*, 16, 3, 199–218.

Parasuraman, A., Zeithaml, V. and Berry, L. (1988) 'SERVQUAL: A multiple item scale for measuring consumer perceptions of service quality', *Journal of Retailing*, 64, 1, 12–40.

Schultz, R. and Evans, K. (2002) 'Strategic collaborative communication by key account representatives', *Journal of Personal Selling and Sales Management*, 22, 1, 23–32.

Selnes, F. (1998) 'Antecedents and consequences of trust and satisfaction in buyer–seller relationships', *European Journal of Marketing*, 32, 3, 305–322.

Shapiro, B.P. and Moriarty, R.T. (1984) 'Organising the national account force', working paper, Marketing Science Institute, MA.

10 Customer relationship management

Learning objectives

After reading this chapter, you should be able to:

1. Define customer relationship management (CRM).

2. Analyse the differences between the mainstream practitioner and academic approaches to CRM.

3. Identify and discuss requirements for successful implementation of CRM.

Introduction

This chapter begins by pointing out the differences in interpretation and definition of customer relationship management (CRM). It adopts the definition that CRM is technology-enabled RM, and puts forward some of the criticisms levelled at the practitioner approach to CRM. This is followed by a discussion of how CRM works and explanation of such terms as data warehousing and data mining. A strategic approach to CRM is recommended and specific issues such as channel integration, internal marketing, building of trust and cost of systems are then discussed. A check list is provided for those wishing to adopt CRM and, finally, five myths of CRM are exposed.

What is CRM and why has it become popular?

The importation of RM principles from industrial and business-to-business marketing to the consumer services and goods markets has been made possible through utilisation of the vast advances which have been made in recent years in communications and information technology. This is true at least in the case of large retailers whose customers are large in number and often physically at a distance. To most academics *CRM* is technology-enabled RM, or as Payne (2001: 14) defines it, CRM is 'a management approach that seeks to create, develop and enhance relationships with carefully targeted customers'. The practitioner approach and definition are, in most cases, rather different. For example, Deitel *et al.* (2001: 113) define CRM as 'the sum total of a company's customer service solutions'. The difference of opinion and the confusion is basically down to one group of people (mostly practitioners) believing that CRM is an IT project and those (mostly academics and some practitioners) who believe CRM is a strategy to build a long-lasting relationship with customers that is enabled by technology. The approach taken by this book is that of the latter group.

While advances in technology have made CRM possible, the popularity of CRM in the last decade or so stems from the reasons discussed in Chapters one and two; mainly the increase in market competition and the publication of studies showing the benefits of customer loyalty. Another set of reasons is grounded in the changing pattern of consumer behaviour portrayed through:

> An increased pressure on shopping time; a trend towards outsourcing by consumers, such as the increase in ready meals; increased consumer rationality; a fragmentation of consumer markets; and overall, an increase in the consumer's power relative to producers.
>
> (Wilson *et al.*, 2002: 195)

Criticisms of the practitioner approach to CRM

Many practitioners equate CRM with technology and the use of IT to analyse customer behaviour for the purpose of better targeting customers. In this sense, CRM is essentially database or direct marketing. Many of the vast number of articles on CRM in trade papers and journals are written by practitioners, giving a strong impression of CRM as a device, or technology, for customer manipulation and control. It would be more accurate to regard most CRM programmes in industry today as customer management rather than relationship management programmes vis-à-vis the definition of a relationship and characteristics of RM as outlined in Chapter two. This approach means that the prime requirements of RM, i.e. two-way dialogue, parity of power, long-term commitment, mutual value and achievement of objectives, keeping of promises and nurturing of trust get lost amidst the technological terminology and concern for profits in the short-run. Voices of dissent, however, exist among practitioners and future developments will be interesting to witness. The potential exists for CRM to be used as a genuine tool for long-term relationship building with valued customers based on the principles of RM.

How does CRM work?

The tools

A company's CRM embraces a variety of the functions and technologies listed below (though not necessarily all):

- Website(s) (e-CRM)
- Call centre(s)
- Sales force
- Customer service and help desks
- Point of sale terminals
- Voice response systems
- Mobile communication devices (m-CRM)
- Service history
- Analytical and predictive modelling
- Smart cards.

Profiling and customisation

CRM be used as a tool of dialogue and customer research and a valuable source of establishing customer needs and wants on an individual basis. The most valuable customers could be identified and attempts made at building long-term relationships with them. Combining the information gathered through different parts of the CRM systems (call centre, the web, etc.) a profile of the customer can be drawn up. A typical profile produced by CRM systems includes:

- A map of the customer's relationship with the company
- Product and usage summary data
- Demographic and psychographic data
- Profitability measures
- Contact history summarising the customer's contacts with the company across most delivery channels
- Marketing and sales information containing programmes received by the customer and the customer's responses (Laudon and Traver, 2001).

CRM allows for both mass and one-to-one customisation of products and communication and, therefore, has the potential to be a very useful vehicle for RM. CRM systems can also be used for cross-selling of products and allow for interactive communication as well as marketing research openly or discreetly through tracking.

Tracking is the process of keeping track of a customer's activities on the company's websites and studying the customer's pattern of behaviour (time spent, types of products looked at or purchased, etc.) to identify the products that customers are interested in. Thus, tracking enables companies to offer customised products and communication to customers.

CRM systems normally incorporate data warehouses. A data warehouse is a powerful database which combines information from various smaller databases. Data mining is used by suppliers to analyse information held in their data warehouses for the profiling of their customers. Data mining software make it possible to analyse information and identify previously unseen patterns or trends in markets and purchase behaviour of customers (Chaffey, 2002).

Data mining is used because:

1. Relevant data are not always easy to locate in large databases;
2. Data may be held on different databases and data warehouses, data mining helps gather the information buried in different locations;
3. Data mining tools can easily be combined with spreadsheets and other end-user software development tools. This enables quick and easy analysis of mined data;
4. Data mining enables the gathering of five types of information:
   (a) association,
   (b) sequences,
   (c) classifications,
   (d) clusters,
   (e) forecasting.
   (Based on Turban *et al.*, 2000)

Such systems also often incorporate *cookies*. A cookie is a code attached to a file on a customer's computer by the server computer. The cookie resides on the customer's hard drive and becomes activated each time the customer revisits the site or its affiliated sites. This code is different for each customer and enables individual tracking of the activities of the customer on the website of the supplier over time. Thus, it can be used for profiling and targeting of customers.

By using special software CRM operators can identify their most profitable customers and engage in a long-term relationship with them through dialogue and customisation. To enhance the relationship, and to go beyond mere e-marketing, two-way channels of communications must be facilitated and genuine partnerships developed. A website can be designed to contain a personal file for each customer which would contain customised communication, including news and product offers, based on the information learned from the customer on previous visits. For example, Amazon.com makes personalised book offers to its regular customers based on their personal profile. The customer accesses his personal file by using a password. Good sites will have the facility for the customer to automatically update personal details and requirements as and when they change.

As stated earlier, CRM is not confined to the use of the Internet. Call centres are used as interaction or contact centres where the staff answer telephone calls and enter into dialogue with customers. More effective CRM programmes will combine website, e-mail and call centres so as to facilitate customer-to-supplier dialogue and give the customers a choice of method for contacting the supplier. For its successful implementation, CRM relies on up-to-date information about the customer and the availability of this information to the customer-facing staff. The need for up-to-date records must be balanced against pestering customers with calls and e-mails requesting information – information collection must be unobtrusive.

Handled correctly, CRM can have an exciting future, particularly with developments in WAP technology, mobile telephony and hand-held computers, also referred to as mobile CRM (m-CRM), enabling instant communication between suppliers and customers on the move. Leading suppliers of CRM software include E.piphany, eGain, PeopleSoft and Siebel.

The strategic approach to CRM

Successful CRM will depend on treating it not as an add-on to the existing strategy and tactics of the company but as an all-embracing strategy to conduct the company's affairs, taking advantage of technology to achieve the objectives of that strategy. Various models of CRM planning and implementation have been proposed in the past. This book takes the stand that the principles of planning, implementation and control as outlined in Chapters four to seven apply equally here. Adoption of CRM strategy and systems must emanate from a clear appraisal of the company's products, internal strengths and weaknesses as well as a thorough environmental analysis.

The CRM strategy must keep within sight that RM and fostering loyalty amongst customers is dependent on the added value proposition offered by the company in terms of tangible benefits to be gained by the customer from committing to a supplier on the basis of trust. At the same time this must be balanced with the creation of value for other stakeholders too. Major cultural change within the organisation, adoption of a genuine customer orientation philosophy and full training in the operation of the system is required.

Successful implementation of CRM often requires a philosophical and strategic change by the organisation which must ideally be championed by a senior director, questioning and unfreezing existing assumptions and practices, with a team working alongside him to bring about the necessary changes. Change in attitudes as well as continuous training in all aspects of marketing and in the operation of the technology must be effected with a great deal of thought. CRM is an organisation-wide philosophy and strategy which should not be confined to sales or marketing departments. The concept of part-time marketers, or everyone within the organisation being customer and marketing focused applies here.

> If you want to change the business with a major step improvement in the way you interact with your customers, *everyone* in the company must understand the changes being made, why they are being made, what is required from them personally, what it means for the customers, and what the road map of developments and expected results are.
>
> (Osborne, 2001: 34)

Proper consideration ought to be given to the impact of CRM on the employees of the organisation, who need to be prepared for the cultural change that CRM requires. For example, if changes are proposed which mean a move to handling most of the customer services operation on the Internet, then consideration needs to be given to how customer service staff will react. Will they feel their jobs are in danger? (Siragher, 2001: 18). It may be that the reward structures will have to be changed to reward employees for customer keeping, level of service achieved and for cross-selling rather than customer getting and single sales.

Other considerations for a successful implementation of CRM strategy

Integration of channels

Successful operation of CRM requires the seamless operation and multi-channel integration of the processes and the channels involved e.g. e-tailing, m-tailing, call centres, sales force and communication systems. For this purpose IT and data repositories must be used effectively and front office and back office integrated. A data repository contains IT systems, analysis tools, front office and back office applications. Front office refers to the systems and people that the customer interacts with, e.g. marketing, sales, technical support, customer service, etc. Back office refers to the systems and people that deal with technology, software, data, non-payment, product returns, etc. Channel integration, of course, also offers customers the choice of the method of contact with the supplier.

The importance of a strategic approach to CRM and full integration of customer channels is perhaps demonstrated by the results of surveys conducted amongst a variety of commercial sectors. One survey showed that keeping hold of existing customers was the key reason most companies adopted CRM, but that only 6 per cent of the sample felt that they 'had been very successful' at integrating different customer channels. Additionally, only 42 per cent of the respondents felt the use of technology and CRM was delivering sufficient competitive advantage; a similar proportion were unable to make a satisfactory evaluation and 10 per cent felt it was not (Sweet, 2001).

Building of trust

The stance taken in this book has been that trust is the driver of genuine customer loyalty. A visitor to a bricks and mortar retailer does not need to leave any information, or more information than he is willing to, about himself. A customer dealing with a supplier who uses the Internet for trading and CRM can unintentionally leave lots of information behind which can be analysed by the supplier through tracking and mining. Due respect for customer privacy is necessary for CRM to be successful (see Chapter eight for ethical and legal implications).

Customers need to trust not only the supplier but the technology that is the facilitator of the relationship between them and the supplier. The inclusion of reliable security devices and techniques within the CRM systems and clear communication of such measures as well as the company's policy of security and privacy to the customers are important here. Reichheld *et al.* (2000) report on the American company Vanguard who, instead of offering their customers instant access to their website, ask them to wait for a password by mail, and then to take the time to download a special browser. While this might put some customers off, Vanguard is convinced that this careful attention to security is valued by its customers. Vanguard's customers conduct 40 per cent of their business with this one company.

The cost

CRM is a costly multi-million pound business with a large number of companies, such as Siebel, Oracle and PeopleSoft, presenting an array of software programmes to potential customers considering adoption. The industry is growing speedily and is estimated to become worth billions of pounds in the next few years. Hard- and softwares can cost several thousand to hundreds of thousand of pounds to purchase, install and make operational. With continuous developments in technology and improvements to systems and programs those responsible for adoption and implementation of a CRM strategy must think carefully, choosing the right program from the suppliers they can work with. Selecting from a wide range of products can be complicated and should be done through consultation with the employees who will be operating them. It is important to remember that all the various technologies and channels used must integrate and work together in a seamless fashion in order to be effective, to give a unified message and portray a single image of the company.

Companies that find CRM technology too expensive can opt to work with one of a large number of service providers. Service providers can provide a wide range of services from telephone operated call centres to complete CRM packages including equipment, network, data and e-mail, as well as personnel and management services. Due to the high costs, and the large number of failures in implementing CRM strategies, the trend in outsourcing of CRM services is likely to grow (Cheung, 2001).

Finance directors will need to be convinced of the expenditure at the beginning and as the strategy progresses and operations grow. A clear measure of the benefits based on a calculation of the profits of engaging in a relationship and managing a relationship with different categories of customers will need to be made available. According to Stone and Foss (2001: iii–viii) companies need to understand that:

> With good planning, good preparation and good programme management, and good integration of systems – with each other and management activity – CRM can produce greater profits. But without these, it will just be a drain on shareholder value.

The reality, however, is that there is no clear and widely accepted formula to measure effectiveness of CRM. Indeed, it would be fair to say that many companies do not know how to measure customer profitability and cannot even tell whether their CRM programmes are making a positive return.

As mentioned in earlier chapters, relationship building is recommended only with those customers who are willing to enter into a relationship and who are also going to be profitable. Using software to calculate customer life time value and targeting the right customers, CRM can help companies reap the benefits of having loyal customers. Even so, it has been suggested that 'typically, it takes three years for a customer to turn a healthy profit' (Reichheld *et al.*, 2000). So those investing large sums of money in CRM systems must also be prepared to wait and not expect immediate improvements in profitability. The hype from CRM software suppliers must be taken with more than a pinch of salt. One such supplier – Oracle – has placed full page advertisements, for example in *Marketing Business* (December–January 2002) reading: 'Start today and have global CRM in 90 days – Time is money, everything you need, everywhere you operate, in just 90 days!'

Checklist

Those wishing to adopt CRM may find it useful to ask themselves the following questions:

1. Why do we want CRM? Is it because it is trendy to have a CRM system in operation? Is it to cut costs? Or is it because we understand the importance of customer retention?
2. Do we realise CRM is not about technology, but about creating value for customers?
3. Have we carried out a full internal, external and competitor analysis?
4. Have we asked our customers what they think about our plans?
5. Have we looked at different IT systems and software packages and compared them? Have we thought about outsourcing?

6. Do we know the true cost?
7. Do we realise CRM is not an add-on, but a philosophical and strategic orientation to business?
8. Have we given enough thought to internal marketing?
9. Arc we prepared, possibly, to wait two or three years to see any real benefits?
10. Do we realise that the data gathered is of no use unless we properly analyse, interpret and use it?

The myths of CRM

Earlier estimates of how large and fast CRM will grow have turned out to be exaggerated. Many companies investing in CRM have failed to reap appreciable benefits. Recent research suggests that nearly one-third of the sampled consultancies and users of CRM believed that one of the main causes of failure to achieve benefits from CRM investment was organisational. A fifth blamed company politics and inertia, while 20 per cent believed a lack of understanding of CRM was the cause of failure (Siragher, 2001).

This chapter will conclude with a summary of the myths surrounding CRM.

- Myth one – 'CRM means management of the customer'

  The term Customer Relationship Management implies that customers can somehow be managed, i.e. can be manipulated to behave in a certain way. The multitude of alternative products and services and the ease of access to them makes this a naive notion and possibly quite offensive to customers. In reality, it is often the customers who manage the organisation, deciding what to buy, when, how and through which channel.

- Myth two – 'CRM software will solve all our problems'

  Software vendors' message seems to be 'buy our CRM application and all your troubles will be solved'. It is certainly useful to bring all customer information together in one place, but knowing what to do with it is another matter. The information needs to be translated into real customer intelligence and business rules and procedures need to be developed to turn this intelligence into competitive advantage based on customer experience and value.

- Myth three – 'CRM applications will always pay for themselves'

  Evidence of cost benefit for CRM is as yet not totally convincing. This is made more difficult by the fact that CRM investment decisions are often based on vague criteria which are not clearly quantifiable. Customer and business benefits must be clearly and realistically defined.

- Myth four – 'All customers love the new technologies'

  Organisations must be careful with the use of technology for its own sake. This carries the risk of alienating customers if they begin to feel remote and isolated from organisations.

- Myth five – 'Our organisation speaks to its customers with one voice'

  While marketing departments are giving out the message to customers that they are valued and welcomed as lifelong partners, the message from other functional sections, for example customer service, is often 'you are a bit of a nuisance, please go away'. Conflicting objectives and measures for different departments are partly to blame. For CRM to be successful, systems and processes must be evaluated in terms of customer experience (Gould, 2001).

Summary

In this chapter CRM was defined as IT-enabled RM and it was stated that the basic principles of planning, control and measurement as outlined in earlier chapters are equally applicable to CRM. It was pointed out that it would be a mistake to equate CRM to technology; rather, CRM is a business strategy aimed at building long-term relationships with valued customers which is made possible using the latest developments in technology. CRM enables storing of customer data in powerful warehouses. This data can then be mined and analysed to draw customer profiles which may be used for customised communications and product offering. It offers customers a choice of channels and times to contact suppliers from the convenience of their homes, offices or even on the move. It must, however, be realised that not all customers are happy with using technology and some prefer face-to-face contact with suppliers.

Successful CRM planning must include internal marketing and management of cultural change, staff training and embedding of the philosophy of customer orientation within the whole organisation. CRM systems must be designed from the beginning in consultation with marketing and other departments that will use them rather that being designed by IT specialists in isolation.

Case Study   firstdirect

firstdirect was formed in 1989 as a telephone banking service. By 1989, it had 2,300 employees, and today its website boasts over one million accounts (www.firstdirect.com, 14 August 2002). **firstdirect**'s achievements aren't just based on quantity, however; the French-based bureau network Teleperformance gives awards for call handling standards, making 'mystery shopper calls' to 2,000 firms worldwide. In 1998 **firstdirect** scored second highest in the UK, close behind Virgin Direct (Gofton, 1998).

The secret, according to Barratt (2001) is simplicity. The brand theme of 'Black and White' runs through all its communications. Log on to the constantly updated website, for example, and you'll find plain graphics and plain English, offering assurances such as the now historic 'black white promise'. Customers know what to expect, and employees know what must be delivered.

Communicating with employees is an important factor in **firstdirect**'s success, at least according to Sue Pollitt, the bank's Internal Marketing Director. She argues that internal communications should not become too stage-managed. Instead, she aims to create an atmosphere in which people feel that they can have a dialogue with anyone in the company. The creation of good atmosphere requires imagination in the way staff are motivated and rewarded. **firstdirect** gives its meeting rooms over in the evening to hold classes for staff on anything from guitar playing to Spanish. 'We are trying to achieve a bit of wow factor with our internal audience, just as we would like our people to achieve this with our external audience' says Pollitt (in Mazur, 1999). Hiring the right people is also crucial – Pollitt defines 'right' not in terms of skills or experience, but by attitude and personality, stating that **firstdirect** looks for people with 'natural empathy' (Mazur, 1999).

The bank's centralised operating structure probably helps too. With its staff concentrated in two big sites on the outskirts of Leeds and

---

the firstdirect

black & white promise

We recognise that guarantees and promises are all very well, but we have to put our money where our mouth is. At firstdirect, we're keen to do this so:

No quibbles, if we make a mistake in transferring your account you get £20.

We'll even give you £20 if you ask us to transfer your account to another bank and we don't do it correctly.

Glasgow, both internal and customer communications can be managed far more efficiently than in the conventional branch structure. Centralisation is not without its risks – May Day 1999 saw the bank's back office database crash under the weight of bank holiday transactions, leading to delayed payment and unnecessary charges. This came hot on the heels of an error over the Easter break, when 11,000 holders of **firstdirect** visa cards had interest incorrectly added to their bills. Despite these setbacks, the efficiency of the system, and the 24/7 account access provide customer benefits that the high street establishment have found hard to rival.

It is in customer development, however, that **firstdirect** has truly excelled. Its success rate in securing personal loans from direct mail is 8.3 per cent – not impressive, perhaps, unless you know that the industry average is only 1 per cent (Cramp, 1996). Much of this success can

▶

be attributed to **firstdirect**'s use of MIND; a database marketing system, which combines individual purchasing profiles with a predictive model. Data is drawn from a number of sources – not just banking transactions, but also feedback from promotional campaigns, data from other organisations and **firstdirect**'s own, extensive marketing research. Says Peter Simpson, **firstdirect**'s Commercial Director 'We know from paying attention to our customers if they are price driven, service-driven or short of time. This data … helps in predicting the buying behaviour' (In Cramp, 1996).

It appears that there are limits, however, to the extent to which customers will respond to offers of 'total solutions' that anticipate their needs. In 1998, **firstdirect** launched Octopus, an Internet service that promised to unleash the true potential of Internet technology for offering automated, customised information services, initially in response to, but eventually in anticipation of, customer requests. The service gave users access to information on anything from local tide times to suggestions on birthday gifts for their favourite aunt. The idea was to move from the management of customers' money into offering expert guidance on every aspect of their life. At the same time, rival NatWest launched its experimental 'Zenda' service, which offered similar benefits.

Eighteen months later, Octopus was spun off into an independent company, and Zenda was discontinued. It was not clear why these innovations failed. Some observers blamed charging policies – **firstdirect** had charged up to £30 for some services, whereas most people expected Internet information to be free. Others felt that customers simply would not trust the banks to manage their non-financial affairs. Whatever the truth, it was notable that the new, independent Octopus was a lot busier after leaving the control of **firstdirect**, with some people *delegating their lives* to the newly formed company (Maguire, 2000).

It seems then that **firstdirect** should stick to its core business – that customer conservatism may limit the supposed potential of Internet technology to offer 'total lifestyle solutions' cost effectively. It may be, however, that the banks themselves are the real problem, or at least the customers' image of them. Perhaps customers just don't trust banks, even those of **firstdirect**'s calibre, enough to 'delegate their lives' to them.

References

Barratt, M. (2001) 'Direct choice/**firstdirect**', *Marketing*, March, 29, 13.

Cramp, B. (1996) 'Reading your mind', *Marketing*, February, 22, 33.

Gofton, K. (1998) 'A line on quality', *Marketing*, August, 27, 5.

Maguire, C. (2000) 'Two UK banks cancel experiments of catch-all information service', *American Banker*, 165, 159, 1.

Mazur, L. (1999) 'Unleashing employees' true value: employees can be your company's most valuable marketing asset', *Marketing*, 29 April, 22.

Discussion questions

1. What are the hurdles that First Direct must overcome to gain and retain more customers?

2. What benefits does First Direct offer in comparison to a traditional high street bank?

3. How far do you think First Direct can extend the range of services offered to a customer? Do you think there is a future for total solutions services such as Octopus?

References

Author unknown (2001) 'A brighter horizon', *e-CRM Reaching the Customer*, London: *The Times*, April 11.

Chaffey, D. (2002) *E-Business and E-Commerce*, Harlow: Pearson Education.

Cheung, N. (2001) 'Outward bound', *Information Age*, Infoconomy, July, 33–36.

Deitel, H.M., Deitel, P.J. and Nieto, T.R. (2001) *E-Business and e-Commerce, How to Programme*, New Jersey: Prentice Hall.

Gould, R. (2001) 'Myths, legends and truth', *CRM*, 3, 10, 30–32.

Heywood, T. (2001) 'Strategy-industry blank over CRM's effect', *CRM*, 3, 2, 12.

Laudon, K.C. and Traver, C.G. (2001) *E-Commerce-business, Technology, Society*, Boston: Addison Wesley.

Osborne, B. (2001) 'Back to school', *CRM*, 3, 8, 32–34.

Payne, A. (2001) 'Steps to a strategy', *The IT Report for Directors and Decision Makers*, Conspectus, October, 14–16.

Reichheld, F.F., Markey, R.G. and Hopton, C. (2000) 'e-Customer loyalty – applying the traditional rules of business for online success', *European Business Journal*, 12, 4, 173–178.

Siragher, N. (2001) 'Are you ready?' *CRM*, 3, 7, 16–21.

Stone, M. and Foss, B. (2001) 'Where do we go from here', *Marketing Business*, May, iii–viii.

Sweet, P. (2001) 'CRM purse strings tighten', *The IT Report for Directors and Decision Makers*, Conspectus, October, 2–4.

Turban, E., Lee, J., King, D. and Chung, H.M. (2000) *Electronic Commerce – A Managerial Perspective*, New Jersey: Prentice Hall.

Wilson, H., Daniel, E. and McDonald, M. (2002) 'Factors for success in customer relationship management (CRM) systems', *Journal of Marketing Management*, 18, 1–2, 193–219.

Case Study   *Amazon – the world's leading e-tailer?*

In July 1995, a new retailer opened its cyber-doors to e-customers, with the aim:

> ...to offer Earth's Biggest Selection, and to be Earth's most customer-centric organisation, where the customer can find and discover anything they may want to buy online.
>
> (Amazon.com, 2001)

In the mid-1990s, such dreams of world-domination seemed destined to go the way of every Bond villain's. Although founded early enough to earn the title of 'web-pioneer,' the Seattle-based company was by no means the first Internet-based retailer. Others with a far more respectable pedigree had tried, and failed – most notably IBM with its abortive World Avenue shopping mall. Perhaps more importantly, the decision of Amazon's CEO, Jeff Bezos, to confine initial operations to the relatively low-margin sector of book retailing seemed a rather hesitant start to the leadership bid.

Seven years later, the jury is still out on Amazon. Few dispute its claim to be the world's largest book retailer, and one of the world's leading brands. Its size and popularity, however, have yet to produce any net profits. Despite showing its first ever net profit of $5m in the last quarter of 2001, this must be seen in the context of net losses of more than $550m for the year as a whole, and this from net sales of well over $3bn. Investors, analysts and employees alike are asking the same question: is Amazon taking a patient, long-term approach to the creation of a world-beating retailer, or is its business formula essentially untenable?

Company structure and market segments

A major world retailer
On 31 December 2001, Amazon permanently employed some 7,800 full and part-time employees, as well as independent contractors and temporary personnel for seasonal work.

Order fulfilment centres in the US, Europe and Japan gave the company about 4 million square feet of warehouse space (Amazon.com, 2001). Turnover stood at over $3 billion for 2001, more than double the 1997 figure (see Figure A1).

Since January 2001, Amazon has structured its operations around the four principal segments of US books, music and DVD/video; US Electronics, tools and kitchen; services; and international. Each is described in more detail below. Net sales for each segment are illustrated in Figure A2 and gross profits in Figure A3.

US books, music and DVD/video
This segment represents what was traditionally Amazon's core business, consisting of retail sales of books, music and other products through the Amazon.com website, as well as commission of second-hand sales through Amazon Marketplace, where customers can buy and sell second-hand books and other goods. Net sales have risen substantially over the last three years, though 2001 sales were slightly down on the previous year. Gross profit growth for the segment has outpaced sales, as gross margins increased from 20 per cent to 27 per cent over the period. The segment continues to be the mainstay of the company's income, its $453m contribution accounting for nearly 57 per cent of gross profits in 2001.

US electronics, tools and kitchen
Launched in 1999, this segment covers sales of electronics, computers and other home electronics products, as well as various hardware, home ware and leisure ranges. Sales have shown healthy growth in the first two years of operation, with gross profits of $78m. At 14 per cent in 2001, margins are less attractive than the US book segment.

Services
Since 1999, Amazon has been operating websites and managing order fulfilment for

other retailers, as well as several other web marketing and management services. Notable partners include Target, AOL, Virgin Wines and Toys 'R' Us. This segment represents the most profitable arm of the business, with gross margins of 56 per cent, though this figure has fallen from 93 per cent in 1999, as more recent alliances have shifted from high margin marketing and promotional agreements to the more costly business of order fulfilment.

International

This segment comprises retail sales through its four websites in the UK, France, Germany and Japan. Gross profit from all four sites accounted for nearly 18 per cent of the 2001 total, with margins at 21 per cent being slightly worse than those of the US site. It is notable that whilst US margins have decreased significantly, the average figure for the international sites has remained constant.

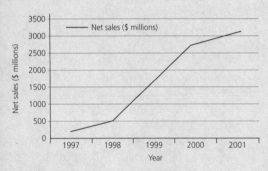

A1 Net sales for Amazon 1997–2001

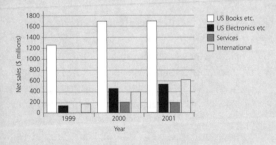

A2 Net sales by segment

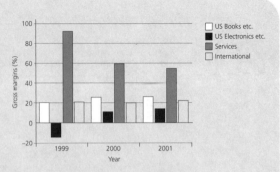

A3 Gross profit margin by segment

Mission and values

The company's 1997 annual report included a letter to its shareholders, which set out the goals and values of the organisation. This has been reprinted in all subsequent reports, and used as a framework for presenting the company's achievements. The key dimensions of the Amazon approach are as follows:

- It's all about the long term: The words 'long term' appear a number of times in all of the annual reports. Underpinning Amazon's whole approach is the principle that superior customer value will lead to customer acquisition and retention and so to profitability and dividends.

- Growth is the key to success: Maintaining its position as market leader is crucial to Amazon's business model, which assumes that market leadership creates higher profitability. Customer retention figures significantly in the company's leadership strategy, with its three primary performance indicators being customer/revenue growth, the amount of repeat business, and brand strength. Word of mouth is said to be *the most powerful acquisition tool* that the company possesses (Amazon.com, 2001).

- Learning and continuous improvement underpin growth: The principle of continuous improvement is implicit in Amazon's business policy. This is reflected in a commitment to innovations which enhance the online shopping experience, in reducing costs and in eliminating the root causes of mistakes. The idea of learning and continuous improvement is not restricted purely to operations – the 1997 letter refers to the need to learn from both successes and failures in its strategic investment decisions.

- Getting the right employees: Amazon professes a commitment to hiring and retaining an employee base that is both talented and motivated.

Perhaps because it was conceived during a time when hopes for the Internet were unrealistically high, Amazon's philosophy carefully stresses the effect of dogged, incremental progress, rather than presenting its retail model as inherently superior to that of its competitors. This is perhaps not surprising, given the company's disappointing financial performance. Although few could question the sense of the philosophy, Warner (2001) echoes the sentiments of many in dubbing Amazon *'a land of eternal hope'* and attributing the company's survival to Bezos' extraordinary talent for attracting investment. So how much real progress has the company made?

Company strategy

A record of innovation

Innovation in the field of e-commerce was a feature of Amazon's early strategy, as the company strove to develop a comprehensive online retailing service (Mellahi and Johnson, 2000). Among its innovations are:

- *Enhanced search facilities*: Amazon was the first company to enable customers to obtain obscure books as easily as best-sellers.

- *One-click shopping*: the 'one-click' format reduced the tedium of order-form-filling by storing customer information, such as addresses and credit card numbers.

- *Collaborative filtering*: this software analyses the customer's past and present purchases, and suggests other books that people with similar purchase histories have bought.

- *E-mail reminders and order tracking*: the company was the first to give their customers reminders and tracking updates through e-mail, rather than requiring them to log onto the retailer's system to obtain such information.

Mellahi and Johnson (2000) observe that the above innovations were relatively easily copied by rivals, though Amazon did derive significant first-mover advantages, such as increased brand awareness and customer loyalty. Nevertheless, 2001 saw a significant shift in its strategic focus, from differentiation to cost leadership.

Cost leadership

Whilst Amazon's initial focus was on developing its product range and enhancing the online shopping experience, 2001 saw a deliberate move to a cost leadership strategy. In Bezos' own words:

> There are two types of retailer – those …that work hard to raise prices, and those …that work hard to lower prices. Though both models can be successful, we've decided to relentlessly follow the second model.
>
> (in Prior, 2002)

Recent initiatives have indicated the potential value of this strategy. The offer of free shipping on orders over $99 last autumn was, according to analysts, a key factor in Amazon's unexpected operating profit for the first quarter of 2002. Customers bought more on each order to qualify for the offer, thus reducing costs per order (Hof, 2002). Bezos has recently extended a 30 per cent discount, previously offered on titles over $30, to those over $15.

Improving operational efficiency

According to Hof and Green (2002), Bezos has some justification for believing his discounting strategy to be sustainable. The company has made great progress in terms of operational efficiency and hence cost reduction. Improvements in inventory software and storage systems have reduced the proportion of incoming inventory stored in the wrong place from 12 per cent to 4 per cent since last year, significantly cutting order-fulfilment expenses. Better demand forecasting by region reduced inventory levels by 18 per cent in the fourth quarter of 2001.

But when will enough be enough? Bezos says that aggressive price cutting is 'something we think we can do for years' (in Hof, 2002), but given the fact that Amazon has yet to show a net annual profit, isn't it time to start enjoying those increased margins? Over-capacity may be the reason – with its distribution centres operating at only 40 per cent of capacity, there's still a lot more room for future growth before Amazon thinks about harvesting (Hof and Green, 2002). In the meantime, the relentless drive for improved operating efficiency not only allows price reductions, but also improves customer satisfaction and stimulates good word of mouth. In 2001 the company gained the highest score ever recorded for any service company in the American Customer Satisfaction Index, conducted by the University of Michigan.

A focus on customer retention and brand value

The Amazon business philosophy places customer retention at the centre of growth and profitability (Amazon.com, 2001). Various commentators have suggested that, in an online purchasing environment, psychological switching costs are high (e.g. Machlis, 1998). This is reflected in Amazon's sales figures, which put repeat purchases as high as 58 per cent in 1997. According to company figures, despite its discounting policy, sales per customer account rose from $117 to $125 p.a. between 1999 and 2001. Amazon's massive growth, therefore, was driven not only by acquisition, but also by increased spending on the part of existing customers.

The assessment of brand value is more difficult, however. Clarke (2001) assessed the brand strength of Amazon late in 1999, finding that awareness of the Amazon name derived more from the company's 'celebrity status' than a true understanding of the values of, and

loyalty to, the brand. Nevertheless, much progress has been made since then, and the customer retention figures suggest that the same measures may now yield very different results.

Strategic alliances

Perhaps the most dramatic shift in Amazon's strategy has been the move towards servicing online operations on behalf of other retailers, rather than developing its own range. This has been heralded by some commentators as a move from 'online department store to retailing back office' (Hof, 2001). However with average margins at least double those of its traditional retailing operations, Amazon probably considers the cash to be worth the indignity. Others see it as only sensible that the company should leverage its hard-won skills in e-tailing and distribution.

The seeds were sown in 2000, when Amazon took over the running of the Toys 'R' Us site, and have grown to include other established retail brands such as Circuit City and Virgin Wines, with the latest strategic alliance being a five year deal with the fashion retailer, Target Corp. Not all strategic relationships have been smooth, however. Earlier this year, online travel partners Expedia Inc. and Hotwire expressed disappointment with Amazon's handling of its online marketing. There is little doubt, though, that e-tailing services will remain a major contributor to Amazon's future growth.

The future

There can be little dispute that Amazon is a remarkable company, having survived in an environment that saw the death of many dotcoms. Its dizzying growth rate and present flirtation with profitability are testaments to the fact that it has learnt quickly, made real operational improvement and generated a degree of customer loyalty in a relatively short period. The fact remains, however, that the company has yet to demonstrate that such loyalty arises from trust and commitment, rather than merely being bought by aggressive discounting. If the latter is the case, it is unlikely that any amount of cost-cutting will generate sustainable competitive advantage in the long term.

It may be, however, that Amazon's future lies not with its own retailing operations, but with the provision of online services for established 'bricks and mortar' retailers. Certainly, it currently has the capacity to offer fulfilment services to a number of partners of Target's calibre, and such a policy would ensure a much better return than Amazon could hope to see from the extension of its own retailing operations. However, this would mean a move away from its core business, and from Bezos' original dream of being the earth's largest retailer. If he wishes to keep his investors, however, he may have to accept that the world is not enough.

Discussion questions

1. Amazon currently operate in two markets: the business-to-business (offering Internet retailing services) and consumer markets (retailing consumer goods). Identify the characteristics of the two types of buyers and markets.

2. Access the Amazon website and evaluate the effectiveness of the site in building long-term relationships with retail customers, and suggest improvements.

3. What lies behind Amazon's success in building business-to-business relationships?

4. To what extent can the skills, resources and processes used by Amazon to build effective relationships with business customers be transferred into consumer environment?

References

Amazon.com (2001) Annual report. www.amazon.com, accessed 1 July 2002.

Clarke, C. (2001) 'What price loyalty when a brand switch is just a click away', *Qualitative Marketing Research: An International Journal*, 4, 3, 160–168.

Hof, R. (2001) 'Amazon: we never said we had to do it all', *Business Week,* 3753, 53.

Hof, R. (2002) 'Jeffrey Bezos: the shipping news', *Business Week,* 3781, 42.

Hof, R. and Green, H. (2002) 'How Amazon cleared that hurdle' *Business Week,* 3768, 60.

Machlis, S. (1998) 'Amazon.com: Wal-Mart pushes web branding', *Computer World,* 32, 32, 13.

Mellahi, K. and Johnson, M. (2000) 'Does it pay to be first mover in e.commerce? The case of Amazon.com', *Management Decision,* 38, 7, 445–452.

Prior, M. (2002) 'Amazon's profit milestone reverses steady 4Q slide', *DSN Retailing Today,* 41, 3, 8.

Warner, M. (2001) 'Can Amazon be saved?', *Fortune,* 144, 11, 156.

Case Study *Tennyson Ltd*

Merryweather Sailing and Tennyson Ski were amalgamated in 2002 to form the activity brand of a major UK tour operator. The new brand, Tennyson, offers a wide range of activities including skiing, snowboarding, sailing, yachting, diving, mountain biking and walking.

For example, Merryweather Sailing had control over the entire holiday experience. They leased their own 80–90 bed hotels near water sport locations which would offer a range of choices for the novice and the experienced sailor but all with prevailing on-shore winds to add safety value. These locations were always some distance away from the heavily commercialised holiday centres, thus presenting a more local experience, and the hotels were leased and staffed entirely by Tennyson employees with the ratio of staff: guest being approximately 1:8. Holidays were booked direct with Merryweather Sailing so that clients could not, by mistake, end up at a resort which would be unsuitable for their sporting ability or personal needs. In essence the service was highly personalised, and care of the customer and service quality were of paramount importance.

Merryweather Sailing's mission was: 'To be the best tour operator to go on holiday with and invest in'. This mission statement has since been adopted for Tennyson Ltd.

Merryweather Sailing believed that their success was largely a result of their marketing culture, which flowed from management to their staff, from staff to customers, and back into repeat bookings. This manifested itself in the company's policy, which encouraged staff to arrange clients' first night meal, a midweek meal and last night barbecue. The company encouraged innovation, opportunity to develop, ownership of problems, enjoyment, the customer being Number One, and doing things right first time.

The snow market is quite different. Tennyson Ski did not have the same level of control over the holiday experience and were, therefore, unable to build up the same kind of relationship with their clients. They operated at destinations where they would have allocations of beds in a large number of properties ranging from chalets and apartments to hotels. Once clients had arrived they might not see a Tennyson Ski representative until their day of departure. On average, the ratio of ski rep: client is 1:30. A large majority of skiing and snowboarding holidays are booked at the last minute, with clients basing their decisions largely on price.

The challenge

Bringing two different cultures and operations together into one seamless brand is no small task. Tennyson needed a new strategy; it needed to undertake a lot of research and look for an innovative way to move forward; it needed to take the best from both systems and look at how it could best improve its relationship with its customers.

The new company had to work hard to develop a strategy which would harness the best of both brands. Tennyson faced two main hurdles. First there was no clear strategy, and second, the non-profitable elements would have to be identified and axed.

A new strategy

To decide on a new strategy, certain questions had to be answered. Tennyson Ski was part of the mass tourism market and Merryweather Sailing was a specialist tour operator – *hot* vs *cold* holidays. Tennyson sought to find answers to key issues such as:

- What are the sources of our future growth?
- What market are we – or should we be – in, specialist vs mass?
- Who is our customer?
- What do we stand for?

Targeting non-profitable elements

To identify and eliminate non-profitable elements, Tennyson had to establish:

▶

- What products or services were falling below an acceptable profit margin;
- What products or services will require a significant investment of resources in the near or long term without a reasonable expectation of return on the investment; and
- What products or services could be eliminated without having an adverse impact on the new strategy.

Brand strategy

Tennyson concluded that what they needed first was a *brand* strategy, so they set about developing this and commissioned assistance from a consultancy firm. The process involved management interviews, consumer feedback, desk research and workshops. The brand strategy elements involved (a) brand essence which asked the questions: Who are we and What business are we in?; (b) brand positioning which seeks to find out what we have to be and (c) brand personality which finds out who our customers perceive us to be.

The success criteria aimed at differentiating Tennyson from its competitors, and making the product relevant to and easily identified by their customers and ownable by Tennyson and only Tennyson.

Consumer intelligence

Information was gathered on the consumers *directly* from current and potential consumers themselves to find out what they liked and disliked across a wide range of topics including service, choice of activities, meals and so on. The company talked to their own customers, to people who had holidayed with competitors and to people who had fancied the idea of an activity holiday but had never taken one. In addition Tennyson looked at consumer trends. Socio-demographic changes showed increasing prosperity in a cash rich, time poor society and a redefining of the family including the increasing proportion of older persons. They found that personal values were evolving; that there was an increased awareness of well-being and a growth in demand for personal enrichment.

Research found that the income profile of both client groups (hot and cold holidays) were very similar. This came as rather a surprise, as it was thought that the Merryweather customers would be far more affluent than their skiing counterparts. Another surprise revealed by Tennyson's research was that only 4 per cent of their hot holiday clients regarded themselves as experts and only 10 per cent of the skiers thought themselves to be in the advanced category. In particular this surprised the ex-Merryweather marketers who, believing their clients to come from an experienced water sports background, had invested in the latest hi-tech equipment.

Tennyson also found that, of the 'hot' holiday customers, 23 per cent also ski or snowboard, that 32 per cent would definitely be taking a ski holiday the same year as their 'hot' holiday, that 12 per cent would holiday with Tennyson and that 60 per cent do not know which company they will ski with next season. Conversely, of the skiers interviewed, 18 per cent go diving, 18 per cent go sailing, 11 per cent go windsurfing, 49 per cent go walking and 27 per cent go mountain biking. Clearly this has significant relevance for marketing.

The Tennyson customer

Tennyson customers are lively and interesting, they want to grow, they want to relax by actively engaging in an activity, and they are discerning, hate inefficiency and are happy to pay for quality.

Brand essence

Customer insight for the brand essence found that active people look for more than just a beach holiday; they like to improve themselves, gain a sense of achievement and be stretched. They want to be able to socialise on their terms with like-minded people and they desire an experience to talk about to their friends when they return home.

Brand position

Tennyson want to present a clear position to trade, customers and investors. Tennyson want to be perceived as the active holiday experts. They are experts in snow sports, water sports and biking. Tennyson want to be known as having great instructors with whom it is a pleasure to learn and develop skills and who uniquely enhance the holiday experience with their knowledge, skills and passion. They want to be recognised by both the travel/retail trade and by the active industry as the experts. They want to be known as the experts for beginners/improvers, groups and families; the only choice for beginners and improvers, from novice to expert.

Brand personality

The brand personality that Tennyson is seeking is simply and purely 'commitment, passion, expertise and enjoyment'.

Changes at Tennyson

Tennyson concluded that a number of changes should be made to achieve their goals. These include a variety of marketing and customer care and service quality issues including:

Consistent delivery to create a uniform template across the business to which customers can relate and depend upon.

Expertise across the business and the drive to shape and share best practice. Tennyson have partnerships with manufacturers of high quality sports equipment including Snow and Rock, Salomon, David Lloyd and Snow Dome, and they are one of the largest RYA school in the world. These partnerships and accreditations pay testimony to Tennyson's standards and quality, which is good both for staff morale and boosting customer awareness.

Staff training and development to include recruitment and development of UK and overseas staff who feel passionate about people, teaching and Tennyson. Training and development should encourage experts in the business and motivate the young upcoming stars and ambassadors of sport. With recognition and a reputation as a leader in the industry, people will want to work with Tennyson and be a part of that quality team. They aim to become the preferred employer.

Customer relationship management to increase customer lifetime value. A major push is to increase guest contact and gain control across the full spectrum of the holiday experience. This involves spreading good practice from the culture of the hot holidays to the cold holidays. Traditionally the water sports holiday operations had involved a higher ratio of staff to customer; contact with customers is more frequent across the hospitality and active sport sides. In part this is due to the nature of the holiday but also because Merryweather Sailing had greater control over all the holiday elements. Tennyson recognise that their success rests not only with the quality of their products at their various destinations but very much with the total customer experience.

To try and redress the balance and increase the client: staff contact, Tennyson are piloting a Ski Guru in four resorts. The brief of these gurus is to ski and socialise with clients with the aim of creating and building a relationship between the customer and the brand Tennyson. This relationship on the 'hot' holiday side is seen by the customers as a major plus. With a lower proportion of staff to clients on the 'cold' holidays this might be a way to achieve a similar result and an increase in repeat bookings.

In short, Tennyson are aiming to provide the 'hot' experience in the winter by:

- Teaching, improving, developing guests' skills:
  - ski gurus
  - Tennyson Ski school and hire shops
  - technique sessions
  - resort 'base' at central properties
  - BASI-endorsed ability system, certificates/grades.

- Increase engagement with the guests:
  - in resort and at home
  - warm-up weekends
  - expert advice (ski boot fittings, latest equipment)
  - recognition of guests on the slopes.

▶

- Programme modification:
  - to fit with strategy
  - more 'club' style 'Tennyson bases'
  - clear and honest classification of resort by ability.

Tennyson is a specialist business and requires specialist skills to look after customers, retain their patronage and encourage new business. Active holidays tend to require the personal touch and expert knowledge.

Marketing Communication

Tennyson have a comprehensive promotional mix which includes:

- Tennyson brochure in 500 Thomas Cook, high street travel agents
- New brochures are mailed out to clients who had booked a holiday in the past two years.
- A quarterly broadsheet is e-mailed to people who have shown an interest in particular activities. It is too early to assess the success of this tactic.
- Advertisements appear in:
  - national press virtually year round; both tabloid and broadsheet.
  - specialist press – e.g. *Yachts and Yachting, Boards and Windsurf, Mountain Bike UK, Total Bike, Outdoor Pursuits, Dive* etc.
  - Internet website – it is not planned to develop online booking because of the complexities of booking appropriate centres ie. beginners vs experienced with the potential problems of clients booking inappropriate locations. Instead – and arguably more customer friendly – is a 'click to call' button. This will allow enquirers to give their telephone number and a best time to be called. The Tennyson automated telephone system ensures that they call the client at that time to discuss their holiday requirements.
  - press releases are written approximately once a month and occasionally special features might tie-in with advertising features.

- early booking brochure – there are now two editions of the brochure which allows prices to be held at previous year's rates if booking before a set date. This first edition can also give information about new activities and destinations which have not been fully developed but will be included in edition two, which is launched at the winter Boat Show. In addition to the generic brochure there are separate activity magazines. These are sent to clients automatically from information held on Tennyson's database.
- press trips for journalists are organised for the national and specialist press. About 15 trips per year are organised with flights and accommodation paid for. Journalists must pay for their extras.
- sponsorship comprises a small part of the overall promotional mix. This takes the form of prizes in return for company logos on equipment to gain media coverage. In addition, they have joined national campaigns such as the national Go Boating Day organised by the British Marine Industries Federation (BMIF).
- exhibitions play another important role. Tennyson exhibits at both the London and Southampton Boat Shows, Sailboat at Alexandra Palace, Bike and Dive Exhibition and Confex (corporate hospitality) at Earl's Court, all the major ski shows as well as adventure and activity shows.
- resort staff promote a 'where to go next' list during the client debrief at the end of their holiday.
- educational visits were arranged for both travel agents and Tennyson's own reservations team to increase product awareness amongst the agents and ensure their own teams have first-hand knowledge of all destinations.

Staying on course

Tennyson Ltd is a successful enterprise in a highly competitive environment. This places enormous pressure on the company and has some interesting ironies. In the world of holiday services, Tennyson cannot sustain its level of success without actually pursuing a higher level of success. It must consolidate its position and at the same time it must expand its operations. It must have a long-term, ambitious business strategy which effectively coordinates measurable activities and focuses them clearly on specific marketing targets, whilst continuously – and ruthlessly – assessing and adjusting short-term strategies to ensure they are actually taking the company where it wants to be. In fact, in the complex race in which Tennyson wants to stay in front, it must continuously make adjustments simply to stay on course!

Case Study by Glynis Young

Discussion questions

1. To what extent do you think Tennyson's product and customer markets offer the potential for a RM strategy? Why?

2. Evaluate Tennyson's attempts at relationship building.

3. How could Tennyson improve their RM strategy? Give your answer using the planning framework in Chapters 4–7.

Case Study *Parker, Downey and Jagger Solicitors*

The firm

Parker, Downey and Jagger (PDJ) are a firm of solicitors who offer a wide range of legal services to private and commercial clients. The firm was established in Southampton in 1878 and enjoys a high reputation locally. PDJ currently employs around 124 staff, comprising 14 partners, 58 fee-earners and 52 support staff. PDJ's annual turnover is approximately £6m.

PDJ has achieved considerable organic growth during the past five years and has seen the number of employees rise from 79 in 1997 to 124 in 2002. As a result PDJ has purchased an additional premises in order to house their expanding number of employees. The new building is situated 100 metres from the flagship building, which was opened in 1997. Both offices are situated at a prestige location in the heart of Eastleigh.

PDJ is one of the leading firms in Hampshire. Over the past three years, a number of small local competitors have been acquired by large national and internationally established practices.

Currently PDJ have no intention to establish any physical presence outside the Southampton region, although the target market covers a 40 mile radius. Also, at present PDJ have no intention of offering European or international service.

Presently, over 94 per cent of PDJ's business comes from referrals (mainly through estate agents, accountants and existing customers) and repeat business (private and commercial). They would like this to continue and to be complemented by an increase in the number of new clients while they seek to increase substantially their market share. The partners believe that the high referral and retention rate is due to the buoyant economic conditions in the region coupled with the firm's reputation for the quality of their expert and friendly service. They do, however, feel that the economic situation could change and would like a relationship marketing programme to be adopted and implemented.

The location

Southampton is situated in the south of England and is one of the biggest container ports in Britain. P&O Cruises' principal port in Britain, Southampton is home to major ocean-liners such as the Oriana and is used by passengers travelling by sea to Europe and beyond. The city's principal source of income is from the port, the Shell oil refinery, vehicle assembly, marine engineering, insurance and financial services. A large indoor shopping centre has recently been opened bringing shoppers from all parts of the region to the city. The University and the city's colleges of higher and further education also play a major role in its economy.

The Southampton region is considered a growth area. In general companies in the area are predicted to grow both in terms of size (staff numbers) and in terms of turnover. Much of the growth in and around Southampton is predicted to come from international and European trade. Southampton City Council is keen on European integration and capitalising on opportunities arising in Europe. The council is working to raise the profile of the city and building networks with other cities within the EU and outside it.

Mission statement

The firm's mission statement is: 'Excelling in legal services, courtesy and value'.

Corporate objectives

The objectives were formulated from a strategic review that was agreed by the partners in July 2001. These were to:

- Excel in the provision of legal services
- Be courteous in the way that we deal with each other within the firm and with our clients and contacts outside the firm
- Give value to our clients and a service that is beyond their expectations
- Increase our profitability and profit

▶

- Pay our staff better than the other firms in our area
- Be able to attract the best new staff, whether lawyers or not
- Have the funds to enable us to expand (where it would increase our profitability) and to provide the fund for investment in our properties and information technology
- Increase the number of staff to 250 in the next five years.

Marketing objectives

Solicitors have only been able to promote to their existing customers since the early 1990s. In November 2001 the Law Society extended and introduced a publicity code to allow solicitors to target non-customers through direct marketing media.

PDJ employ a part-time marketing consultant who has been leading marketing communications developments and tactical promotional initiatives over the past five years.

Currently there are no clear marketing objectives. The main aim is the achievement of the corporate objective of growth. However, the following are thought desirable by the partners.

- Establishing an RM programme
- Improving internal marketing
- Establishing and communicating an appropriate and singular brand image.

Products

The principal areas of work (core products) offered are:

- Property – Commercial and private portfolios, secured lending, retail premises, development and investment property.
- Litigation – Personal injury and agency work.
- Private Client – Family tax and estate planning, divorce, weighty financial relief claims, family mediation and childcare.
- Employment – all aspects of statutory and individual employment law.

No specific profiles of the users of these products have been drawn up.

Competition

Competition has increased in recent years as the region has become more financially prosperous. This has led to the increase of takeovers of independent practices. National firms such as Blake Lapthorne have established a physical presence in Southampton. A number of smaller regional firms, for example White and Bowker, Shoosmiths and Lester Aldridge, are investing in marketing and expanding both physically and through the creation of partnership arrangements within the region.

Branding

Research conducted amongst the employees of PDJ has revealed that 35 per cent of employees believe that the firm's brand image is:

- Well known locally
- Expensive
- Knowledgeable

The remaining 65 per cent have differing opinions, none of which include any of the above.

A majority of respondents believe that the values of the brand lie in tradition and the ability to respond to a large variety of legal matters quickly and expertly.

PDJ employees identify their main competitor to be Blake Lapthorne and the majority of them associate this firm's brand image with:

- Well-known
- National firm status
- Proactive in targeting

Fifty-six per cent of respondents suggest word of mouth as the best means of communicating the brand externally.

Internal marketing

The partners and the marketing consultant believe that internal marketing should play an increasingly prominent role within the firm. Research shows that, as with many firms in the sector, there is confusion amongst the staff as to the meaning and implications of internal marketing. The answers which were obtained without any prompts by interviewers are demonstrated in the diagram below.

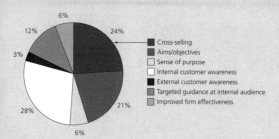

Cross-selling
Aims/objectives
Sense of purpose
Internal customer awareness
External customer awareness
Targeted guidance at internal audience
Improved firm effectiveness

What do you understand by the term internal marketing?

Further research relating to internal marketing shows that 81 per cent of employees attend Monday morning briefings on a regular basis. The three most popular uses for the briefing were thought to be:

1. To understand aims and objectives of PDJ
2. Relationship building
3. To understand employees' role within PDJ.

Eighty-one per cent of fee earners attend fee-earner lunches. The top three benefits of these were believed to be:

1. Networking
2. Understanding employees' role within PDJ
3. Meeting partners.

Additionally, a number of events are organised on a fairly regular basis by the firm. The event and the percentage of employees who normally attend them is illustrated below:

Event	% of participants
Networking opportunities	88
Social events	88
Internal/external presentation	56
Lunch with partners	56
Lunch with clients	56
Team building	50

Asked about the effectiveness of internal marketing activities and a few suggestions for additional activities the respondents' views were:

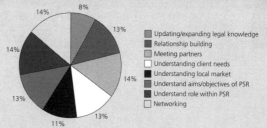

Updating/expanding legal knowledge
Relationship building
Meeting partners
Understanding client needs
Understanding local market
Understand aims/objectives of PSR
Understand role within PSR
Networking

How useful do you find this in terms of …

Marketing communications

Traditionally, law firms in Britain have not engaged in any serious marketing activity and only recently have they been allowed to advertise. Although the larger national firms have started to employ full time marketing specialists, PDJ have some way to go to establish a significant marketing department. Currently employing one part-time marketing consultant, the marketing budget including communications budget stands at £110,000 per annum, which represents 1.8 per cent of the firm's turnover. The majority of the marketing activities are communication/promotion related. These are mainly in the form of seminars on various law topics, e.g. employment law, to business customers, sponsorship of local organisations, e.g. Southampton football club and Mayflower the local theatre, limited advertising in the local press, yellow pages and business directories, the legal directories, on line websites and printed brochures for business and private clients.

There is no clear marketing communication objective at present.

Case Study by Matt Helstrip and Ruth Tudor

Discussion questions

1. Carry out a SWOT analysis for PDJ.
2. Evaluate the mission statement, corporate and marketing objectives and communication

strategy of PDJ and suggest if these need to be amended and/or written differently.

3. Evaluate the branding and internal marketing strategies within PDJ.

4. Who are the main stakeholders of PDJ, and how can a relationship marketing programme benefit the firm? What would be the value proposition offered to these stakeholders?

5. Suggest a strategic relationship marketing plan spanning the period 2003–2007.

Case Study   *Energy Saving Trust*

TransportAction: CleanUp Haulage

Background

The Energy Saving Trust (EST) was established as part of the government's action plan in response to the 1992 Earth Summit in Rio de Janeiro, which addressed worldwide concerns on environmental issues such as climate change and global warming. The UK government acknowledges that one of the greatest challenges of the future is to protect and safeguard the environment through sustainable development policies and it has therefore established targets of reducing carbon dioxide emissions by 20 per cent and sourcing 10 per cent of electricity from renewable sources by 2010.

Today, the Trust is the UK's leading organisation working with business partners to deliver energy efficiency to households, small businesses and to corporate and local authority fleets to promote the use of cleaner road vehicles. It is a non-profit distributing company set up by the government and major energy companies. The Trust's vision is: 'Working through partnerships towards the sustainable and efficient use of energy'.

The Trust's current priorities are:

- Stimulating energy efficiency and the use of clean fuel vehicles (CFVs) in UK households to achieve social, environmental and economic benefits;

- Creating a market for CFVs in order to help deliver local and global environmental benefits including improved air quality;

- Making a difference through energy efficiency programmes targeted at small businesses, schools and business lighting; and

- Signposting consumers towards credible renewable energy supplies.

Programmes

The Trust administers a broad range of programmes that are designed to achieve the strategic vision outlined above. TransportAction is one of the Trust's two main divisions. It is essentially a business-to-business operation which delivers innovative solutions, programmes and information to reduce the damaging effects of transport on the environment and seeks to promote sustainable mobility.

Road transport is one of the major and fastest growing sources of airborne pollution, contributing to both poor local air quality and global warming. Action in the area of road transport is a high priority for TransportAction whose challenge is to develop relationships with all its target audiences to achieve a sustainable position for cleaner fuelled vehicles.

Objectives of the CleanUp haulage programme

TransportAction's two main initiatives are the PowerShift and CleanUp programmes. PowerShift's focus is on the development of markets for alternative fuel cars and light commercial vehicles running on cleaner fuels including liquified petroleum gas (LPG), natural gas and electricity. CleanUp is aimed at improving air quality through emissions reduction technology on heavy-duty diesel vehicles (trucks, buses and coaches). CleanUp Haulage is part of the overall CleanUp programme but with specific ring-fenced funds to encourage the take up of emission control equipment (chiefly catalytic converters and particulate traps) to older vehicles that operate in pollution 'hot spots'; it also targets the most polluting commercial vehicles in English cities that have a significant impact on local air quality. CleanUp Haulage's challenge is to attain 10 per cent penetration of CFVs in the UK's 422,000-strong commercial vehicle park.

It is perceived that smaller truck operators run fleets that are older and emit higher pollutant levels. This is in contrast to larger fleet operators who typically employ shorter fleet

▶

replacement cycles and whose vehicles are likely to be the cleanest and most efficient. Therefore, the government's focus is on smaller operators, although CleanUp Haulage's remit is to target operators of all sizes.

Among the road haulage's main trade associations are the Road Haulage Association (RHA) and Freight Transport Association (FTA) (see Appendix 1) and both organisations are keen for their members to be 'green' and have communicated this to their respective membership bases.

In terms of new vehicles, manufacturers such as Scania and Iveco have led the way in developing new low emission vehicles which have been promoted to companies upgrading their commercial vehicle fleets. These new vehicles meet the Euro II and Euro III emission standards, posing less of a pollution problem. However the capital expenditure is significant, placing new vehicles out of the reach of most small operators.

Companies who run used or second hand trucks can benefit from investing in retrofitting technology. Technology suppliers including Eminox and Dinex have been actively marketing oxidation catalysts and particulate traps which can be retrofitted to vehicles to reduce emission levels. These vehicles are re-marketed by manufacturers or dealers to fleet operators with the vehicle possessing a Reduced Pollution Certificate. Running cleaner vehicle fleets can provide hauliers with a competitive advantage as it gives them the ability to negotiate with customers whose contracts contain environmental conditions, and allows them to widen their customer base and potentially increase profitability.

Financial resources

The Government's Road Haulage Modernisation Fund allocated £100m to road haulage over ten years. TransportAction's overall budget was £16m in 2000/1 and £35m in 2001/2. The 2002/3 grant implementation target for CleanUp Haulage is £5.8m.

Key relationships

The primary target audience for the CleanUp Haulage programme is road freight transport and distribution companies (logistics and distribution operators, own account operators, and hire or reward operators in the food and beverage distribution, retailing, express parcels and distribution and freight forwarding sectors) as well as construction and plant hire companies that operate commercial vehicle fleets. Managing these relationships is a considerable task for the Trust, particularly as the road freight transport market is highly fragmented. Sixty per cent of road freight transport companies have annual turnovers of less than £100,000 and typically these companies run small, ageing fleets with 41 per cent of all commercial vehicles over ten years old.

Direct marketing is used to communicate with end-user customers, utilising direct mail and telemarketing, to raise awareness, stimulate demand and generate leads for grant funding. TransportAction's field-based Account Managers also help fleets through the decision-making process and provide practical guidance. Fleet operators, including Safeway and Sainsbury's, also benefit from direct advice and support from the Account Managers who undertake regular face-to-face visits and assist these customers through the grant application procedure.

TransportAction also provides grant funding indirectly to end-user customers through block grant funding allocations made to intermediaries, including commercial vehicle manufacturers and technology manufacturers. Industry trade associations (see Appendix 1), vehicle funders (such as finance houses, commercial vehicle short-term rental and contract hire and leasing companies) and professional associations are also influencers of the end-user customer. Therefore, it is also critical for TransportAction to develop and manage relationships with these organizations.

Other major relationships are held with government ministers, senior civil servants, the media (particularly commercial vehicle trade press such as *Commercial Motor, Motor Transport* and *Truck and Driver*), technology consultants and advisers and non-governmental organisations (e.g. Transport2000).

Market definition

TransportAction's aim is the establishment, where practical, of a UK market running the cleanest fuel commercial vehicles. These CFVs are heavy duty commercial vehicles over 3.5 tonnes, defined as follows:

- Adoption of natural gas vehicles
- Diesel vehicles fitted with the latest particulate trap technology
- Diesel vehicles fitted with the latest oxidation catalyst technology.

The fund

CleanUp Haulage has £30m allocated over the next two years to support the retrofitting of technologies, including particulate traps and oxidation catalysts, to light and heavy commercial vehicles in England. A 75 per cent grant will finance the capital cost plus fitting of emission control equipment to commercial vehicles over 3.5 tonnes. Particulate traps or conversion to gas (which must be done by approved CleanUp suppliers) should qualify the vehicle for a reduced pollution certificate (RPC) which would attract up to £500 annual vehicle excise duty (VED) rebate.

Conditions for grant eligibility

In order for a vehicle to be eligible for a grant, the vehicle's supplier, vehicle make and model, or the converter must be listed on the CleanUp Register of approved suppliers. Grants are based on four bands that take into account the vehicle's emissions performance compared to its petrol equivalent and vary depending on whether the vehicle is Euro II or Euro III compliant. The bandings are as follows:

	Euro III*	Euro II**
Band 1 – emissions not proven	0% of premium costs	0% of premium costs
Band 2 – Euro III	40% of premium costs	30% of premium costs
Band 3 – Euro IV	60% of premium costs	40% of premium costs
Band 4 – Euro IV – 30%	75% of premium costs	50% of premium costs

*Euro III (some vehicles registered in 2000 and nearly all vehicles registered after January 2001)

**Euro II (mostly vehicles registered after Jan 1997 but before Dec 2000)

Benefits to the vehicle manufacturer

Euro IV demands particulate traps fitted on heavy goods vehicles, anticipated from 2004/2005. CleanUp Haulage will give truck operators the opportunity to put a toe in the water, even if the fleet is not currently particularly green. For commercial vehicle manufacturers this is positive news which provides them with a longer-term marketing opportunity as second hand vehicles can return to the commercial vehicle fleet market as they are refurbished with original RPCs. It also offers manufacturers additional control over the routes to market for used vehicles.

Benefits of running low emissions commercial vehicles

- Competitive advantage for truck operators from an environmental perspective that can assist when bidding for public sector/local authority business, in environment-sensitive business areas and in achieving ISO14001;
- RPC providing potential VED rebate of £500 annually;
- London congestion charging will provide natural gas vehicles with free daily access or yearly registration;
- Potential vehicle access to low emission zones (LEZs) and potentially an exclusive customer base acquired at minimum cost. A national standard of vehicle technologies for LEZs is due to be established by the end of 2002. National LEZs are expected to follow suit in major cities including York, Bristol, Bath and Nottingham;

- Opportunities to generate fleet/brand awareness through enhanced PR opportunities and provide consumer/public perception of a 'cleaner, greener fleet';

- Traditional trucks without clean technology may also run the risk of losing access rights and being turned away from access to a LEZ.

Deterrents to rapid adoption of low emission truck technology
Particulate traps/oxidation catalysts

- Even with a CleanUp grant, hauliers have to make an initial capital investment (of particular concern for smaller companies whose businesses operate at fine profit margins);

- Payback for using a particulate trap may not be achieved in many cases. At low vehicle weight, the financial benefits of reduced VED are very small;

- There is no payback scenario for the use of an oxidation catalyst (no reduction in VED is granted);

- The perceived increase in fuel consumption if particulate traps are not properly maintained (which is untrue and TransportAction's payment of maintenance can help overcome this);

- Additional vehicle down time during retrofitting and equipment maintenance, and the associated costs.

Natural gas

- Inadequacy of refuelling structure potentially restricting truck movements;

- Limited choice of natural gas vehicles;

- Capital investment required, even with a CleanUp grant, to establish a refuelling station (£500k plus);

- Maintenance costs of conversions or new vehicles;

- Lack of vehicle choice for new natural gas vehicles;

- Consistency of the tax structure associated with natural gas i.e. the tax differential is currently in favour of natural gas but scepticism exists in the market that this will change with natural gas eventually reaching a price parity with fossil fuels.

The grant application process
TransportAction-based Account Managers are on hand to help major fleets through the decision process and provide practical guidance. A dedicated hotline is also available to provide help and advice to smaller operators.

Benefits of the CleanUp application process include a fast turnaround. Application to decision status takes no longer than ten working days. The invoice for retrofitting work can be directly processed by CleanUp for 75 per cent of the payment aiding the applicant's financial position. This promotes good cash flow management.

In an increasing number of cases application for a grant by the operating or purchasing company is not necessary. A fast-track grant applications process is in place where customers can contact their commercial vehicle manufacturer, vehicle manufacturer dealership or the technology suppliers and receive equipment priced net of the grant. No paperwork is required on the part of the operator but is completed by the supplier company.

Positioning
TransportAction is the established authority on sustainable road freight transport. Through established programmes such as CleanUp, TransportAction can help truck and commercial vehicle operators on best practice for emission control seeking to improve local air quality and reduce global warming gases.

Communication programme activity
1. From purchased data, initial data cleansing is undertaken via telephone to acquire or confirm correct key purchasing decision-makers and influencers for the direct mail/telemarketing phases of the campaign.

2. Direct mail is then undertaken via the database, which is segmented by vehicle fleet size. Direct mail is targeted towards a combination of decision-makers and

influencers highlighting a range of key messages addressed to the range of audiences but all designed to raise awareness of the TransportAction and CleanUp Haulage programmes.

3. A telemarketing campaign then targets key decision-makers to gain interest and commitment and to obtain telephone appointment leads.

4. A follow-up call is made to answer any specific queries and to encourage/assist with grant applications.

5. Regular face-to-face updates are held with TransportAction Account Managers for follow-up site visits with key leads generated from the above activity.

Case study by Lesley Macdonald

Discussion questions

1. What is the value proposition offered by TransportAction to its target markets?

2. Identify the key relationships that TransportAction must manage in pursuit of its clean up programme.

3. Suggest improvements to the mechanisms by which the relationships identified above are managed.

4. Do you think that strategies employed will have to be different for the organisation's intended expansion into consumer markets? Explain your answer.

Appendix 1

Road Freight Transport Trade Associations
Association of International Courier and Express Services
www.aices.org
British Association of Removers (BAR)
www.barmovers.co.uk
British International Freight Association
www.bifa.org.uk
Cold Storage and Distribution Federation
www.csdf.org.uk
Freight Transport Association
www.fta.co.uk

Institute of Grocery Distribution
www.igd.com
Institute of Logistics and Transport (Freight Transport Special Interest Group)
www.iolt.org.uk
Movers Institute Council (affiliated with BAR)
www.barmovers.co.uk
Road Haulage Association
www.rha.net
Timber Packaging and Pallet Confederation
www.timcon.org

Appendix 2

Low emissions technologies
Two types of systems are currently approved and eligible for grant funding by CleanUp Haulage and are a popular solution for hauliers. They are the CRT oxycat and particulate trap system, designed and developed by Johnson Matthey and provided through Eminox (which has an extensive licence for the canning and fitting of equipment in the UK), and the Engelhard DPX system marketed by Dinex.

Particulate traps
These are very effective in reducing emissions with 95+ per cent particulate reductions and reductions in hydrocarbons and carbon monoxide of 80+ per cent.

Oxidation catalysts
Particulates (PM)	25% – 50%
Hydrocarbons (HC)	approx. 80+%
Carbon monoxide (CO)	approx. 80+%

There are currently four suppliers approved by Transport Action to provide particulate traps and oxidation catalysts for the haulage market. Each technology works slightly differently and will provide differing additional benefits.

Conversion to natural gas
This is an alternative to diesel retrofitting attracting a grant of up to 75 per cent of the conversion cost dependent on emission performance. Cummins and Detroit Diesel offer gas engines that fit a number of truck manufacturer chassis.

Iveco offers manufacturers' production built gas-powered models.

Gas powered engines virtually eradicate particulates and greatly reduce oxides of nitrogen tail pipe emissions compared to diesel. In addition, a feature of all gas versus diesel is the reduction in engine noise and Scania models have been tested for TransportAction and have achieved up to 50 per cent reduction in noise. Although there are no standard environmental targets for noise reduction, local authorities have the ability to set night curfews for restriction of deliveries in built-up areas. Relaxation of these curfews can be made for natural gas fuel vehicles for night-time deliveries. Gas fuelled vehicles therefore may provide an added value element for some haulage operators.

Appendix 3

Energy Saving Trust web references
www.est.org.uk
www.transportaction.org.uk
www.saveengergy.co.uk

Index

Guildford College
Learning Resource Centre

Please return on or before the last date shown.
No further issues or renewals if any items are overdue.
"7 Day" loans are **NOT** renewable.

-7 OCT 2004

2 2 FEB 2005

-6 JUN 2005

28/7/05

1 9 APR 2007

2 7 NOV 2007
3 1 JAN 2008

-5 JUN 2009

2 5 FEB 2010

1 0 MAY 2010
0 7 JAN 2011

-9 MAY 2011

1 3 MAR 2012

3 0 MAY 2012

Class: 658.812 LIT

Title: RELATIONSHIP MARKETING MANAGEMEN

Author: LITTLE, Ed